East Asian Multilateralism

T0355558

Forum on Constructive Capitalism
Francis Fukuyama, *Series Editor*

East Asian Multilateralism

Prospects for Regional Stability

•　　•

Edited by

KENT E. CALDER

and

FRANCIS FUKUYAMA

The Johns Hopkins University Press
• BALTIMORE •

© 2008 The Johns Hopkins University Press
All rights reserved. Published 2008

Printed in the United States of America on acid-free paper

9 8 7 6 5 4 3 2 1

The Johns Hopkins University Press
2715 North Charles Street
Baltimore, Maryland 21218-4363
www.press.jhu.edu

Library of Congress Cataloging-in-Publication Data

East Asian multilateralism : prospects for regional stability / edited by Kent E. Calder
and Francis Fukuyama.
   p. cm.—(Forum on constructive capitalism)
   Includes bibliographical references and index.
   ISBN-13: 978-0-8018-8848-9 (hardcover : alk. paper)
   ISBN-13: 978-0-8018-8849-6 (pbk. : alk. paper)
   1. East Asia—Economic integration.   2. East Asia—Foreign economic relations.
3. United States—Foreign relations—East Asia.   4. East Asia—Foreign relations—
United States.   I. Calder, Kent E. II. Fukuyama, Francis.
HC460.5.E2754   2008
337.1'5—dc22   2007037718

A catalog record for this book is available from the British Library.

*Special discounts are available for bulk purchases of this book. For more information, please
contact Special Sales at 410-516-6936 or specialsales@press.jhu.edu.*

The Johns Hopkins University Press uses environmentally friendly book materials, including recycled text paper that is composed of at least 30 percent post-consumer waste, whenever possible. All of our book papers are acid-free, and our jackets and covers are printed on
paper with recycled content.

Contents

Part II • COUNTRY PERSPECTIVES

Part III • POLICY IMPLICATIONS

Acknowledgments

THIS VOLUME grew out of the 2005 Bernard L. Schwartz Forum on Constructive Capitalism held at the Johns Hopkins Paul H. Nitze School of Advanced International Studies (SAIS) and co-sponsored by SAIS's Edwin O. Reischauer Center. The editors thank Bernard Schwartz, former chairman and CEO of Loral Space and Communications, for his generous support of the conference and the forum as a whole.

This book would not have been possible without the work of a number of people. Peter Beck of the International Crisis Group; Kurt Campbell, then of the Center for International and Strategic Studies; Dean Jessica Einhorn of SAIS; Lyric Hale of Hale Associates; Chen Jian of the University of Virginia; Michael Swaine of the Carnegie Endowment for International Peace; Kathryn Weathersby of the Woodrow Wilson Center; and our SAIS colleagues Karl Jackson and David M. Lampton all took part in the original conference. Hiromi Murakami and Levi Tillemann-Dick took time out of their graduate studies to help edit the volume. Cynthia Doroghazi and Robin Washington, on behalf of the Bernard L. Schwartz Forum, and Mayumi Tani and Juri Yamazaki of the Reischauer Center helped organize the conference and assisted in the production of the book.

Abbreviations

6PT	Six-Party Talks
ABF	Asian Bond Fund
ABF2	Asian Bond Fund Initiative, second stage
AMF	Asian Monetary Fund
ANZCERTA	Australia New Zealand Closer Economic Relations Trade Agreement
APEC	Asia-Pacific Economic Cooperation
APT	ASEAN Plus Three
ARF	ASEAN Regional Forum
ASEAN	Association of Southeast Asian Nations
ASEAN PMC	ASEAN Post-Ministerial Conference
ASEM	Asia-Europe Meeting
ASPAC	Asia and Pacific Council
BSA	bilateral swap agreement
CSCAP	Council for Security Cooperation in the Asia Pacific
DMZ	demilitarized zone
EAEC	East Asian Economic Caucus
EAEG	East Asian Economic Grouping
EAS	East Asia Summit
EASG	East Asia Study Group
EAVG	East Asia Vision Group

ECA	Economic Cooperation Administration
EFTA	European Free Trade Association
EVSL	Early Voluntary Sectoral Liberalization
FDI	foreign direct investment
FTA	free trade agreement
GATT	General Agreement on Tariffs and Trade
IEA	International Energy Agency
IMF	International Monetary Fund
KEDO	Korean Peninsula Energy Development Organization
METI	Ministry of Economy, Trade, and Industry (Japan; formerly MITI)
MFN	most favored nation
MITI	Ministry of International Trade and Industry (Japan)
MOFA	Ministry of Foreign Affairs (Japan)
NAFTA	North American Free Trade Agreement
NATO	North Atlantic Treaty Organization
NMD	National Missile Defense
ODA	overseas development assistance
OECD	Organisation for Economic Co-operation and Development
PECC	Pacific Economic Cooperation Council
PRC	People's Republic of China
PTA	preferential trading agreement
ROK	Republic of Korea
SCO	Shanghai Cooperation Organization
SEATO	Southeast Asia Treaty Organization
UN	United Nations
USSR	Union of Soviet Socialist Republics
WTO	World Trade Organization

Notes on Foreign Names and Transliterations

A VARIETY OF ROMANIZATIONS are available for Chinese, Japanese, and Korean names. In this volume the following conventions will generally be employed.

Japanese names will be transliterated using a modified Hepburn *romaji* system that omits macrons and circumflexes for the sake of convenience.

Unless historical usage dictates otherwise, Mandarin Chinese names and transliterations will be rendered using the Pinyin system. Mandarin names will be parsed into two words (e.g., Hu Jintao). Some names with commonly accepted romanizations are excepted from this convention (e.g., Chiang Kai-shek).

There is no broadly accepted convention for the transliteration of Korean names, and such matters are usually left to the personal preference of the individual. For the sake of consistency, this volume will follow the convention of parsing Korean names into two words and hyphenating the given name (e.g., Kim Jong-il).

Exceptions to these rules are made in three cases: (1) when a contributor or scholar has manifested a clear preference in the transliteration of his or her own name (e.g., Cheng-Chwee Kuik); (2) when a widely recognized historical name follows conventions that differ from those employed by the editors of this book (e.g., Syngman Rhee); or (3) when there is another reasonable precedent for following alternative conventions.

Transliterations from other languages will follow the conventions established by individual chapter authors.

East Asian Multilateralism

Introduction

Kent E. Calder and Francis Fukuyama

OVER THE PAST GENERATION, East Asia has become increasingly afflu-
ent, industrialized, and economically integrated. Indeed, Japan, China,
and South Korea alone currently account for nearly 20 percent of global
GDP, or two-thirds that of the European Union.[1] And the ratio of their
trade to their GDP is nearly a third, compared to 70 percent in the European Union, 17 percent in the countries bound together by the North
American Free Trade Agreement, and 55 percent for the world as a whole.[2]

In other parts of the world, economic interdependence has typically
correlated strongly with formal transnational multilateral economic organization. That has paradoxically not been true in Northeast Asia. Despite
its high level of internal economic integration, East Asia has long suffered
from an "organization gap"—a paucity of multilateral organization, particularly formal organization—that is pronounced in comparison with the
situations in other global regions.[3] For example, in 2005 Europe participated in seven regional trade agreements, Latin America in five. East Asia,
by contrast, was part of only two, and both were limited to Southeast Asia.[4]
Northeast Asia had none at all.[5]

An East Asian organization gap, of course, has major implications for
the United States. It makes it harder for East Asians to convert their rising
economic influence into geopolitical power that could potentially chal-

lenge Washington, should they desire to do so. Yet the gap also complicates East Asian efforts to address common problems, increasing intraregional security tensions and threatening the possibility of financial chaos in the absence of stabilizing outside interventions.

The existence of a multilateral organization gap in East Asia, especially pronounced in the northeastern part of the continent, has important historical origins. No serious regionwide organization to speak of has existed since the collapse of the wartime Japanese Empire in 1945. In recent years, smoldering historical resentments have been fueled by populist nationalism. Urbanization and democratization have expanded the political area, even as patriotic education has intensified local consciousness of longstanding wrongs allegedly committed by neighboring states. The outcome has been a lamentably slow evolution of regional institutions. Whatever utility East Asian divisions once had in sustaining American Cold War influence in the region is now outweighed by the geopolitical dangers and the senseless obstacles to economic progress that rampant nationalistic rivalries have created.

Aside from presenting omnipresent dangers of nationalism and financial instability, East Asia's organization gap is inconvenient from a political-economic point of view because the region confronts unique capital-intensive developmental challenges. These challenges mandate a deeper net of regional organizations to neutralize geopolitical risk and simultaneously deal with common security and economic challenges. For example, most of the region's nations suffer from a severe shortage of readily accessible domestic energy reserves. They also confront inadequate transportation and communications infrastructure, as well as integrated regional capital markets that might harness the area's massive financial surpluses to the tasks of local regional development. Besides, needless to say, there are likewise dangers of nuclear proliferation, against which systematic regional cooperation is urgently needed.

Although a multilateral organization gap is currently a prominent characteristic of the East Asian regional political economy, seen from a comparative perspective, the region is by no means devoid of regional architecture per se. Indeed, a well-developed "hub-and-spokes" system of bilateral security relationships centering on Washington, D.C., was created in the early 1950s and continues to prevail. Some equivocal attempts to forge a broader multilateral system were made before then, yet the overall paucity of multilateral organization continues, and major supplements to the hub and spokes have emerged since. In the next few pages we will outline how these efforts to forge a broad Pacific regional architecture have progressed, what embedded heritage they have left for the future, and finally how a prospective further evolution of multilateralism in Asia might affect American interests.

The Tortured Course of Multilateralism in Asia

A perverse, hegemonic form of regional architecture existed from 1895 to 1945 in the form of the Japanese Empire. In 1895, Japan annexed Taiwan through the Treaty of Shimonoseki, beginning its course of regional conquest. In 1905, it added the southern half of Sakhalin and established a protectorate over Korea, which it annexed in 1910. After adding Manchuria in 1931 as the puppet protectorate of Manchukuo, Japan drove deep into China after 1937 and into Southeast Asia after 1940–41, amassing the Greater East Asia Co-Prosperity Sphere. In all, well over 30 million Asians—fewer than a tenth of them Japanese—died in these intermittent imperial wars, which severely inhibited economic growth across most of the region for more than half a century.

Following Japan's collapse in 1945, ending World War II, many of East Asia's boundaries remained ambiguous and bitterly disputed amid the turbulence of the early postwar transition. For example, days after the conflict had formally ended, in the last two weeks of August 1945, the Soviet Union abruptly occupied the southern Kurile Islands just north of Hokkaido, creating a "Northern Territories" dispute with Japan that continues to this day. Similarly, South Korea occupied the Takeshima/Tokdo Islets in the middle of the Sea of Japan, while U.S. forces based in Japan occupied the rocky Senkaku/Diaoyutai Islets in the East China Sea near Taiwan. All these island territories came to be disputed, with even their names a subject of controversy, giving birth to bitter, enduring conflicts within the region.

The United States had overwhelming political-military influence in Northeast Asia during the early postwar years, having vanquished the Japanese Empire and then occupied both Japan and South Korea. It was also, of course, the dominant global political-economic superpower, with a monopoly on nuclear weapons and a powerful economy that comprised nearly half of global GDP. Yet the United States, which clearly could have healed or suppressed most of the early postwar intra-Asian rivalries, made little attempt to do so.

The role of John Foster Dulles, U.S. Secretary of State Dean Acheson's special representative to the treaty negotiations, seems to have been especially crucial.[6] Dulles, determined not to turn defeated Japan into another embittered Weimar Germany, was the architect of a well-institutionalized

U.S.-Japan relationship that has persisted as the pillar of American interests in the Pacific to this day. His efforts with respect to intra-Asian issues were less vigorous and impressive.

The San Francisco Peace Treaty of September 1951, formally ending the war with Japan, resolved few of the deep, contentious territorial and political ambiguities left by the Japanese Empire's collapse. Korea became independent, of course, but its frontiers remained unclear. It was not represented at the conference, did not receive reparations for its 40 years of colonial occupation by Japan, and refused even to reestablish diplomatic relations with Tokyo until 1965. It did not establish relations with the Union of Soviet Socialist Republics (USSR) until 1990, or with China until 1992. Japan's ties with China and Russia, also fraught with political and territorial ambiguity, remained similarly unresolved for even longer.[7]

Dulles forced Japanese Prime Minister Shigeru Yoshida to recognize Taiwan as the legitimate government of China, and Japan did not recognize the People's Republic of China until October 1972. Japan normalized its relations with the USSR in 1956, but has not resolved its Northern Territories dispute with Russia to this day.

In the Cold War years, such divisions within Asia often worked demonstrably to America's benefit. They estranged rising Japan and South Korea, in particular, from old interlocutors on the continent, turned communist, which otherwise could have benefited from their technology and political-economic support. The intra-Asia divisions also inhibited the pan-Asianist sentiments that had been pronounced early in the century, and constrained any prospective conflictual tendencies that America's Northeast Asian allies might otherwise have had.[8]

To be sure, the hub-and-spokes system did give rise to some inconvenience for American diplomacy as occupation and colonial rule gave way to independence.[9] It accented the hierarchical nature of regional security affairs, in which all roads led to Washington, and inhibited the development of intraregional ties. For many new nations in Asia, such as India, Indonesia, Malaysia, and even Singapore, nominal nonalignment was preferable to formal asymmetric bilateral security ties with the United States.

Of course, vestiges of the Cold War remain. China and Korea remain divided across the Taiwan Straits and the demilitarized zone, respectively, although the shadows of reunification are lengthening in both cases as economic interdependence increases. Japan and Russia are estranged by the Northern Territories dispute, Japan and Korea by a dispute over the status of Takeshima/Tokdo in the Japan Sea / East Sea, and China and Japan by conflict in the East China Sea.[10] These conflicts and the underlying geostrategic anxieties that they reflect have inhibited the emergence of a cohesive East Asian regionalism. Such regionalism has a more substantive formal institutional history, however, than the conventional wisdom suggests, frequent American ambivalence notwithstanding.[11]

The Origins of East Asian Multilateralism

East Asia's postwar attempts to establish a formal regional architecture appear to have begun with the Pacific Pact discussions of 1949–51. The concept of such a pact was first broached in January 1949 by Philippine Foreign Secretary Carlos Romulo in New Delhi as a means of achieving diffuse pan-Asian political-economic agreement. In March 1949, just after the release of the text of the new North Atlantic Treaty Organization (NATO) agreement in Europe, in an effort to gain U.S. support, Philippine President Elpidio Quirino gave the pact concept a more explicitly military dimension, stressing the need for a Pacific defense agreement to fight communism in the Far East. China's Chiang Kai-shek and Korea's Syngman Rhee were favorably inclined, and India's Jawaharlal Nehru favored the general concept of Asian collective action, although he preferred an economically oriented Marshall Plan for Asia to Quirino's NATO-like conception.

The United States adopted a wait-and-see stance, but encouraged the Philippines to organize a union of other Asian nations, which was explored at the Baguio Conference of six key Asian nations in April 1950. Following the outbreak of the Korean War, the United States apparently considered the collective security concept implicit in the Pacific Pact and went so far as to have a draft pact prepared and internally discussed, but ultimately decided against the notion following the intervention of Chinese Peoples' Volunteers in the war. The Pentagon, sobered by the force of the Chinese intervention, felt that it could not ensure the defense of Hong Kong under any such collective defense pact, and the British, in turn, opposed the creation of any multilateral pact to which they were not a party, fearing that it would direct Chinese pressure against their Asian possessions, including Malaya and Singapore, as well as Hong Kong.

The Divisive Hand of Dulles

During the 1950s, the driving force for actually creating a Pacific regional architecture was clearly the United States. John Foster Dulles, author of the San Francisco Peace Treaty of 1951 before serving as President Dwight Eisenhower's secretary of state (1953–59), was a nephew of former president Woodrow Wilson's secretary of state, Robert Lansing, and had been a junior delegate at the Versailles Peace Conference of 1919, which had officially ended World War I. Because of his memories of the vindictive 1919 settlement against Germany, he strongly believed in the importance of a settlement that would do three things: (1) link Japan securely to the United States, (2) give it ample opportunity to prosper economically, and (3) leave lingering ambiguities in its relations with its neighbors that would reinforce Japan's dependence on the United States.

Dulles sowed ambiguity in Japan's relations with Northeast Asia through the San Francisco territorial settlement, as noted earlier. He linked Tokyo securely to the United States through the U.S.-Japan Mutual Security Treaty, signed at the Presidio in San Francisco within hours of the peace treaty itself. And he aided Japan's economic recovery through both ensuring access to the U.S. market and encouraging rapprochement with Southeast Asia through a series of U.S.-inspired reparation agreements between 1954 and 1963.[12]

Following a series of bilateral hub-and-spokes security arrangements between the United States and Australia, Japan, New Zealand, the Philippines, South Korea, South Vietnam, and Taiwan across the early and mid-1950s, the next concrete step in the formulation of a regional security architecture was the establishment of the Southeast Asia Treaty Organization (SEATO) in 1955. This collective security arrangement, with its secretariat in Bangkok, was intended to buttress the noncommunist nations of the region in the wake of the Indochina War. Along with the Philippines and Thailand (though not Japan due to its "no-war" constitution, which proscribed collective security arrangements), SEATO included Western powers, which undermined its broader legitimacy in Asia.

The Advance of Subregionalism

During the 1960s, one of the major themes of regional organization, apart from American efforts to maintain Cold War solidarity, was the attempt of Southeast Asian nations themselves to attain some regional coherence amid the continuing conflict in Vietnam. In 1961, the Association of Southeast Asia was initiated by Malaysia, followed by the Philippines and Thailand. This was succeeded in 1963 by Maphilindo, a loose confederation of the Malay peoples that included Indonesia in place of Thailand in an effort by Indonesia to forestall the creation of Malaysia.[13]

Maphilindo collapsed amid the "*konfrontasi*" against Malaysia that followed its establishment in 1963, but was superseded by an even more ambitious organization, the Association of Southeast Asian Nations (ASEAN), in 1967. ASEAN included Singapore and Thailand as well as the Maphilindo nations, and it served as a nonprovocative display of solidarity against communist expansion in Vietnam and against insurgency within the borders of its member nations. Tacitly supported by the United States but not including that nation, other Western powers, or controversial governments of Indochina, ASEAN had a relative neutrality that would sustain it across the turbulent decades that were to follow, reinforced by its cardinal principle of nonintervention in the internal affairs of members.[14] Its membership steadily expanded from the original five nations with the inclusion of Brunei (1984), Vietnam (1995), Laos and Myanmar (1997), and Cambodia (1999). Today its ten members have a population of well over 550 million people and a GDP in excess of U.S.$2 trillion.

There were also initiatives by Northeast Asia to add to a regional architecture that met with mixed success. In 1965, the Asian Development Bank, originally a Japanese initiative, was founded, but with its headquarters in Manila. The latter development was markedly contrary to the strong desires of the Japanese Finance Ministry, which had already selected a headquarters building in Tokyo. In 1966, Korean President Park Chung-hee initiated the Asia and Pacific Council (ASPAC) to unify Asia against the Chinese, but U.S. President Richard Nixon's visit to China fundamentally undermined its rationale, and ASPAC collapsed in 1974. The "Asia-Pacific Sphere of Cooperation," another Tokyo-inspired concept, was also a failure.

Non-American leaders in the Pacific fared better in establishing lower-profile policy networks than in trying to change the formal architecture of the region. The Pacific Basin Economic Council and the Pacific Economic Cooperation Council (PECC), composite business-government bodies with Track II functions,[15] were founded in 1967 and 1980, respectively; they have been relatively successful, with PECC admitted to formal observer status with the Asia-Pacific Economic Cooperation (APEC). The Pacific Trade and Development Conference, a transnational network of economists founded in 1968, has also played an important role in agenda-setting within subsequently founded regionwide organizations.[16]

APEC and Its Alternatives

An important watershed in the evolution of a regional architecture was the establishment of APEC in January 1989 on the initiative of Australia and Japan. The first APEC Leaders' Meeting was held in 1993, when U.S. President Bill Clinton, seeing an opportunity to bring the derailed Uruguay Round of trade talks back on track, invited the leaders of member economies to Blake Island, Washington. Since then, the pattern of annual regional summits has continued, but APEC has met with uneven success as a policy coordination and formulation body. The 1994 Bogor summit adopted an ambitious program of reducing tariffs to between 0 and 5 percent for member industrialized economies by 2010 and for developing economies by 2020, and the 1996 Subic Bay summit secured agreement to abolish most information industry tariffs. Yet many observers feel that APEC lost policy momentum in the latter half of the 1990s and has been notable mainly as a high-level networking forum.

Since 1990, the struggle to develop a regional architecture has been dominated by the effort, long spearheaded by former Malaysian Prime Minister Mohamad Mahathir, to establish a discrete intra-Asian organization not involving the United States. Mahathir proposed an East Asian Economic Grouping in 1990, but Indonesia, Japan, and other nations declined to endorse the concept, under strong pressure from the United States. Mahathir's notion resurfaced as the East Asian Economic Caucus concept in 1993, and the Asian Monetary Fund concept, a similar, albeit more specialized vehicle, was proposed by Japanese Vice Minister of Finance for International Affairs Eisuke Sakakibara during 1995–96. This notion, in the modified guise of an interlocking set of swap quota arrangements,[17] was finally realized in the Chiang Mai agreement of May 2000, with the Asian financial crisis of 1997–98 having served as a catalyst.

In December 2005, the first East Asia Summit was held, fittingly in Kuala Lumpur, Mahathir's capital, although he had retired as Malaysian prime minister in 2003. Although the summit's principals did not include an American representative, they did include leaders from Australia, India, and New Zealand, with Russian observers also present. Many questioned how much cohesion or ability to innovate such a diverse group might have in the future.

Functionalist Multilateralism

Although the development of a regional architecture has not progressed substantially at the macro level, as evidenced by the East Asia Summit, it has become denser and more effective in more specialized spheres. In finance, the May 2000 Chiang Mai Initiative established a bilateral swap agreement (BSA) network, to be installed by 2003. As of May 2006, the BSA network had already traded as high as $75 billion.[18] The ASEAN Plus Three summit mechanism,[19] established in 1997 (also at Kuala Lumpur), spearheaded the development of an Asian Bond Fund as well.[20] Routine consultations among regional ministers of finance and central bankers have also become common, reducing the future prospects of another Asian financial crisis like the traumatic one of 1997–98.

Specialized regional multilateral consultations are also becoming more common in the field of energy. The most dynamic body in the energy area appears to be the APEC Energy Caucus, chaired by Australia. Northeast

Asian think tanks are also meeting routinely to perform studies on the feasibility of regional energy infrastructure projects such as the building of pipelines and plants for the gasification of liquefied natural gas, as well as the most efficient applications of nuclear energy.

Minilateral organizations are also emerging, although they have a mixed track record. One of the most conspicuous has been the Korean Peninsula Energy Development Organization (KEDO), founded in 1995 by Japan, South Korea, and the United States to provide nuclear reactors and heavy fuel oil to North Korea in accordance with the Agreed Framework between the United States and the Democratic People's Republic of Korea, which ended the 1994 North Korean nuclear crisis. Although KEDO became largely inactive in 2006, following the termination of its light-water reactor project in North Korea, the model of mixed government and private sector multilateral interaction among a limited number of countries with respect to a narrowly focused problem will likely have further applicability in the future. Certainly the "six-party process," which during the period 2005–8 conducted negotiations on an end to the North Korean nuclear program, was well configured for broader intraregional policy coordination as well.

Across the half century and more since the Pacific Pact proposals inaugurated efforts toward Asian regional organization after World War II, the United States has almost always been an important element in the mix. It decisively shaped the San Francisco Peace Treaty of 1951 and the hub-and-spokes system of bilateral political-economic ties that flowed from it. During the Cold War, it saw the bilateralist structure and the continuing estrangement of Asian states from one another across the Cold War divide as the best guarantee of regional stability.

As we have seen, the United States has rarely been in the forefront of postwar multilateralist ventures in Asia. It did consider the Pacific Pact, but the notion was aborted by the Korean War. It backed SEATO and ASEAN in their early days, but expended little effort on their behalf. Multilateralist overtures, such as that represented by APEC itself, invariably came from elsewhere.[21]

Changing Imperatives?

Now the calculus has arguably changed. The Pacific and indeed the world have grown more interdependent economically and financially, necessitating much tighter political-economic coordination than has previously been the case. The volatility of global finance, along with Asia's crucial role in that context as the dominant global creditor, brings special urgency to the task. The clear dangers for financial stability of a Washington-centric hub-and-spokes configuration that lacks a clear conception of Asia's complexities have been manifested in the 1997 Asian financial crisis and in uncertainties a decade later relating to the unwinding of the yen carry trade.

New developments in energy markets have also arguably enhanced America's national interest in considering new, more multilateral frameworks at the regional as well as the global level. Asian nations, led by China, India, and Japan, are becoming some of the largest and most insistent consumers in global markets. China and India, in particular, have insufficient buffer stockpiles and remain outside global contingency planning regimes. Because they do not qualify, on nonenergy grounds, for membership in the Organisation for Economic Co-operation and Development (OECD),[22] the traditional prerequisite for membership in the International Energy Agency, other frameworks, possibly regional, will be needed to coordinate their collective consumer action in energy, as in finance, in the coming years.

Between mid-2005 and late 2007, the ongoing Six-Party Talks periodically taking place in Beijing on the North Korean nuclear issue showed the potential fruitfulness of this multilateral approach, together with some inherent limitations. In September 2005, the talks secured North Korea's agreement in principle to abandon its nuclear program. February 2007 brought an agreement to cease operations at the Yongbyon nuclear facility, and in October 2007 an understanding was reached on North Korea's dismantling its nuclear facilities in return for economic assistance, albeit one that left important ambiguities with respect to monitoring and implementation.

Security is a final area—arguably the most important—in which national interest clearly requires that the United States think more seriously about multilateral frameworks in Asia, even as it shows up prevailing bilateralist structures like the U.S.-Japan alliance. The troubling evolution of Pyongyang's nuclear program, culminating in the 2006 nuclear test, is only the most dramatic manifestation of the importance of this area. Developments in chemical and biological weaponry, missile proliferation, missile buildups, the emergence of active ballistic missile defense countermeasures, piracy, and drug smuggling all present urgent, deepening collective action challenges to Asian stability and prosperity, whose active multilateral management is made ever more urgent by rising interdependence.

The specter of geopolitical instability on the Korean peninsula, through scenarios ranging from a sudden collapse of a North Korea with ambiguous nuclear capacity to the outbreak of civil warfare there, continues, apparent progress in nuclear negotiations notwithstanding. Beyond the nuclear crisis itself, further creative thinking is needed, oriented toward collective multilateral action, on such issues as how to manage and then abolish North Korean nuclear capacity amid a national political transition, how to minimize the impact of prospective changes in Korea on Japan's security posture, and how to confront the implications of advancing missile technology for East Asian security. In the nascent Six-Party Talks, a process and interpersonal network for coping with Northeast Asia's dangerous organization gap are gradually being built. Yet the substantive policies that will animate this new soft multilateralism, and the institutions that will enable it to endure into the future, are yet to be fully conceptualized.

How have conditions changed since the early days of the hub and spokes? Do developments within Asia, in the shadow of the North Korean nuclear crisis, or with respect to America's role in the world now suggest an increasingly positive approach to multilateralism? If so, what form of such region-building will serve America's interests best? These are some of the pressing policy-relevant questions that we pursue in this book, after first reviewing the heritage of the past.

Notes

1. World Bank, *World Development Indicators,* available at http://devdata.world bank.org/. Figures are for 2005.
2. World Bank, *World Development Indicators,* available at http://devdata.world bank.org/ and Organisation for Economic Co-operation and Development (OECD), *OECD Statistics,* available at http://new.sourceoecd.org/. Figures are for 2004.
3. On the concept of the organization gap, see Kent Calder and Min Ye, "Regionalism and Critical Junctures: Explaining the 'Organization Gap' in Northeast Asia," *Journal of East Asian Studies* (Spring 2004): 191–226.
4. See Jo Ann Crawford and Roberto Fiorentino, "The Changing Landscape of Regional Trade Agreements," discussion paper, World Trade Organization, 2005, available at www.wto.org.
5. Ibid.
6. See Kent Calder, "Securing Security through Prosperity: The San Francisco System in Comparative Perspective," *Pacific Review* 17 (2004): 135–57.
7. Japanese Prime Minister Shigeru Yoshida was forced by John Foster Dulles to recognize Taiwan as the legitimate government of China, and Japan did not reestablish diplomatic relations with mainland China until October 1972. Japan established diplomatic relations with the USSR in 1956, but has not resolved its Northern Territories dispute with Russia to this day.
8. These were a concern of American commentators in the 1970s. See Zbigniew Brzezinski, *The Fragile Blossom: Crisis and Change in Japan* (New York: Harper and Row, 1972); Albert Axelbank, *Black Star over Japan: Rising Forces of Militarism* (New York: Hill and Wang, 1972); and Isaac Shapiro, "The Risen Sun: A Gaullist Japan?" *Foreign Policy* (Winter 1980–81): 62–68. On the complex early evolution of Japan's relationships with Taiwan and with mainland China, see John Dower, *Empire and Aftermath: Yoshida Shigeru and the Japanese*

Experience, 1878–1954 (Cambridge, Mass.: Council on East Asian Studies, Harvard University, 1979).

9. Burma, India, Indonesia, Japan, Korea, Pakistan, and the Philippines all recovered self-determination during the first decade after World War II.

10. On the latter issue, see Kent E. Calder, "China and Japan's Simmering Rivalry," *Foreign Affairs* (March–April 2006): 1–11.

11. Peter Katzenstein, for example, argues that East Asian regionalism is largely an agglomeration of informal personal networks, in contrast with a much more formal and legally based European pattern, and his general review remains highly influential. See Peter Katzenstein and Takashi Shiraishi, eds., *Network Power* (Ithaca, N.Y.: Cornell University Press, 1997).

12. See William S. Borden, *The Pacific Alliance: United States Foreign Economic Policy and Japanese Trade Recovery, 1947–1955* (Madison: University of Wisconsin Press, 1984).

13. Matthew Jones, *Conflict and Confrontation in Southeast Asia: Britain, the United States, and the Creation of Malaysia* (Cambridge: Cambridge University Press, 2002).

14. Amitav Acharya, "Ideas, Identity, and Institution-Building: From the ASEAN Way to the Asia-Pacific Way?" *Pacific Review* 10 (1997): 319–30.

15. "Track II" organizations are unofficial bodies, often think tanks, university research institutes, or informal assemblies of former officials and other specialists, who shadow the formal policy-making process and periodically provide input.

16. See Hugh Patrick, *From PAFTAD to APEC: Economists' Networks and Public Policymaking,* APEC Studies Center Discussion Paper 2, January (New York: Columbia University, 1997).

17. "Swap quotas" are ceilings for amounts of local currency that a government agrees to lend to a contractual partner (normally another government) for purposes of foreign exchange intervention.

18. Japan's Ministry of Finance Web site: www.mof.go.jp/jouhou/kokkin/cmi01 .htm.

19. ASEAN Plus Three is an Asian regional grouping including the ASEAN nations along with Japan, China, and South Korea.

20. Japan's Ministry of Foreign Affairs Web site: www.mofa.go.jp/mofaj/area/ asiakeizai/asean_3ci.html.

21. On the evolution of APEC, see John Ravenhill, *APEC and the Construction of Pacific Regionalism* (Cambridge: Cambridge University Press, 2001).

22. Article 2 of the OECD Convention requires that members liberalize capital movements, including restrictions on foreign direct and portfolio investment, conditions that China and India do not fully meet. See OECD, *Convention on the Organisation for Economic Co-operation and Development,* available at www.oecd.org.

Part I · Beyond the Hub and Spokes

CHAPTER 1

Critical Junctures and the Contours of Northeast Asian Regionalism

Kent E. Calder

TO UNDERSTAND THE FUTURE, insofar as it is humanly possible to do so, it is crucial to understand the forces that drive change in human affairs. Clearly, the future does not precisely replicate the past. Yet it must take as its point of departure the institutions and the perceptions it has inherited.

How and why patterns of regional organization *change* in Northeast Asia is the central concern of this chapter. It takes an eclectic historical approach to that subject, focusing on the periods of regional political-economic history since World War II that have been most important in generating distinctive patterns of Northeast Asian regional relationships. Most striking in cross-regional comparative terms have been (1) the pronounced "organization gap" in Northeast Asia, especially in the first 45 years after the Korean War; (2) its gradual erosion since then; and (3) the rising importance of multilateral institutions in regional organization. It is on this triad of historical dynamics that this chapter concentrates, with special attention to the balance of multilateral and bilateral structures that have emerged.

Central to my analysis is the notion of "critical juncture" as a key explanatory variable.[1] I argue that developments during climactic periods, often relatively brief, account for a large share of the variance in institutional structure over time. My hypothesis is that history moves *discontinuously*. Therefore, to understand prevailing institutional and policy profiles at any given point in time—both longitudinally and cross-regionally—it is productive to focus on the intensive political-economic interactions of the periods in which those patterns were born.

Theoretical Background of the Critical Juncture Framework

The critical juncture concept is not frequently employed in the study of regionalism. Yet a variant of the concept has frequently been productively applied to explain domestic institution-building. In particular, many seminal works on nation-building find national policies and leaders' choices at critical decision points crucial in determining the form and function of subsequent institutions.[2]

Crises reduce the incongruence between state structures and the domestic environment by ushering in structural change that is responsive to the environment. Yet during subsequent periods, institutions created to resolve the incongruence take on a life of their own. Institutional structures reproduce themselves without necessarily matching societal changes, leading to increased tensions that eventually precipitate further crises. This dualism of change and continuity is crucial in understanding the significance of crisis-created critical junctures in political development.

Without rejecting alternative formulations, the critical juncture framework explains many dynamics and consequences of regional political development. Domestic institutions are the product of interactions among interests groups, organizations, administrative branches, and even individual leaders, undertaken in an effort to tackle common crises. Regional cooperation is therefore the product of dynamic interactions among countries with different interests and resources that are seeking to solve emergent common problems or to fill a power vacuum.

Key Features of the Critical Juncture Model

A critical juncture can be defined as a historical decision point at which there are clear alternative paths to the future. Specifically, for a decision point to be a critical juncture, certain defining features are both necessary and sufficient:

- There is usually a *crisis* that calls the legitimacy of current arrangements into serious question. A crisis can be strategic, economic, or a mixture of the two. Examples include the Cuban missile crisis of 1962, the breakdown of the Bretton Woods system in 1971, the oil shocks of 1973 and 1979, the collapse of Soviet satellites in Eastern Europe in

1989, the collapse of the Soviet Union itself in 1991, and the Asian financial crisis of 1997.

- Crisis breeds *stimulus for change.* It also generates a parallel need for collective action to address a *common problem,* although it may take a substantial period of time for full resolution to occur.
- There is intense *time pressure* on the parties involved. Such time pressure makes interactions hard to routinize and constrains the time available to search out options. As a result, decision making is conducted under severely bounded rationality. As the concept of the "fog of war" suggests, decision makers are forced into sudden, high-stakes decisions under extreme circumstances, often with remarkably little information given the consequences of their actions.[3]

Players at critical junctures are the individual *leaders* in charge of problem solving during and in the immediate wake of crises. They can be, but need not be, heads of government. When the Korean War erupted, U.S. State Department adviser John Foster Dulles was the key player in negotiating with Japan and other countries to secure regional arrangements across Asia in the context of a World War II peace settlement. Prime Minister Shigeru Yoshida of Japan and President Syngman Rhee of Korea were also major players at the critical juncture leading to a settlement, but they were less influential than Dulles. In confronting the Asian financial crisis of 1997, the respective heads of state of the affected countries themselves, rather than any advisers, were the driving force in launching policy initiatives.[4] The locus of decision-making power and of potential leadership thus varies with decision-making circumstances. Yet *leadership* of some sort is crucial.

The Link between Critical Junctures and East Asia's Profile of Regionalism

Answers to three key questions are crucial to understanding the current profile of East Asian regionalism, or indeed regionalism more generally: (1) What accounts for the organization gap—that is, for the lack of regional organizations, despite a manifest need for coordination? (2) What accounts for the modest profile of international organization, both bilateral and to some extent multilateral, that has emerged? (3) What accounts for the rising salience of multilateral organizations in East Asia?

These are the questions that this chapter addresses. It does so through a central focus on two critical junctures: (1) the period of the Korean War (1950–53), which aborted budding support for a multilateral Pacific Pact concept and gave birth to a bilateralist "San Francisco System," and (2) the crucial three years following the Asian financial crisis (1998–2000). These junctures, together with the one that led to the founding of the Asian Development Bank, have been the *only* instances of clear success in Pacific regional institution-building since World War II. Twenty other such junctures, including those that gave rise to the Asian Pacific Economic Community, the Association of Southeast Asian Nations (ASEAN) Regional Forum, and the Southeast Asia Treaty Organization, have either abjectly failed or succeeded only modestly.

The Korean War Origins of the Organization Gap

In accounting for the East Asian organization gap it is crucial to understand the tumultuous circumstances under which the system of international relations that emerged in the Pacific after World War II was initially forged. In the process one needs to look into the black box of national decision making to examine how the nations of the Pacific responded, and thus how Northeast Asia's distinctive profile of regionalism actually came to be. Two regionalist concepts in particular emerged shortly after the fall of China in 1949 and were fatefully refashioned by the ensuing critical juncture initiated by the Korean War: the Pacific Pact and the San Francisco System.

The Pacific Pact concept was originally an Asian collective security notion conceived by America's anti-communist Asian allies to cushion the regional impact of the Chinese Civil War of 1946–49. It was first presented formally by Philippine Foreign Minister Carlos Romulo at the New Delhi conference on Indonesia in January 1949 and conceived as a league of Asian nations working to promote mutual economic as well as security interests under U.S. auspices, with a small permanent secretariat.[5] Prime Minister Jawaharlal Nehru of India, however, opposed such a grouping. World opinion, he argued, could easily interpret it as anti-West.[6]

Later in 1949, following the establishment of the North Atlantic Treaty Organization (NATO), as the prospect of revolutionary triumph on the Chinese mainland grew stronger and stronger, the Pacific Pact idea became a vehicle for containing China. The strongest early proponents were the Philippines, South Korea, and Taiwan. The notion was of a multilateral military alliance, analogous to NATO, centering on the United States and directed toward containing a revolutionary and prospectively militant People's Republic.

The San Francisco System was an alternative architecture for the regional security of the United States and its Pacific allies. Like the Pacific Pact notion, it was developed during 1950–51 in the wake of the fall of China. Following China's late 1950 intervention in the Korean War, it gained particular currency as a second-best alternative to the Pacific Pact concept as a means of coping with practical political difficulties in realizing the Pacific Pact and of stably incorporating a post-occupation Japan into the Pacific order of international affairs.

The San Francisco System idea abandoned multilateralism. It conceptualized Pacific security as a series of "spokes"—American bilateral understandings with various Pacific allies—radiating out from the hub of Washington, D.C. The system, as fashioned by U.S. diplomat John Foster Dulles, had four basic traits:[7]

1. A dense network of *formal bilateral security alliances,* including U.S. mutual security treaties with Australia–New Zealand (July 1951), the Philippines (August 1951), Japan (September 1951), South Korea (November 1954), and the Republic of China or Taiwan (December 1954).
2. U.S. *military basing rights* throughout the region.
3. Relatively *limited reconstruction aid* compared to that given Western Europe.
4. Gradual integration of allied economies on *preferential terms* into the bilateral-internationalist *trade and financial order* fostered by the United States.

In contrast to the architecture of the Pacific Pact concept, that of the San Francisco System thus included an explicit economic dimension.

Ultimately, a Korean War critical juncture played a central role in both the failure of the Pacific Pact and the establishment in its place of the "second-best" San Francisco System.[8] Through these dual developments the profile of regional organization in the region was established and perpetuated for the balance of five decades. In exploring the process of stabilization, one can also test the theoretical framework of critical junctures.

The Momentous Early Postwar Years

August 1945, of course, brought the end of World War II in the Pacific, and with it the Japanese Co-Prosperity Sphere. Globally, the cessation of hostilities with the Axis powers led rapidly to the Cold War. In Asia, as Akira Iriye suggests, this transition produced what might be called a "Yalta system of international relations": a condominium of U.S. and Soviet power,[9] established at the Yalta conference of February 1945 among Britain, the Soviet Union, and the United States, in which China's role was fundamentally ambiguous.

By the end of 1949, after an epic struggle, the People's Liberation Army was triumphant on the Chinese mainland, sending shock waves across both Northeast Asia and the broader world. At the regional level, the Yalta system of fragile East-West entente in the Pacific, contrasting with still more confrontational politics in Europe, stood at a delicate crossroads. For America and its allies, there was also, to be sure, some vacillation as to the appropriate parameters of their future defense line. U.S. Secretary of State Dean Acheson, for example, famously excluded Korea in a fateful statement that apparently convinced both Stalin and Kim Il-sung that a U.S. intervention in response to a North Korean attack would be unlikely.[10]

There was considerable diplomatic maneuvering on relations with China. Britain actually recognized the People's Republic of China (PRC), Japan wanted to do so, and American diplomats and politicians were divided. Yet the likelihood of escalating future tensions with China was a matter of broad agreement in the American foreign policy community; the major question was the *form* that the U.S. response should take. The Pacific, in short, lay at the cusp of a critical juncture.

At this crucial turning point between the "fall of China" in late 1949 and major Chinese intervention in the Korean War a year later, many key decision makers in both the United States and allied Pacific nations seriously considered the concept of the multilateral Pacific Pact. For the smaller allies, such as the Philippines, South Korea, and, of course, Chiang Kai-shek's Taiwan, which were among the earliest and most vociferous backers, a Pacific Pact afforded both assurance of American support against the newly emerging Chinese communist colossus and more leverage with the United States than a purely bilateral relationship might provide. For the United States itself, a multilateral Pacific Pact could potentially provide diplomatic advantages superior to those of unilateralism or bilateralism, although the relative weakness of Pacific allies made multilateralism less attractive in Asia than in Europe.

The Pacific Pact concept was first broached in January 1949 by Philippine Foreign Secretary Romulo in New Delhi as a diffuse pan-Asian political economic conception. On March 21, 1949, just three days after the text of NATO was released, Philippine President Elpidio Quirino gave the Pacific Pact concept a more explicitly military dimension in an effort to gain U.S. support. Citing NATO and U.S. leadership in Europe as precedents, Quirino advocated the formation of a similar Pacific defense pact to fight communism in the Far East.[11] Several influential American commentators, including Harold Noble in the *Saturday Evening Post* and Daniel Poling in *Look* magazine, took up the cause.[12]

During the summer of 1949, as the People's Liberation Army surged across the Yangtze into South China and toward victory, there was a flurry of diplomatic activity in Asia in support of the pact. In July, Chiang Kai-shek met with Quirino of the Philippines to discuss it, and the Chinese

Nationalist Cabinet in Canton supported the concept,[13] immediately drawing a vitriolic response from Radio Beijing. Australia was also actively promoting the idea.[14] In August, Generalissimo Chiang went to Chinhae, on the southern coast of Korea, for a meeting with President Syngman Rhee to discuss the pact. Nehru, although he opposed the pact, called for collective action in the form of a Marshall Plan for Asia.

During 1949 the U.S. government adopted a wait-and-see approach both to the pact and to China policy, as epitomized in the State Department's white paper on China, published in August 1949. Yet as the new PRC government adopted an increasingly anti-American stance, U.S. interest in more formalized collective security in the Pacific gradually increased. In January 1950, U.S. Ambassador-at-Large Philip Jessup gave assurances during a Manila visit of America's sympathy with any efforts by the Philippines to organize a union of other Asian nations to "preserve the democratic way of life."[15] In April 1950, encouraged by this American show of support, the Philippines hosted six key nations in a discussion of regional cooperation at the Baguio Conference.[16]

The Emergence of Critical Juncture

Two months later, in June 1950, North Korean forces burst across the 38th parallel, drastically altering the Asian security equation and inaugurating a historic critical juncture for the region. The Pacific Pact notion continued to be considered, albeit in a different light, as the crisis on the Korean peninsula deepened. Within the U.S. government, a complete Pacific Pact was drafted in early 1951 and seriously discussed.[17] In the draft the United States stipulated that such a multilateral security arrangement would be terminated only if the United Nations adequately covered the area or a broader, more formal framework was created into which the Pacific Pact could be merged.[18] Clearly, the United States was groping for a viable Pacific collective security concept, and it was evidently willing to explore a multilateral formulation.

Dulles's fateful Pacific trip in January and February 1951, however, was undertaken in an extremely delicate period of U.S. Pacific diplomacy. Washington had just been traumatized by the intervention of close to 300,000 People's Liberation Army "volunteers" in Korea. That sudden attack trapped more than 150,000 UN troops, many of them American, on the frozen battlefields of North Korea just after Thanksgiving 1950.

When Chinese troops entered the fighting in the fall of 1950, there were even more intense calls for Japan to embrace neutralism and distance itself from the United States.[19] As U.S. policy makers fully realized, oppo-

nents of the pro-American Yoshida conservatives were using Japan's formal lack of sovereignty as a vehicle for attacking the U.S.-Japan relationship from both the left and the right. This situation made every escalation
of the Korean War a more compelling reason for the United States to conclude an early peace treaty with Japan, which it had tentatively decided to
do in September 1950.[20]

As Dulles embarked on his Pacific tour in January 1951, he wanted,
above all, a *rapid* resolution to the broad range of troubling geopolitical
uncertainties across the region. These were ever more deeply linked to one
another—and rendered more urgent—by both the conflict in Korea and
the related imperative of peace with Japan. Both developments mandated
the creation of a credible Pacific security framework as rapidly as possible.
The time pressures were overwhelming and helped create the bias toward
bilateralism that finally emerged in the wake of the Korean War.

Toward a Second-Best Solution:
How Bilateralism Actually Emerged

A detailed empirical examination of critical junctures and their consequences needs to begin with a heuristic test: that of the historic origins
of the Northeast Asian organization gap in the tumultuous early period of
the Korean War. This was when the idea of the multilateral Pacific Pact
failed and the bilateralist San Francisco System of international relations
in the Pacific fitfully emerged. To a remarkable degree, the San Francisco
System has persisted to this day.

Looking at the preferences of countries involved in the postwar negotiation of a peace settlement in Asia, it is clear that indeterminate prediction and bilateralism were decidedly not the best options for the parties
involved, as suggested in Table 1.1.[21] Between the Chinese Revolution of
1949 and the Chinese intervention in the Korean War late in 1950, as noted
earlier, Japan seems to have preferred a multilateral security arrangement
in East Asia to a narrowly bilateral one, and the U.S. State Department, the
principal American actor, also found multilateralism congenial. Other important American allies in Asia likewise applauded the idea of a multilateral Pacific Pact, driven by simultaneous uncertainties regarding the political futures of both China and Japan.

The critical juncture of the Korean War fundamentally transformed
the equation, most importantly by introducing the Pentagon as a central
policy actor. American military leaders were most immediately concerned
about untrammeled U.S. access to bases in Japan. They saw a bilateral

Table 1.1 The Second-Best San Francisco System: Preference Structure during the Korean War, 1950–1951

United States	Multilateralism >	Bilateralism >	No treaty
Australia	Multilateralism >	Bilateralism >	No treaty
Britain	Bilateralism >	Multilateralism >	No treaty
Japan	Multilateralism >	Bilateralism >	No treaty
South Korea	Multilateralism >	Bilateralism >	No treaty
Taiwan	Multilateralism >	Bilateralism >	No treaty

Source: Michael Schaller, "Japan and the United States Reconsidered," available at www .econstrat.org.

Note: > indicates preference ordering, with declining preferences from left to right.

understanding with Japan on bases as a high priority and were not convinced that a multilateral regional security pact would be either necessary or sufficient to achieve such an understanding.

In the shadow of Chinese intervention in the Korean War, the Pentagon also feared the thorny collective security issues that multilateralism in Asia raised, such as a prospective defense of British Hong Kong against China, which the sudden surge of People's Volunteers across the Yalu had transformed into a disturbingly real possibility. In addition, multilateralism in the Pacific offered few concrete military dividends in reinforcing U.S. political ties across Asia, however attractive it might have been diplomatically. Any potential Asian allies were simply too weak, and too vulnerable to mainland Chinese pressure, to offer much tangible military support. While the diplomatic calculus arguably outweighed the military before the onset of war, the tables were turned as the conflict in Korea deepened.

The British opposed the concept of U.S.-led Pacific multilateralism on many grounds, especially after the Chinese People's Volunteers crossed the Yalu. The United Kingdom was moved, most importantly, by the troubling prospect that a U.S.-led Pacific Pact would exclude Hong Kong from security guarantees. The British were understandably reluctant to see the emergence of a pact that either excluded them or failed to provide such guarantees. They felt that the omission would undermine the security of not only Hong Kong, but also their other colonial possessions in the region, such as Malaya, Sarawak-Brunei, and Singapore.[22]

In the face of the complex counterpressures outlined earlier, which came to a head in late January 1951, the United States retreated from the Pacific Pact concept. As late as August 1952, both the Philippines and South Korea were still enthusiastically promoting the idea, and the Truman administration, sensitive to political accusations that it treated Asians as "second-class expendibles," was publicly continuing to entertain it as a possibility.[23] However, serious momentum had been interrupted by the stark imperatives of war 18 months earlier.

As the process outline presented here so clearly illustrates, the bilateralist San Francisco System, with its enduring legacy of a Northeast Asian organization gap, was the product neither of geopolitical power alone nor of preexisting institutions nor of collective identity. *Process* played a subtle yet crucial role that less empirically grounded analysis has unfortunately ignored.[24] To be sure, power, institutional environment, and identity influenced the interests and preferences, both conscious and intersubjective, of the parties to negotiation—namely, the United States and its allies.

Neither interests nor preferences nor identity alone, however, shaped the key actors' ultimate decisions. The interests and preferences of the key nations involved were ultimately refashioned in a critical juncture created by the Korean War. During the first traumatic year of the Korean conflict the structure and rules of the bargaining games among the United States, Japan, and other major nations in the Pacific were profoundly transformed as the critical calculus shifted from diplomatic to military and early prospects for multilateralism were destroyed.

Fighting Financial Dangers: Asian Crisis and Regional Integration

The critical juncture of the Korean War, as just discussed, crucially shaped the political-economic profile of Pacific relations during the early years after World War II. It created a bilateralist "hub-and-spokes" framework, with Washington as the hub; a complementary network of bilaterally oriented economic ties; and, within Northeast Asia itself, an organization gap involving virtually no multilateralist dimension, which persisted for a remarkably long time. Only momentous developments at the global level in the 1980s and 1990s, driven in part by economic globalization, had any serious impact on this durable bilateralist structure.

Three driving forces have begun to encourage regional integration with a multilateralist bias in recent years, moving beyond the Washington-centric hub and spokes. Those forces are (1) *local economic pressures;* (2) *leverage seeking,* especially by developing countries frustrated with American unilateralism and the market fundamentalism of institutions like the International Monetary Fund; and (3) *counter-regionalism.* Developing economies, including those of Asia, have become anxious to consolidate their own cohesion as a counterweight to the growing unity of both Europe and the Americas.

These broad global forces, simultaneously facilitating regional integration due to strong intraregional complementarities, were greatly enhanced in Asia by the 1997 financial crisis, just as they had been in Latin America by earlier regional financial earthquakes. Clearly, Asia's financial crisis was a watershed in the economic growth and the political mentality of the region. The stinging affront that it presented to nations long used to economic success, which collectively hold two-thirds of the total foreign exchange reserves on earth, was a particular stimulus to new regionalist approaches. To ensure the broadest possible cooperation, these approaches tended to be multilateral.

The crisis, with all its trauma, galvanized national governments to action. It also spurred a growing realization among both political and business leaders in Northeast Asia of the need for formal mechanisms to cope with similar crises in the future.[25] It provided, in short, a catalyst for major change. In contrast to the Korean War crisis, this catalyst produced momentum for *intraregional* organization to make Asia more independent of Washington.

The significance of the 1997 financial crisis as a critical juncture can be clearly demonstrated through a brief survey of regionalism before the crisis. As the next section shows, before 1997 the countries of Asia had been, at most, bound together in a rather loose, network-style, open regionalism. To be sure, there had been efforts—many of them quite determined and persistent—to achieve greater cohesion, including cohesion independent of the United States. Yet most attempts to establish formal multilateral institutions in the region had nevertheless failed, with the exception of the one that resulted in the formation of the Asian Development Bank (1966). Even this institution, however, was the product of unusual circumstances: a conducive regional and international environment (including close collaboration between Japan and the United States) and a critical juncture at the onset of the Vietnam War.

Pre-Crisis Regionalism in Asia

Compared to the dynamic economic growth and market-oriented trading relations that prevail across most of Asia, the weakness of formal intraregional institutions is striking. Time and again since the 1950s, attempts by Japan, South Korea, and others to promote multilateralism have experienced a series of false starts. Only when critical junctures have been present have multilateral arrangements emerged that have shown substantial subsequent promise.

During the 1950s, the San Francisco System of asymmetric trans-Pacific political-economic relations, established as a result of the Korean War critical juncture, perpetuated the old hub-and-spokes relationships between the United States and its Asian allies. Bilateralism prevailed, and for three decades multilateralist initiatives produced little more than "minimal open regionalism"—a shallow form of integration involving only limited institutional development. The most elaborate manifestation of this pattern was the Asia-Pacific Economic Cooperation (APEC), which began evolving only in the late 1980s.[26]

Some actors, especially in Japan, have wanted to see a richer multilateralist structure. During the early 1960s, the Japan Economic Research Center served as an active forum for discussions of regional integration that brought Japanese scholars and officials together with representatives from the Australia, Canada, New Zealand, and the United States. Subsequently, Saburo Okita, later Japan's foreign minister, articulated the superficially promising concept of Pacific Economic Cooperation (PEC). Okita proposed annual meetings among representatives of these five countries to discuss economic, cultural, and other issues of common concern. Yet this Japanese initiative, like virtually all Japanese proposals of this era apart from that of the Asian Development Bank (1966), never went anywhere. Neither did multilateralist initiatives proposed by South Korea (the Asia and Pacific Council, 1966) and Thailand (Western Pacific Economic Cooperation, 1988).

Gradually, proposals for Asian multilateralism did achieve some modest successes, albeit only those that *included* the United States. In 1989, responding to an initiative from Prime Minister Robert Hawke of Australia, APEC was created. This broad regional grouping originally brought together governmental and nongovernmental representatives from Japan, the United States, Canada, the Republic of Korea, Australia, New Zealand, and the five member states of ASEAN.[27] The PRC, Hong Kong, and Taiwan joined in 1992; Mexico and Papua New Guinea in 1993; and Chile in 1994.

With a budget of only U.S.$2 million and a small secretariat located in Singapore, however, APEC has only limited administrative capacity even today, relying mostly on technical working groups. It also has the fateful political drawback, during China's "peaceful rise," of including Taiwan (in the guise of "Chinese Taipei") as a member. This atavistic reality, which Beijing reluctantly agreed to in its days of diplomatic vulnerability during the early 1990s, recently caused the PRC to devalue APEC as a serious vehicle for regional integration.

Since 1993, APEC has held annual national leaders' summits that have given it prominence as a high-level networking mechanism. Yet it remains a purely consultative forum bounded by the constraints of routine consensus decision making, despite persistent business pressure for deeper integration.[28] At times it has had greater aspirations, with the United States among its most enthusiastic backers.[29] In the years to come, APEC may well remain a meaningful forum for debating trade and investment liberalization, but it will not be a forum for operationalizing actual economic integration unless it is reshaped in the grip of a fateful critical juncture.

In contrast to the proposal for APEC, proposals for smaller and more exclusively Asian organizations failed miserably in the decade prior to the 1997 Asian financial crisis. In the late 1980s, the East Asian Economic Grouping (EAEG) was first proposed by Prime Minister Mohamad Mahathir of Malaysia at the time of a seemingly faltering global Uruguay Round. From the outset, Mahathir's regionalist proposal was attacked by the United States, which was not to be included in Mahathir's design. Japan proved reluctant and wary of antagonism from Washington, indicating that it would wait for an ASEAN decision before clarifying its stance. And Indonesia, the largest member of ASEAN, was cool to Mahathir's controversial idea.

In sharp contrast to its 1991 hesitation to enter the proposed EAEG, Japan itself conceived an even more controversial multilateral proposal for an Asian Monetary Fund (AMF) shortly before the onset of full-scale financial crisis in 1997.[30] The AMF was officially proposed at the Group of 7 International Monetary Fund (IMF) meetings in Hong Kong in September 1997, with Japan offering to create a U.S.$100 billion fund to stabilize exchange rates in Asia. Japan differed sharply with U.S. views about curtailing the financial crisis, reflecting Japan's deep frustration with the IMF. If realized, the AMF would have allowed Japan to shape policy outcomes more effectively, in line with its preferences toward easy credit and looser conditionality. Additionally, the AMF could have helped provide a greater headline figure for the bailout package, thus helping to calm markets and to disburse funds more flexibly.

In fact, the AMF received a warm initial reception in virtually every Southeast Asian capital. Taiwan and South Korea were also favorably disposed.[31] The United States, however, strongly opposed the plan, and lobbied China to oppose it as well, invoking the specter of "Japanese hegemony."

Ultimately, the AMF proposal was rejected, despite support from ASEAN and South Korea. In place of the ambitious AMF draft came a substantially downgraded "Manila Framework," which quietly dropped the AMF's most controversial features.

In sum, there were clear multilateralist aspirations in Asia before the 1997 Asian financial crisis, but they were loosely structured and lacked many binding commitments. One assumption implicit in the region has long been that regional endeavors should be subordinate to national interests and independence.[32] Supranational authorities of the European pattern have never been accepted.

Relations with the United States have also been an inhibiting factor, particularly for Japan, itself a potential leader of a regionalist movement. Asian countries have responded to the complex mélange of crosscutting interests by supporting "soft" institutional proposals. Those proposals have both lacked binding formal rules and failed to exclude non-Asian nations and interests, even when those diverged from the concerns of Asian parties themselves.

All these assumptions and structures were challenged during the Asian financial crisis. The following section recounts how the crisis occurred, how it affected the Asian countries, and how it forced them to act together in the common interest. Only through such a crisis, at a critical juncture in their development, were they able to achieve the cohesion necessary to stabilize their region in the face of the financial hurricanes gusting across the globe.

Coming Closer to Crisis

Since the early 1970s, the Asian nations have grown more integrated with one another economically. Despite their lack of political ties, a quiet engine of change has incessantly corroded the long-immutable hub-and-spokes bilateralist order: the power of global finance. Two forces have been at work: finance itself has been changing profoundly, and Asia's role in that arcane but crucial world has been changing as well.

By 1997 as much as U.S.$2 trillion in transactions daily was surging across the financial markets of the world, exerting intense pressure on governments and corporations even under routine circumstances. The volatility of global financial flows had already provoked the Latin American debt crisis of 1982, the European exchange rate crisis of 1992–93, and the Mexican foreign debt crisis of 1994–95. Yet Asia had lain remarkably unscathed until the summer of 1997.

Due to an apparently benign macroeconomic environment, capital flowed into Asia in massive amounts in the early 1990s. In Thailand, for example, average capital inflows averaged 10.3 percent of GDP throughout 1990–96. Confident that the future looked bright, Asian firms borrowed heavily in risky dollar-denominated short-term capital markets because interest rates were lower there.

By September 1997, for example, South Korea owed foreign banks more than U.S.$114 billion, of which nearly $78 billion was short-term debt. Korea's own foreign exchange reserves were only $31 billion, or barely a quarter of the debt outstanding. Indonesia and Thailand were in similar circumstances. Much of the dollar lending was to finance real estate and other projects denominated in local currency, exposing the borrowers to foreign exchange risk. As is well known, the international claims by foreign banks from 1995 to 1997 represented massive potential risk to the region.

Reaping the Whirlwind: The Coming of Critical Juncture

Thailand's decision to float the baht on July 2, 1997, aroused a storm that almost no one, even those most specialized in Asian finance, anticipated. On the first day of the float, the baht fell 15 percent. Within a month it had lost 40 percent of its value, and in another two months it had fallen a further 20 percent. Before long, all the Southeast Asian countries and Korea were in the throes of a historic international monetary crisis. Within a year, the exchange rates of Indonesia, Korea, Malaysia, the Philippines, Singapore, and Thailand had dropped massively against the U.S. dollar, making the massive dollar-denominated foreign debts difficult to repay and spurring fears of contagion.

American hesitance to go to Thailand's aid, despite Washington's political-military standing at the hub of the bilateralist order, also emboldened hedge funds and other speculative investors. They saw clearly the broad currency misalignments across the region and the general lack of political will to defend the status quo. When Indonesia was forced to devalue its currency in August 1997, responding to pressure from international funds, speculation began against Korea, whose banks were heavily invested in Indonesia and which was itself heavily leveraged. The February 1997 collapse of the Hanbo Group—the first of 8 of Korea's top 30 *chaebol* to fail by December 1998—and Korea's rising current account deficit indicated that it might be vulnerable as well. There was clearly blood in the water.

A sharp 9 percent drop in Hong Kong's Hang Seng index on October 20, followed overnight by the largest point fall ever in New York's Dow Jones average,[33] stoked fears in Washington and among leaders throughout Asia that the Southeast Asian crisis might well become global. Now etched in history and in the consciousness of a generation of Asians are the events of the following months—a capital outflow of U.S.$12 billion from Asia as a whole during 1997; a collapse of the Korean won, which lost 60 percent of its value in six months, leading to a massive Korean financial crisis and a humiliating $57 billion IMF bailout package; and the downgrading of Indonesian, Korean, and Thai sovereign debt to junk bond status by Moody's.[34]

Japan and China, although less directly touched by the crisis than their neighbors, also felt its trauma. Despite Japan's position as a long-standing U.S. ally, with the largest foreign exchange reserves on earth and a GDP comprising 15 percent of the global total, it was summarily lectured by U.S. financial officials and its proposal for an AMF rejected, as noted earlier. With Asia taking over 35 percent of its exports—significantly more than the United States—Japan also suffered economically from the macroeconomic downturn that followed the crisis.[35]

China's Move toward Multilateralism

China, while siding with the United States in rebutting Japan's AMF initiative, also slowly began to see the substantial dangers of the emerging regional financial disaster. For example, it provided U.S.$1 billion of the Thai support package proffered in August 1997—$1 billion more than the United States—although its delegation was not able to announce its contribution before consulting with Beijing after the meeting of the support group.[36] This was the first time that China had made a substantial contribution to a country hit by a currency crisis, and in this sense it represented the country's debut in international currency crisis diplomacy.

China's policies further evolved in the direction of intra-Asian financial cooperation during 1998. That year, at the Hanoi meeting of the leaders of ASEAN Plus Three,[37] with the region still deep in the shadow of the financial crisis, China proposed that central bank governors and the deputies of finance ministers throughout the region meet regularly to explore possibilities for further multilateral cooperation. At the Manila leaders' meeting in 1999, Prime Minister Zhu Rongji himself played a leading role, together with Japanese Prime Minister Obuchi Keizo, in finalizing the currency-swap quota arrangement that led to the historic May 2000 Chiang Mai agreement.[38]

In addition to actively participating in cooperative financial initiatives in the region, China was also growing more responsive to Southeast Asian security concerns. On July 27, 1999, China signed the Southeast Asia Nuclear Weapon Free Zone treaty and concluded the Treaty of Amity and Co-operation with Southeast Asia. For several years, ASEAN had been trying to persuade nuclear powers to accede to the protocol, so China's gesture was welcomed by these nations. China also became more conciliatory in its dealings with ASEAN on South China Sea maritime issues.

China's gradual historic move toward multilateralism was thus driven by a complex mixture of four different motives, all related to the critical juncture of the Asian financial crisis:

1. *A deepened sense of its own vulnerability to international monetary developments.* Between 1982 and 1997, Chinese foreign debt had risen five-fold, to U.S.$10 billion, excluding foreign direct investment and bonds.[39] China had also assumed responsibility for a global financial center with the July 1997 reversion of Hong Kong.
2. *A rising sense of its own long-term economic sustainability and diplomatic strength.* By the latter part of 1998, it was clear that the Chinese economy itself had successfully weathered the crisis, although vulnerabilities remained in the region as a whole.
3. *Its perception of competitive dynamics within the region.* While Beijing undoubtedly felt empowered by the events of 1997–98, as suggested earlier, it was also stirred by defensive impulses, particularly in the face of initiatives from Tokyo.
4. *Its deepening intraregional networks in international finance, particularly with Japan and Korea.*

Collectively, these four motives, all flowing from a critical juncture, catalyzed a major transformation in China's relationships with Asia. Before the crisis, China had tended to pursue a narrow, mercantilist definition of national economic interest that was destabilizing to the broader region, as manifested in the 1994 devaluation of the renminbi. This tendency evolved, in the heat of the financial crisis, into a broader and more mature sense of responsibility—not only for China's own growth, but for regional stability as a whole.

By early 1999, Asia had begun to leave its financial crisis behind. In Korea, which led Asia out of the crisis, GDP growth surged to 10.9 percent in 1999 and 8.8 percent in 2000, driven by both consumer spending and heavy new foreign investment.[40] Yet the scars of the crisis remained, and it was all the more traumatic because it had been unexpected and, in the view of many Asians, unjustified.

Given the intense, plausible fear of renminbi devaluation and the lack-luster regional economic recovery, many Asian nations feared that financial chaos might recur if no regional institutional arrangements were established to defuse that grim prospect. This persistent sense of urgency and time pressure, flowing from the critical juncture of the 1997 financial crisis yet persisting at least two years thereafter, encouraged Asian collective action to build regionalist financial understandings. America's hesitance to act proactively itself in the early stages of the crisis made this Asian regionalist determination all the stronger.

The Road to Chiang Mai: A Model for the Future?

In November 1999 the ASEAN Plus Three heads of state met in Manila and declared that monetary and financial cooperation had become priority areas of shared concern for them. Six months later, in May 2000, the ASEAN Plus Three finance ministers gathered in Chiang Mai, Thailand, to announce that they would create a network of bilateral currency-swap agreements so as to prevent future currency crises such as they had suffered in 1997–98. Neither the United States nor Australia and New Zealand were included in the arrangements, and the IMF did not endorse them until a year later.

Within four years of the Chiang Mai meeting, 15 bilateral swap arrangements had been put in place, involving standby credits of nearly $35 billion. The Chiang Mai framework, as indicated later in greater detail, clearly represents an intensification of regionalism in Asia, with a multilateralist cast despite the bilateral machinery involved. It has exclusively Asian nations as members. Although the swap agreements are thus far technically bilateral, the basic configuration of the agreements was decided multilaterally at Chiang Mai. And the prospect that this network of bilateral understandings will morph into a regionalist institution is real and expected.

The Chiang Mai agreement thus represents a substantial advance in East Asian—particularly Northeast Asian—regional cooperation, independent of the United States and U.S.-influenced multilateral organizations such as the IMF. This advance came in the wake of numerous futile attempts to advance such regionalist cooperation, as noted previously, including the proposals for an East Asian Economic Caucus, EAEG, and AMF.

The Chiang Mai model of regional policy innovation has five distinctive characteristics that are especially noteworthy:

1. *The noninvolvement of the United States and global multilateral institutions.* Chiang Mai, the first substantive agreement on Asian regional finance, was achieved in a forum that did *not* involve these actors.
2. *The sequence through which deepened regional integration proceeds:* substantial *trade interdependence,* leading to a substantive *regional integration* proposal (the AMF concept of the early 1990s), followed by a *crit-*

ical juncture that opens a "policy window" of prospective innovation, an indeterminate moment for *leadership decision making,* a concrete *regional agreement,* and ultimately *international post facto acceptance.*

3. *The key role of political leaders* such as Kim Dae-jung, Obuchi Keizo, and Zhu Rongji in spurring policy innovation, in place of bureaucrats.
4. *The concentration of policy innovation in the financial area rather than trade,* which drove the European integration process through innovations such as the European Coal and Steel Community.
5. *The limited nature of constraints on national sovereignty.* The swap quotas authorized under the Chiang Mai agreement do not constrain the prerogatives of national governments, in contrast to most steps toward regional integration in Europe, for example.

The success of the Chiang Mai agreement in the wake of the Asian financial crisis demonstrates the potential importance of critical junctures as a mechanism for overcoming collective action problems in Asia. As Sidney Tarrow observes:

> Movements are created when political opportunities open up for social actors who usually lack them. They draw people into collective action through known repertoires of contention, and by creating innovations around their margins. . . . Triggered by the incentives created by political opportunities, combining conventional and challenging forms of action and building on social networks and cultural frames is how movements overcome the obstacles to collective action and sustain their interactions with opponents.[41]

Of course, regional integration in Asia has advanced further since Chiang Mai. In trade a rash of free trade agreements (FTAs) have been proposed, most conspicuously Zhu Rongji's dramatic suggestion of an FTA between China and ASEAN, to be effective by 2010. Yet the quality of the FTAs proposed has been uneven, and they are by no means primarily intraregional.

Finance has been an area of deeper and more meaningful cooperation than trade, building on the momentum of the Chiang Mai agreement and fueled by common regional interest in a safety net to defuse the risks to stability implicit in China's rapid ongoing economic growth. Financial cooperation has also been primarily multilateral in character, as opposed to the pervasive bilateralism in trade.

In June 2003, the Asian Bond Fund (ABF) was inaugurated, investing $1 billion in U.S. dollar–denominated bonds issued by borrowers in eight member economies. This was complemented soon thereafter by an Asian Bond Market Initiative to coordinate technical changes in the tax treatment of bonds and related matters. In 2004 a second stage of the Asian

Bond Fund Initiative (ABF2) announced a framework for investing around U.S.$2 billion denominated in domestic currency bonds in member economies during 2005.[42] Through such measures ASEAN and the nations of Northeast Asia have been working to diversify the risks implicit in East Asia's traditional high-leverage, bank-based patterns of economic growth by nurturing capital markets, building on their painful experiences during the critical juncture of the Asian financial crisis.

Energy has also been an area of policy innovation, particularly as energy prices have risen. The January 2007 Cebu Declaration on Energy Security, for example, committed members to a broad program of regional energy cooperation, including expansion of renewable energy systems and biofuel production. It included agreement on a system of periodic meetings among energy ministers to enhance cooperation. Within ASEAN Plus Three, energy cooperation has been active since 2004.[43]

Transcending the sector-specific initiatives, the nations of Asia have also inaugurated an annual East Asia Summit, first convened at Kuala Lumpur in December 2005. The 16 national participants include the 10 members of ASEAN and the 3 major Northeast Asian powers (China, Japan, and South Korea), plus Australia, India, and New Zealand. Since 2006 the summit has begun to take on significant policy agenda–setting functions in such areas as energy conservation, discussed earlier, the handling of pandemics, and the creation of a consolidated East Asian free trade area.

Conclusion: The Past and Future of Asian Regionalism

The countries of East Asia generally, and Northeast Asia in particular, showed enormous variation in the degree of economic and political integration that they manifested over the course of the twentieth century. As the century opened—and indeed, through virtually the entire first half of that century—it was possible to travel seamlessly and rapidly overland, from Japan across the entire Korean peninsula to Manchuria and beyond, in 24 hours or less. Yet the second half of the century was a much more complex proposition, despite vast improvements in transportation technology, due to the radical, albeit felicitous, transition from forced assimilation within the Japanese empire to independence.

To understand the future, as noted at the outset of this chapter, it is clearly important to understand the forces that drive change in human affairs. I have argued that *political crises*, responding episodically, discontinuously, and yet systematically to underlying economic logic, have heavily influenced complex and subtle contours of regionalism in East Asia. The dual experiences of the Korean War and the Asian financial crisis have accounted more significantly than any other considerations of the past 60 years for the current contours of East Asian political-economic integration.

The Korean War and the shadows of World War II before it, as we have noted, largely explain the profile of the distinctive organization gap that has estranged the fractious nation-states of the region. They explain why the fledgling multilateralism of the Pacific Pact initiative did not succeed, despite greater interest in the concept before the Korean War than is generally realized. And the aftershocks throughout Asia of China's sudden strike across the Yalu in late 1950 gave birth to the bilateralist, U.S.-centric San Francisco System, which has structured security affairs in the Pacific to this day.

Similarly, the Asian financial crisis of the late 1990s galvanized important new intraregional political and financial networks within East Asia, catalyzing fledgling new forms of economic multilateralism, such as the Chiang Mai currency-swap arrangements and the ABF. Bypassing the United States, this new crisis-inspired framework combined with economic forces driving the rise of China to bias regional organization in an entirely new and more multilateralist direction. For the first time in half a century, the movement was *away from* a Washington-centric bilateralist hub-and-spokes framework and *toward* increased intra-Asian political-economic integration, with multiple leading players in finance.

The logic of this chapter, extrapolating from past to future, is no doubt somewhat unsettling to believers in the stable evolution of Northeast Asian solidarity. However substantively important multilateralism may be in muting the systemic impact of nationalism and power transitions within East Asia, it does not emerge spontaneously of its own accord. Really substantial policy innovation, it suggests, including new multilateralist frameworks, tends to be born of crises, and during crises policy makers often do not make optimal decisions. Furthermore, the parameters they are forced to consider are often different from those of noncrisis periods, and not necessarily conducive to multilateralism. Technocrats can certainly refine the broad outlines of crisis-dictated initiatives, but it is often political leaders, devoid of personal expertise or adequate time to reflect, who must make the fateful choices on which systemic change is based.

Although history shows how hard it is to directly adopt pre-crisis plans as guides to policy, history also highlights the manifest *dangers* of inattention to preexisting realities, especially the deep and persisting mutual paranoia with which Northeast Asian countries regard one another. Incrementalism, networking, and dialogue on a multilateral basis may not be able to *transform* the region or deter aggression, but they are vitally important as a safety net in the face of unanticipated disasters. The "trust gap" among the "spokes countries" in the persisting San Francisco System is intense, as manifested in the explosive Sino-Japanese and Japan-Korea confrontations of 2005–6.[44] And given the persisting hub-and-spokes framework of Pacific affairs, it is difficult for these spokes countries to resolve their troubling differences without a proactive stance toward multilateralism, however informal, on the part of the United States.

History thus provides important perspectives on the long-term utility of multilateral diplomatic constructs like the Six-Party Talks as vehicles for real institution-building. They are clearly useful in the short run as static devices for promoting transnational communication and minimizing the very real dangers of misperception and paranoia that pervade the region. Yet their long-run importance is most likely in a different sphere: the role they may play in forging enduring personal networks and drafting creative, future-oriented proposals for the turbulent, unanticipated future that is almost certainly to come. For it will be that turbulent future—likely a short, sharp, critical segment of it—that will most crucially determine the long-run geoeconomic course of this region, with fateful implications for the future course of the rest of the world.

Notes

1. For a fuller exposition of this concept, see Kent Calder and Min Ye, "Regionalism and Critical Junctures: Explaining the 'Organization Gap' in Northeast Asia," *Journal of East Asian Studies* (Spring 2004): 191–226.
2. See Leonard Binder, ed., *Crises and Sequences in Political Development* (Princeton, N.J.: Princeton University Press, 1971); Stephen Krasner, "Approaches to the State," *Comparative Politics* (January 1984): 223–46; Nelson Polsby, *Political Innovation in America: The Politics of Policy Innovation* (New Haven, Conn.: Yale University Press, 1984); Peter Gourevitch, *Politics in Hard Times* (Ithaca, N.Y.: Cornell University Press, 1986); and Stephen Skowronek, *Building a New American State* (Cambridge: Cambridge University Press, 1982).
3. Graham Allison and Philip Zelikow, *Essence of Decision,* second ed. (New York: Longman, 1999).
4. Yoichi Nemoto, "An Unexpected Outcome of the Asian Financial Crisis," Program on U.S.-Japan Relations Occasional Paper (Princeton, N.J.: Princeton University, June 2003), 14.
5. Milton Walton Meyer, *A Diplomatic History of the Philippine Republic* (Honolulu: University of Hawaii Press, 1965), 142–43.
6. Meyer, *Diplomatic History.*
7. On this concept and its relationship to broader international relations theory, see Kent E. Calder, "The San Francisco System in Comparative Perspective," *Pacific Review* (January 2004): 135–57.
8. On the international and domestic Korean events surrounding this Korean War critical juncture, see, for example, Bruce Cumings, *The Origins of the Korean War,* Vols. 1 and 2 (Princeton, N.J.: Princeton University Press, 1981

and 1990); Chen Jian, *China's Road to the Korean War: The Making of the Sino-American Confrontation* (New York: Columbia University Press, 1994); John W. Garver, *The Sino-American Alliance: Nationalist China and American Cold War Strategy in Asia* (Armonk, N.Y.: M. E. Sharpe, 1997); and William Stueck, *Rethinking the Korean War: A New Diplomatic and Strategic History* (Princeton, N.J.: Princeton University Press, 2002).

9. Akira Iriye, *The Cold War in Asia: A Historical Introduction* (Englewood Cliffs, N.J.: Prentice-Hall, 1974), 93–97.

10. See Sergei N. Goncharov, John W. Lewis, and Xue Litai, *Uncertain Partners: Stalin, Mao, and the Korean War* (Stanford, Calif.: Stanford University Press, 1993), Chap. 5.

11. Meyer, *Diplomatic History,* 143.

12. Robert T. Oliver, *Syngman Rhee and American Involvement in Korea, 1942–1960* (Seoul: Panmun, 1978), 255.

13. Meyer, *Diplomatic History,* 147.

14. Oliver, *Syngman Rhee,* 233.

15. Meyer, *Diplomatic History,* 151.

16. The seven participants, including the Philippines, were Australia, Ceylon, India, Indonesia, Pakistan, and Thailand. As indicated earlier, South Korea and Taiwan were also highly supportive of regional cooperation, including that in the security sphere. See Meyer, *Diplomatic History,* 153.

17. U.S. Department of State, *Foreign Relations of the United States (FRUS): East Asia and the Pacific,* Vol. 6, Part 1 (Washington, D.C.: U.S. Government Printing Office, 1983), 133–34. Among the officials to whom copies were sent were Dean Rusk, assistant secretary for Far Eastern Affairs, and Paul Nitze, director of policy planning.

18. See U.S. Department of State, *FRUS: East Asia and the Pacific,* Vol. 6, Part 1, 136.

19. Steven Hugh Lee, *The Korean War* (London: Longman, 2001).

20. Dean Acheson, *Present at the Creation: My Years at the State Department* (London: Hamish Hamilton, 1969), 426.

21. For the idea of indeterminate prediction of regional institutions, see Steve Weber, "Shaping the Postwar Balance of Power," *International Organization* 46 (Summer 1992): 633–80.

22. U.S. Department of State, *FRUS: East Asia and the Pacific,* Vol. 6, Part 1, 143–44.

23. John M. Allison, *Ambassador from the Prairie* (Boston: Houghton Mifflin, 1973), 199–205.

24. See, for example, Peter Katzenstein and Christopher Hemmer, "Why Is There No NATO in Asia? Collective Identities, Regionalism, and the Origins of Multilateralism," *International Organization* (Fall 2002): 575–88.

25. See Kevin Cai, "Is a Free Trade Zone Emerging in Northeast Asia in the Wake of the Asian Financial Crisis?" *Pacific Affairs* 74 (Spring 2001): 11.

26. Saori Katada, "Japan and Asian Monetary Regionalization: Cultivating a New

Regional Leadership after the Asian Financial Crisis," paper presented at the ISA Annual Meeting, New Orleans, March 24–27, 2002.

27. When ASEAN was founded in 1967, its original five members were Indonesia, Malaysia, the Philippines, Singapore, and Thailand.

28. The so-called Pacific Business Forum, formed in 1994 to represent regional business interests, meets routinely, for example, before APEC summit meetings, to prepare road maps designed to guide APEC toward free trade. Since 1995, business interests have also been represented in the APEC Business Advisory Council. They have pushed for such measures as common product standards, harmonized customs procedures, common rules on the protection of intellectual property, and an APEC business visa. See Walter Mattli, *The Logic of Regional Integration: Europe and Beyond* (Cambridge, England: Cambridge University Press, 1999), 171–72.

29. In 1994, for example, the APEC leaders' summit at Bogor, Indonesia, set an ambitious target of zero tariffs throughout the Pacific by 2020, with advanced APEC members to meet this target by 2010. By 1996, however, the momentum embodied in the Bogor Declaration had disappeared.

30. Well before the onset of the Asian financial crisis, the AMF idea had been promoted actively, albeit informally, by Japanese economists and politicians, including personally by Eisuke Sakakibara, the vice minister of finance for international affairs.

31. Eric Altbach, "The Asian Monetary Fund Proposal: A Case Study of Japanese Regional Leadership," *Japan Economic Institute Report* 47a (Washington, D.C.: Japan Economic Institute, December 19, 1997), 10.

32. Saori Katada, "Japan and Asian Monetary Regionalization: Cultivating a New Regional Leadership after the Asian Financial Crisis," paper presented at the International Studies Association Annual Meeting, New Orleans, March 24–27, 2002.

33. The Dow Jones average fell by 7.2 percent—the largest fall ever in terms of absolute points, but only 7.2 percent, as opposed to a 22.6 percent fall on October 19, 1987, in response to the U.S.-German financial dispute.

34. Robert Garan, *Tigers Tamed: The End of the Asian Miracle* (Honolulu: University of Hawaii Press, 1998), 165.

35. In 1999 Asia received 37.3 percent of Japan's exports, compared to 30.7 percent received by the United States. See Asahi Shimbun Sha, *Japan Almanac, 2003 ed.* (Tokyo: Asahi Shimbun Sha, 2002), 90.

36. Nemoto, "Unexpected Outcome," 14.

37. By this time ASEAN had expanded beyond the original five members to include Brunei, Cambodia, Laos, Myanmar, and Vietnam. ASEAN Plus Three added three members from outside ASEAN: China, Japan, and South Korea.

38. This arrangement provided for the participating nations to borrow the currencies of other members for intervention purposes when needed, up to a

specified ceiling, so as to stabilize overall foreign exchange relationships in the region.

39. James Laurenceson, "External Financial Liberalization and Foreign Debt in China," Discussion Paper 304, School of Economics (Queensland, Australia: University of Queensland, 2002).

40. Edward M. Graham, *Reforming Korea's Industrial Conglomerates* (Washington, D.C.: Institute for International Economics, 2003), 111.

41. Sidney Tarrow, *Power in Movement* (London: Cambridge University Press, 1994), 1

42. Jennifer Amyx, "What Motivates Regional Financial Cooperation in East Asia Today?" *Asia-Pacific Issues* (February 2005): 5.

43. See, for example, "The Joint Ministerial Statement," ASEAN, China, Japan, and Korea Energy Ministers' Meeting, June 9, 2004.

44. For suggestions on moderating these tensions, see Yoon Young-Kwan, Security in Northeast Asia: A South Korean View, address given at the Reischauer Center for East Asian Studies, April 2005, and Kent E. Calder, "China and Japan's Simmering Rivalry," *Foreign Affairs* (March/April 2006): 1–11.

CHAPTER 2

The History and Practice of Unilateralism in East Asia

Bruce Cumings

IN SEPTEMBER 2005, the Six-Party Talks held in Beijing yielded a set of agreed "principles" for denuclearizing the Korean peninsula,[1] which the North Koreans waited about one day to denounce. Two months later, the parties met again in Beijing for three more days of talks at which, as far as anyone can tell, nothing happened. Close on the heels of these talks came the Asia-Pacific Economic Cooperation (APEC) forum in Pusan, South Korea. The forum convened amid worries about China's rise to economic power (and future primacy), a deepening estrangement between Seoul and Washington, the never-ending crisis over North Korea's nuclear program(s), and Japanese nationalists' both busily rewriting the postwar peace constitution and finding innovative ways to ignore and disparage their neighbors.

President George W. Bush passed through the APEC meeting en route to China, where the biggest news from his Beijing visit, at least for the *New York Times,* was a pratfall: three front-page color photos depicted Bush trying to exit a news conference through a locked door, then mugging for the press while yanking on the doorknob, and finally exiting through an open hallway.[2] Nor did the APEC meeting generate any news beyond reports of anti-Bush protests by Korean students and journalists' wondering how the Pusan of Korean War fame had become "Busan." In other words, the meeting provided another boring and predictable iteration of a truism: multilateral diplomacy in East Asia is something of a joke, to the extent that it even exists.

The fundamental reason that multilateralism is so weak in East Asia goes back to the settlements after World War II and the Korean War, as do the roots of the contemporary problems mentioned earlier. Japan's constitution, its rising nationalism, and its failure to seriously confront its wartime crimes in China and Korea, and the resulting regional enmity, may be traced back to the soft peace that the United States enforced during its unilateral occupation of Japan from 1945 to 1952 and to the bilateral peace treaty that ended the state of war between Japan and the United States, but not its neighbors. That treaty left many knotty problems from the Pacific War (1931–45) unresolved.[3] South Korean estrangement from the United States is embedded in six decades of general American preponderance going back to September 1945, when American commanders took over the former Japanese Yongsan Garrison, which sits in downtown Seoul; U.S. troops have yet to evacuate the facility. This estrangement also goes back to July 1950, when Americans took over operational command of the South Korean armed forces. (In November 2005 President Roh Moo-hyun asked the United States to terminate this arrangement, a demand met in Washington with deafening silence.) The North Korean nuclear threat ultimately dates back to the barely voiced fact that the United States stationed nuclear weapons in South Korea from 1958 to 1991 and in contemporary war games routinely simulates using such weapons against the North. The only anomaly in the past 60 years is China, whose growth was unleashed in 1979 both by its own reforms and by the one important breach in the structure and logic of American Cold War power in the region—the opening to China begun by U.S. President Richard Nixon and continued by President Jimmy Carter.

Otherwise, Cold War divisions hindered (and often completely blocked) horizontal relations and communications among the East Asian countries. Most diplomatic communication was vertical, that is, from the foreign ministry in Tokyo, Seoul, Manila, or Taipei to Washington and back again. This vertical diplomacy was punctured horizontally by economic forces that since the 1960s have eroded and bypassed Cold War boundaries, bringing former adversaries together, but primarily through business contacts and pop culture rather than through multilateral institutions. China's opening to the world economy and its rapid growth are the best expressions of this tendency today, but China is also replicating what Japan, South Korea, and Taiwan did in the past. Although the first phase of the Cold War emphasized security considerations and divided the region and the second phase exemplified the ascendancy of economic development and accelerated regional integration, it is important to remember that both these tendencies were primarily the result of basic shifts in American foreign policy and the resulting pressures on East Asian states. Contemporary obstacles to deeper integration in the region may also be traced back (although not exclusively) to Washington. Rightly or wrongly, the United States still holds the key to East Asian regional security and cooperation.

The beginning of the end of the Cold War in East Asia came during the early and mid-1970s with Nixon's opening to China and the conclusion of the Indochina War. Only in the 1990s, however, did a real horizontal diplomacy start to develop between China and its neighbors, especially the Republic of Korea (ROK). Meanwhile, Japan's diplomacy remains weak and is often resisted by its neighbors. Though the Democratic People's Republic of Korea has made strides since January 2000 in opening relations with European and former British Commonwealth nations, its efforts have been stymied by continuing Cold War barriers (most of them home grown, others external) in developing relations with its near neighbors, especially Japan. In short, the past still hangs heavily over everything in the region except business transactions.

Since 1991, however, there has been a promising development of regional tendencies: the emergence of APEC, the deepening influence in Southeast Asia of the Association of Southeast Asian Nations (ASEAN), the increasing inclusiveness of the ASEAN Regional Forum (ARF), the peaceful and (so far) successful return of Hong Kong to China in 1997, and the major gains achieved in trying to reconcile the two Koreas from 1998 to 2005. (As we will see, President Kim Dae-jung was a major catalyst in this, and in garnering support from the administration of U.S. President Bill Clinton.) However, none of this is terribly important compared to the continuing salience of the American-built postwar security structure, and all of it, save China's emergence, is reversible. We see this potential for reversibility when we look at the progress that occurred in Korean reconciliation when Washington, Seoul, and Tokyo worked together in 1997–2000 and the nearly instant regress that took place as President George W. Bush took office in 2001. The crisis that reemerged over North Korea's nuclear installations in October 2002 and a more general "diplomacy by dereliction" have allowed some of the earlier gains to slip away and nearly all of them to be weakened. As a result, Korea remains as it has been since 1945: divided, and thus a serious obstacle to peace in the region. There is a distinct possibility it will return to what it was throughout the Cold War: the linchpin of regional division.

Europe and East Asia in the Postwar Settlement

The postwar settlement of the late 1940s remains the determining mechanism in explaining why Northeast Asia, compared to Europe, has so few multilateral institutions and mechanisms of cooperation and conciliation today, and had even fewer through most of the immediate postwar period. There was and is no North Atlantic Treaty Organization (NATO) in the region. There once was a Southeast Asia Treaty Organization, but it never amounted to much, never spawned a Northeast Asia Treaty Organization, and died after two decades. There was a rump Marshall Plan (the Economic Cooperation Administration, or ECA, which aided South Korea and Taiwan from 1947 onward). Like the Marshall Plan itself in Europe, the ECA was superseded by the revival of the advanced industrial economies, in this case the only one in the region, Japan. Nothing like the Commission on Security and Cooperation in Europe (CSCE) emerged; the Organisation for Economic Co-operation and Development was remote; and the theoretically all-inclusive United Nations (UN) was essentially an American operation in East Asia (U.S. troops in Korea still sit under the blue flag of the United Nations Command). Though the United States pursued multilateral, cooperative policies in Western Europe after World War II, a pattern of unilateralism has prevailed in East Asia, and by now it has almost become rote. For instance, in the same month that APEC met in Pusan, the Korean government requested the return of the joint military command of U.S. and Korean forces assumed by the United States during wartime, but the Americans protested that this would break the structure of deterrence. Japan wants a seat on the UN Security Council, and the U.S. ambassador to the United Nations, John Bolton, supported this request in principle, but also told reporters that no one is going to do anything about it. Japan wants to be a "normal" country, but in that country comic books full of racist depictions of Koreans and Chinese climb the best-seller charts. Pundits say China's diplomatic outreach to the region may crowd out the United States, but the Bush administration is paying no attention because it has taken the unilateral pattern of American power in East Asia and spread it throughout the globe.[4]

Compared to the travails of East Asia since 1945, the historical process of regional consolidation in Europe appears almost seamless. By and large, the Allied victors (except the Soviet Union after 1946) cooperated in orienting the Federal Republic of Germany dramatically away from its former dominance in Eastern Europe, turning it around to "face West" and reconciling it with long-time enemy France.[5] Critically placed American officials like George Kennan, Dean Acheson, and especially U.S. High Commissioner to Germany John J. McCloy pushed and prodded the Germans to refashion themselves as good citizens of the European community in return for agreeing to remove sharp limits on the revival of German heavy industries, thus making West Germany an engine of regional and global growth. The famous Schuman Plan, made public in May 1950, symbolized this fundamental shift in German orientation, bringing European coal and steel production together under a transnational authority. This created "the political and economic bases for a final settlement between the Germans and their former enemies in the West."[6] NATO emerged to give a distinctly multilateral quality to military influence, even though the United States dominated it for decades. In spite of many twists and turns, particularly involving the French, one can trace a reasonably straight line from the Schuman Plan and NATO forward to the emergence of the European Union that we see today.

The outcome in East Asia was very different. The region was split dramatically both by the end of the Pacific War and by the emergence of anticolonial revolutionary-nationalist movements in China, Korea, and Vietnam. In contrast to the multilateral occupation of Germany, the American military unilaterally occupied Japan in 1945. This was followed within five years by a general division of the region into bipolar structures shaped by the Cold War. On August 15, 1945, General Douglas MacArthur issued General Order 1, which excluded Allied powers from the occupation of Japan except in fig leaf form, divided Korea at the 38th parallel and Vietnam at the 16th parallel, and sought to unify China under Chiang Kai-shek's rule by requiring Japanese soldiers in China to surrender to nationalist forces. The only part of that East Asian military division that did not hold was that in China, and as the communists cleared the mainland in 1948–49 a new division took place: that between Taiwan and the People's Republic of China (PRC). MacArthur ruled Japan as a benevolent emperor, while Americans policed the fault lines of the great power conflict in China and Korea.

The Korean War erupted in June 1950, resulting in a vastly deepened division of Northeast Asia. A heavily fortified demilitarized zone (DMZ) replaced the 38th parallel and remains to this day as a relic of the Cold War, and the two Koreas remade themselves as garrison states, with very high ratios of military forces to civilian population. For a generation, China was excluded from the postwar global system by blockade and bellicose threats. Japan also remilitarized, if modestly, as a result of the Korean War. Lingering long after this war was an archipelago of American military installations throughout the noncommunist part of the region, bases like those in South Korea and Japan (especially Okinawa), which have 100,000 troops among them but are rarely discussed in the literature of international relations. Yet they are the coercive structure that locked in the American position in Northeast Asia, offering a diffuse leverage over allies. As in Europe, the trade-off was the revival of Japanese heavy industries and continuous American pressure from 1947 onward to reintroduce Japanese economic influence in East and Southeast Asia.[7] The difference was that, unlike in the case of Europe, no one asked the Chinese or the Koreans whether they supported such policies; this was yet another reason for the continuing estrangement between Japan and its neighbors.

The long-term result of this American unilateralism in East Asia was essentially a "hub-and-spokes" system in which the capitalist countries of the region tended to communicate with each other *through the United States*. This vertical regime was solidified by bilateral defense treaties (between the United States and Japan, the Philippines, South Korea, and Taiwan) and conducted by a U.S. State Department that towered over the foreign ministries of these four countries. Each of them became a semisovereign state deeply penetrated by American military structures. For instance, they ceded operational wartime control of the South Korean armed forces to the United States, acquiesced to patrolling of the Taiwan Straits by the U.S. Seventh Fleet, created defense dependencies, and accepted military bases on their territory. This left them incapable of anything resembling independent foreign policy or defense initiatives. The countries of the East Asian region might as well have been "hermit kingdoms" vis-à-vis each other, if not in relation to the United States: China did not talk to Taiwan or the ROK, not even personal mail passed between the two Koreas, both Koreas hated Japan, and Japanese diplomacy looked to the United States, Europe, and Southeast Asia, but not its near neighbors.

The capitalist countries "communicated" with the communist countries primarily through the American military, a relationship symbolized by the military talks at Panmunjom, minicrises like those over Quemoy and Matsu in the Taiwan Straits, the developing war in Vietnam, periodic fracases with North Korea (e.g., the seizure of the USS *Pueblo* in 1968, the downing of an EC-121 plane in 1969, and the "tree-cutting incident" in 1976), and the all-around containment of the (relatively weak) Soviet position in Northeast Asia. There were minor démarches through this curtain of military division beginning in the mid-1950s, such as low levels of trade between China and Japan or between Japan and North Korea. But the dominant tendency until the 1970s was a unilateral American regime heavily biased toward military forms of communication, and correspondingly biased against the multilateral mechanisms that emerged in Europe. Even businessmen were blocked from traveling through the region. Until the mid-1960s, the East Asian political economy was primarily bilateral with the United States, with the smaller countries sustained by American bulk aid grants. For example, in the late 1950s five-sixths of ROK imports came from aid, and Taiwan was similarly dependent. These two countries had relatively little economic exchange with Japan. There was next to no economic exchange with the communist countries of East Asia; instead Japan and the smaller economies were dependent on exporting to the vast American consumer market.

The Beginning the End of the Cold War in East Asia

The decade of the 1960s was a watershed in beginning the transformation back to "normalcy" in the Northeast Asian system. Thenceforth and down to the present, economic exchange was the driving force restitching ties among the nations of the region. The administration of U.S. President John Kennedy was pivotal, inaugurating many policies directed toward deemphasizing the multifurcated military structures and bringing into play new economic relationships. For the first time, Japan was asked to "share burdens" in defense.[8] Kennedy also came to office hoping to normalize relations with the PRC, and W. Averell Harriman, assistant secretary of state for Far Eastern affairs, secretly developed a plan for withdrawing U.S. troops from Korea. In some ways this was a fulfillment of Dean Acheson's political economy, that is, his "great crescent" conception linking Tokyo, "island Asia," and Middle Eastern oil, which was under way by 1948 but temporarily demolished by the North Korean invasion in 1950.[9] In other ways, Kennedy's changes anticipated policies later implemented by the Nixon administration, especially the Nixon Doctrine and the opening to China.[10]

The leitmotif of Kennedy's strategy, one scripted by Special Assistant for National Security Affairs W. W. Rostow, was to bring Japan's economic influence back into the East Asian region as a way of jump-starting growth in the ROK and Taiwan. This resulted in the normalization of Japan-ROK relations in 1965 (under enormous American pressure and despite strong resistance by Korean dissidents), and both South Korea and Taiwan began industrializing under the banner of export-led development, typically using obsolescent Japanese light industrial technology.[11] Then the International Monetary Fund (IMF) and the World Bank became involved in a kind of transnational planning and cooperation that was particularly evident in the case of South Korea's second five-year plan in the mid-1960s, its recovery from export-led doldrums in the mid-1980s, and the IMF bailout in 1997–98. Nixon opened relations with China in 1971–72, initially to draw down American involvement in the Vietnam War and to contain communism with communism. But after the Sino-American normalization of relations and the epochal reforms instituted by Deng Xiaoping (both policies were decided in December 1978), the economic interactions of China with East Asia and the world economy became dominant in its foreign policy, to the point that China was finally allowed to join the World Trade Organization (WTO) after 15 years of trying. The past decade has seen the economic inclusion of Vietnam, culminating in a major trade agreement with the United States in November 2001, and an attenuation of North Korea's economic isolation through joint ventures with South Korean firms, extensive foreign aid, and limited foreign investment. Since the mid-1960s, in short, economic forces have driven past or run roughshod over the previously impervious security barriers hardened by the Korean War, but they have not knocked them down. The American military structure of the Cold War era still underpins regional security, even as the Cold War's abrupt end fades into the distant past.

In spite of the growing prominence of summit meetings between the leaders of China, Japan, and the ROK, when compared to Europe, Northeast Asia still lacks intense horizontal contact and continues to do without analogous multilateral institutions. APEC made a big splash in the headlines with its founding. The various heads of state have met annually since 1993, and its members account for 40 percent of world trade. Perennial photos showing these leaders communing in the informal dress of whatever country is hosting the summit (Bush, along with Korea's Roh Moo-hyun, Japan's Junichiro Koizumi, and China's Hu Jintao, donned traditional Korean robes in Pusan) give APEC a certain symbolic weight. But it remains a merely consultative group, a weak assemblage of 18 countries that do not interact with each other well or often. Malaysia's championing of an exclusive regional economic group in the 1990s generated considerable heat and attention, but the effort has gone nowhere, except for attracting the occasional support of Japanese nationalists. There is no regional equivalent to the North American Free Trade Agreement (NAFTA), but if a "NEAFTA" comes into being it will most likely be in the form of an enlargement of NAFTA to include selected Northeast Asian or Pacific Rim economies. Despite incremental progress in the past decade, Aaron Friedberg is still right in saying that the Asian "web of interdependence" is weak, that "Asia appears strikingly under-institutionalized" without the "rich 'alphabet soup' of international agencies."[12] There is nothing like the European Customs Union, the European Parliament, or the CSCE (although many advocates of a CSCE-like forum have come forward in the past decade). Some observers also thought they saw a coalescence of the small states of ASEAN against Chinese military expansion in the form of ARF. Although ARF is more inclusive today than it was before, as a security organization it is still relatively ineffective.[13]

Today the main organization linking the Northeast region together is still the private business firm, and it is business firms that drive the dynamics of the region. For example, a decade ago a huge coalition of American firms ended the Clinton policy of linking most favored nation status for China to its domestic human rights situation, just as an ever more influential business coalition counsels moderation in Bush's approach to China. In the 1997–98 financial crisis the IMF and large American banks rode herd on the rescheduling of debt throughout the region, and American and other multinational corporations gave huge amounts of support to China's entry into the World Trade Organization. Travel is no longer restricted for businessmen traversing the East Asian region, and increasingly businessmen are voting with their feet by moving firms, and sometimes even their homes, from Taiwan or South Korea to China.[14] Although economic forces remain weak in helping to bring South Korea and North Korea together, they have become the most important forces promoting Korean reconciliation.

External observers might think that China, Japan, and Korea are linked by a common written language using Chinese ideographs, but in fact the common language of the region is English. China uses simplified characters, whereas Taiwan does not, Japan uses a Sino-Japanese script, South Korea has assiduously sought to substitute its native *han'gul* script for the previously used Sino-Korean script, and North Korea made that change in 1948. Meanwhile, the Vietnamese language, likewise laden with heavy Chinese etymology, is written in the Roman alphabet. The situation is similar to what would happen if the European countries were to contrive ways to make the Latin alphabet unreadable across national boundaries. Furthermore, if Japanese and Korean are close grammatically, Chinese is as different from them grammatically as two languages can be; by comparison, French, Italian, and Spanish seem like dialects of English.[15] Even the presumed common cultural background in Confucianism does not create cultural ties between, say, Japan and Korea or China and Japan; the lingering divisions of colonialism and war, combined with the dominance of American-spawned mass culture, tend to override this traditional heritage and to make Northeast Asian popular culture a hodgepodge of national constructions united only by pop songs and videos—although some of them, like those of the recent "Korean wave," find favor in neighboring countries.

Neuralgic animosities tracing back to colonialism and war remain a major obstacle to regional cooperation, yielding almost daily slights, insults, and brouhahas, and occasional pandemonium. A dramatic example is the backsliding in relations between Japan and the ROK. In late 1998, Korean President Kim Dae-jung visited Japan and made unprecedented progress toward reconciliation, arguing that, as the new century dawned, the conflicts of the twentieth century should be relegated to the past; both peoples should move forward with optimism that their mutual difficulties could be overcome. No Korean president had ever said anything like that, and Japanese leaders were deeply appreciative. In the next two years, Tokyo and Seoul worked closely with Washington to fashion common policies toward denuclearization and reconciliation with North Korea, and plans were even developed for the Japanese emperor to visit Seoul. Before long, however, the news media in Tokyo and Seoul were talking about little else but the issue of textbook revision (which softened the passages relating to Japan's past aggressions in Asia) and Prime Minster Junichiro Koizumi's many visits to the Yasukuni Shrine, where war criminals are enshrined.[16] Although Koizumi's successors, Shinzo Abe and Yasuo Fukuda, refrained from visits to the shrine, rising Japanese nationalism and the strength of the right wing in both the ruling and the major opposition parties continued to make for delicate relations between Japan and its neighbors China and Korea.

In other words, as years pass in the new century, East Asia remains more divided than united, and American unilateralism continues to be the dominant tendency. The multilateralism of the Clinton years made for good, hands-on diplomacy and achieved a major success in freezing North Korea's Yongbyon plutonium facility in 1994, but this diplomacy was often just for show. When serious issues divided Washington and the capitals of the region, problems were usually solved on a bilateral basis. The Asian financial crisis of 1997–98 was mediated and manipulated by the IMF, which was in turn little more than a creature of top American economic advisers such as Treasury Secretary Robert Rubin and his deputy (and successor) Lawrence Summers.[17] Washington continues to shape China's emergence into the world economy while trying to contain any hint of Chinese military expansion. This is remarkable considering that Clinton deployed two aircraft carrier task forces to Taiwan's eastern waters in 1996 during a crisis over Beijing's missile tests near the island, and Bush came into office calling China a "strategic competitor." A singular exception to this rule was the multilateral backing for Kim Dae-jung's Sunshine Policy, which came to include not just Washington, Seoul, and Tokyo, but also strong support from China, the European Union, and, from time to time, Vladimir Putin's Russia. But all that was rendered meaningless by the Bush administration's renewal of hostility toward Pyongyang.

Sunshine or Thunder?

Kim Dae-jung was the primary and most assiduous backer of reconciliation with the North, and a brief consideration of his tenure helps us see both the possibilities of forward-looking diplomacy and the latent influence of the region's Cold War–forged structure. At his inauguration in February 1998, Kim pledged to "actively pursue reconciliation and cooperation" with North Korea and declared his support for Pyongyang's attempts to better relations with Washington and Tokyo. This position was in complete contrast with those of his predecessors, who had chafed mightily at any hint of such rapprochement. Kim explicitly rejected West German–style "unification by absorption" (which had been the de facto policy of his predecessors) and in effect committed Seoul to a prolonged period of peaceful coexistence with the North. He underlined his inaugural pledges soon thereafter by approving large shipments of food aid to the North, lifting limits on business deals between the North and Southern firms, and refusing to be provoked by North Korean hardliners. In general, Kim rejected the decades-old "tit-for-tat" process by which any positive or negative movement by one Korean side had had to be reciprocated by a comparable movement on the other side, thus ensuring that no real progress would ever occur. Kim was also the first Korean president to recommend (during a visit to Washington in June 1998) lifting the 50-year-old U.S. economic embargo on North Korea, arguing that, as long as the embargo continued, one could hardly expect the regime of the North to change its economic policies and open up. Kim's "Sunshine Policy," widely reviled as appeasement, was actually based on two principles of realpolitik. It was his (correct) belief that North Korea was not likely to collapse (and thus had to be dealt with as it was) and also that the North would *not* oppose a continuing U.S. troop presence in the South if Washington pursued engagement with Pyongyang rather than confrontation and normalized relations. U.S. troops would be useful in policing the border, that is, the DMZ, ensuring that the South's superior armed forces would not swallow the North, and in keeping China and Japan at bay. Kim's program thus constituted the first attempt in 50 years to achieve North-South reconciliation *within* the existing Northeast Asian security structure.[18]

Until 1999, Kim's efforts met with indifference from Washington and with ill-concealed contempt from national security managers. Slowly but surely, however, Kim led Washington toward a major reevaluation of its Korea policy. Bill Clinton's ambassador-at-large for Korea, William Perry, shepherded a major review of Korea policy through the State Department and the National Security Council in 1998–99; his efforts culminated in his own report, issued in September 1999, airing many of the changes embodied in a new "engagement" strategy. The report was premised on dealing with North Korea "as it is, not as we might like it to be."[19] Washington, Tokyo, and Seoul developed an effective multilateral consultation mechanism in support of Kim Dae-jung's new strategies, and the North responded by transforming its diplomacy: from January 2000 onward the North opened diplomatic relations with nearly every important U.S. ally save Japan. Kim Jong-il welcomed Kim Dae-jung to Pyongyang for a historic summit in June 2000 and also welcomed Secretary of State Madeleine Albright in October 2000.

Ambassador Perry's review and the new Clinton policies toward the North nearly culminated in a missile deal that was profoundly in the interest of both America and East Asia. By November 2000 the stage was set for a Clinton visit to Pyongyang that would result in the mothballing of North Korea's missile program and an exchange of diplomatic missions, if not necessarily embassies, by both sides. Pyongyang had already indicated that it was prepared to forgo construction, deployment, and international sales of all missiles with a range of more than 300 miles. If Clinton did Kim Jong-il the favor of a presidential visit, American negotiators were convinced that Kim would also agree to enter the Missile Technology Control Regime, which would limit all North Korean missiles to an upper range of 180 miles, removing a threat felt deeply in nearby Japan. In return, the United States would provide around $1 billion in food aid to the regime for an undetermined number of years.[20] But then something utterly unexpected happened, something beyond all possibility of prediction: a fluke produced the closest presidential contest in American history. President Clinton wanted to go to Pyongyang; indeed his negotiators on Korea had their bags packed for weeks in November 2000. But as Clinton's national security adviser, Sandy Berger, later put it, it was not a good idea for the president to leave the country when he did not know "whether there could be a major constitutional crisis."[21] After the Supreme Court stepped in to give the election to George W. Bush, it was too late for Clinton to go to North Korea.

The Bush Difference

Whatever their critics may think, Bill Clinton and the two Korean leaders did more to lessen tensions in Korea than every head of state going back to the country's division in 1945. This statesmanlike approach on all sides showed how much could be accomplished by *diplomacy,* which by and large had been a concept alien to East Asia. But today much if not all of this progress is threatened. President Bush called Kim Jong-il a "pygmy" and told author Bob Woodward that he "loathed" Kim and wanted to topple his regime. He also, of course, included the North among the countries he termed an "axis of evil." The Bush administration has lurched from gratuitous epithets to crisis over the North's alleged highly enriched uranium program, to apparent indifference and absentmindedness because the Iraq war has overwhelmed Bush's foreign policy, to half-hearted participation in the Six-Party Talks. Today's fragile progress is uncertain, and, with six years of enmity separating the Bush White House and Kim Jong-il's regime, it may be too little, too late. The denuclearization of the Korean peninsula may no longer be feasible.

Meanwhile, in U.S. relations with other countries of East Asia, business intercourse with China carries everything else in its wake, and it is not obvious what the Bush policy is toward China. Bush took a stab at the "strategic competitor" idea and then dropped it; at one point he appeared to be ready to defend Taiwan if the PRC attacked, but backpedaled into the accustomed realm of ambiguity that has shadowed this subject; summits of dubious purpose come and go, but otherwise drift, and indifference marks Bush's approach toward China. This administration considers Japan the darling of the region. On the one hand, this has been a Republican tendency going back to the years of President Ronald Reagan. But on the other, the Bush administration has shown far more support than any previous administration for Japan's increasing nationalism and its desire to be a "normal" country with a formidable military. This tendency in U.S. relations toward Japan tends to push the entire region back to its state in 1945: at odds and divided, with the unilateral hub (Washington) manipulating the multilateral spokes.

The Bush administration signaled its intentions with regard to Japan and East Asia in a report issued in October 2000, the same month Madeleine Albright visited Pyongyang, under the direction of Richard Armitage, who later became Colin Powell's deputy in the State Department.[22] In the usual ocean of doublespeak, the report came to two important conclusions: (1) It argued vigorously for maintaining a heavy presence of U.S. forces in Japan, without stating what the overarching strategic objective of such a presence might be in the post–Cold War period. (2) It discussed "footprint reductions" to deal with recent troubles between the U.S. Marines and the people of Okinawa while arguing that Okinawa was the key to American security in East Asia. The report stated that "in matters of security, distance matters. Okinawa is positioned at the intersection of the East China Sea and the Pacific Ocean—only about one hour's flying time from Korea, Taiwan, and the South China Sea." The Armitage report also viewed Article 9 of the Japanese constitution, the "peace clause" that forswears the use of force abroad as a matter of state policy, as an unfortunate "constraint on alliance cooperation" and advocated getting rid of it.[23] In other words, the report concluded that a Japanese constitution written by Americans in 1947 was now deficient. Perhaps this was so according to Americans and right-wing nationalists, but it was not the case for a Japanese public that overwhelmingly supports Article 9. In short, the Armitage report was a blueprint for deepening instead of reconsidering an American military deployment and security structure that had begun in the 1940s and that had lost its fundamental rationale when the Soviet Union collapsed. The report was unlikely to reassure East Asians save for a small cadre of Japanese nationalists and reactionaries, who were vastly emboldened by it and by subsequent support from the Bush administration.

When Kim Dae-jung showed up in Washington in March 2001 as the first foreign head of state to greet President Bush in the Oval Office, he was a freshly minted Nobel laureate. Bush told President Kim that he did not trust Kim Jong-il (inadvertently raising the question "Who does?"), and he argued that the North was not likely to keep its agreements. On the day before this visit, Secretary of State Colin Powell had told reporters that he would pick up where Bill Clinton had left off in working toward a deal that would shut down North Korea's missile program. But Bush's hard line on North Korea forced Powell to backtrack. President Kim had traveled halfway around the world only to receive a rude welcome from Bush, returning home empty handed; this was a clear harbinger of things to come.

In the aftermath of Kim Dae-jung's disastrous visit, the Bush administration said it would have to conduct a thorough review of Korea policy before deciding what to do about the North. Yet Clinton had already conducted the first post–Cold War overhaul of Korea policy under William Perry's direction. By the summer of 2001, the latest review was finished, and the Bush administration announced that it would begin negotiations with Pyongyang. But the review had also raised a number of new issues, such as North Korean deployment of its conventional forces, and Bush's advisers continued to maintain that their pet National Missile Defense (NMD) project, begun under President Reagan and then widely referred to as "Star Wars," was directed particularly at North Korea's missiles. Getting North Korea into the missile control regime under Clinton's plan would have solved the missile defense problem at a cost of $1 billion annually in food aid and an exchange of diplomatic missions. NMD had already cost $60 billion by that time,[24] and under Bush the sky was now the limit.

In October 2002, James Kelly, assistant U.S. secretary of state for East Asian and Pacific affairs, journeyed to Pyongyang to accuse the North of having a second nuclear program to build bombs using highly enriched uranium. As a result of this accusation, made a month after the Bush administration had set forth its doctrine of preemptive attack (with North Korea high on the list of potential targets), it was entirely predictable that the North would return to what it knows best, back-to-the-wall confrontation and belligerence. Within a few weeks of Kelly's visit, the North had kicked out UN weapons inspectors (on the ground at Yongbyon for eight years), withdrawn from the Nuclear Non-Proliferation Treaty, reopened its plutonium facility (frozen for eight years), and begun reprocessing the plutonium in some eight thousand fuel rods (encased in concrete for the previous eight years). It was now alleged to have the wherewithal to build six to eight atomic bombs instead of the one or two that the Central Intelligence Agency had estimated in the previous decade. These actions were the one clear result of Kelly's October 2002 confrontation.

The Six-Party Talks on solving the North Korean nuclear problem represent a strong, indeed unprecedented, assertion of Chinese diplomatic muscle, the clear emergence of regionwide horizontal and multilateral interaction, and Washington's acquiescence in this new forum, if not its avid support. This six-way framework may suggest how twenty-first-century multilateralism might finally emerge in the East Asian region, and it may serve as a kind of template for that future.[25] Numerous informal policy and social networks have also sprung up among China, Japan, South Korea, and even North Korea to a modest extent. These did not exist 10 years ago, and they also augur well for the future. But as of this writing these talks are essentially a Chinese simulacrum for bilateral talks between Washington and Pyongyang, and to the extent that either party does not want to deal with the other, the talks collapse.

Conclusion: Back to the Future

The term that summarizes the Bush foreign policy is *unilateralism,* which merely gives a name to a banal truism. But this term takes us back to the beginning of this chapter and the post-1945 East Asian system. Although unilateralism has been a Republican tendency for decades, beginning with the "Nixon shocks" that reverberated in Japan 35 years ago and continuing through the pursuit of the "Star Wars" fantasies of the Reagan era, a new unilateralism has had far worse effects in East Asia. Unilateralism has been the norm in East Asia since Douglas MacArthur's arrival in Tokyo in September 1945. Bush's first secretary of defense, Donald Rumsfeld, apparently wanted to go back to this future. He may have become a subject of ridicule for talking about "old Europe," but in 2001 he presided over a highly secret reworking of the Pentagon's Quadrennial Defense Review, which signaled a major shift in emphasis from Europe to Asia and, more broadly, a recasting of East Asian–style unilateralism to the rest of the world. Rumsfeld and his allies are said to have been worried about the rise of China, of course, but also about nuclear rivalry between India and Pakistan and about North Korea's intentions, while much less worried about events in the region of America's traditional allies in Western Europe.

The November 2000 election fluke that brought a manifestly inexperienced and unprepared man to power—one nonetheless surrounded by experienced, heavy-hitting Republican foreign policy hands like Rumsfeld and Vice President Dick Cheney—occasioned a retreat toward the historic unilateralism that has long underpinned American strategy in East Asia. Through a dangerous alliance with the Japanese right wing, it even heralds a redivision of the region—that is, a return to hostile relations between Japan and its neighbors. Relations between Washington and Pyongyang are as bad as they have ever been, with a new war easily imaginable, just as it was at any point between 1945 and 1998. Reconciliation between the two Koreas has advanced markedly since 1998, but at the cost of a major estrangement between Seoul and Washington—and if the old ruling party were to return in the December 2007 Korean elections, all the progress could disappear. China policy waffles between containment and engagement, with the American business community's ravenous appetite for the China market underpinning engagement. But that could quickly change in a crisis over North Korea or Taiwan. A deepening reconciliation between North and South Korea would vastly benefit the making of an East Asian community, just as the vast economic exchange between China and Taiwan holds out the hope of a slow withering of their historic differences. But today the continuing division of the Korean peninsula and dangerous tensions between China and Taiwan pose perhaps the largest stumbling blocks to East Asian peace, cooperation, and regional exchange. These two conflicts just happen to be the critical ones that first divided the region in the aftermath of World War II.

All this underscores the degree to which the United States remains the key enabler of either multilateralism or unilateralism in East Asia, with the evidence today indicating that the Bush administration prefers to remake the East Asian pattern into the template for its dealings throughout the world. Perhaps this is fated because the United States is the world's only superpower, instead of simply the sole superpower in East Asia. Former UN chief Boutrous Boutrous-Ghali correctly identified the deepest contemporary truth about the American role in the world: "Like in Roman times," he said, the Americans "have no diplomacy; you don't need diplomacy if you are so powerful."[26] Or perhaps the situation could change with a new administration in Washington. Either way, East Asian leaders are still on the outside looking in.

Notes

1. These talks, which have involved China, Japan, the two Koreas, Russia, and the United States, have been convened periodically in Beijing to resolve the North Korean nuclear question and related issues.

2. *New York Times,* November 21, 2005, A-1.
3. See Herbert Bix, *Hirohito and the Making of Modern Japan* (New York: Harper-Collins, 2000).
4. Norimitsu Onishi, "Ugly Images of Asian Rivals Become Best Sellers in Japan," *New York Times,* November 17, 2005, A-1.
5. Chancellor Konrad Adenauer exemplified the tendency to turn toward the West in his own person and leadership.
6. Michael Hogan, *The Marshall Plan* (Cambridge: Cambridge University Press, 1987), 378; see also 286–92 and 366–78. Kai Bird, *The Chairman: John J. McCloy and the Making of the American Establishment* (New York: Simon and Schuster, 1992), 336–44.
7. See Bruce Cumings, *The Origins of the Korean War,* Vol. 2 (Princeton, N.J.: Princeton University Press, 1990), 49–58.
8. Senator Frank Church's speech of April 22, 1963, was probably the opening curtain in this long-running drama. See Makato Momoi, "Basic Trends in Japanese Security Policies," in Robert Scalapino, ed., *The Foreign Policy of Modern Japan* (Berkeley: University of California Press, 1977), 353.
9. Cumings, *Origins of the Korean War,* 45–54 and 168–75.
10. The Nixon Doctrine, first presented on Guam in July 1969, held that thenceforth the United States expected its allies to assume responsibility for their own military defense. This doctrine advocated a partial withdrawal of U.S. forces from East Asia and led to the departure of the U.S. Army's Second Division from Korea.
11. See the analysis of documents from the Kennedy Library in Jung-en Woo, *Race to the Swift* (New York: Columbia University Press, 1991). A neglected older source on this period is Kim Kwan Bong's *The Korea-Japan Treaty Crisis and the Instability of the Korean Political System* (New York: Praeger, 1968).
12. Aaron L. Friedberg, "Ripe for Rivalry: Prospects for Peace in a Multipolar Asia," *International Security* 18 (Winter 1993/94): 19–23.
13. Takashi Inoguchi offers some additional cogent reasons for the lack of regional integration in Northeast Asia in "Dialectics of World Order," in George Sorenson and Hans-Henrik Holm, eds., *Whose World Order? Uneven Globalization and the End of the Cold War* (Boulder, Colo.: Westview, 1996), 10–12.
14. Tens of thousands of Taiwanese businessmen and entrepreneurs now live in China, especially Shanghai.
15. I have a strong recommendation for furthering regional communication and integration: let everyone go back to extensive use of Chinese characters, in nonsimplified or standard form.
16. In side talks at the recent APEC meeting in Pusan, Roh Moo-hyun again asked Koizumi to stop these visits and got nothing but prevarication in return.

17. See Bruce Cumings, "The Asian Crisis, Democracy, and the End of 'Late' Development," in T. J. Pempel, ed., *The Politics of the Asian Economic Crisis* (Ithaca, N.Y.: Cornell University Press, 1999), 17–44.
18. I have written more extensively about this aspect of Kim's policies in the journal *Ch'angjak kwa Pip'yông* (Creation and criticism) (Seoul, Spring 2001). During the June 2000 summit, Kim Jong-il said he agreed with Kim Dae-jung's strategy of keeping U.S. troops in Korea as reconciliation proceeds.
19. I met with Perry's group as an outside expert at the State Department in May 1999 and was told that the review had been going on for six months (since the fall of 1998), resulting in the most important changes in U.S.-Korea policy since the Korean War.
20. See Michael R. Gordon's investigative report "How Politics Sank Accord on Missiles with North Korea," *New York Times,* March 6, 2001, A-1 and A-8. Gordon determined that Clinton's trip to Pyongyang was delayed pending the outcome of the election in Florida, and after the U.S. Supreme Court decided the election in favor of Bush in early December, it was too late.
21. Quoted in Gordon, "How Politics Sank Accord," A-8.
22. The Armitage report represented the views of a 16-member study group; Democrat Joseph Nye was a member, but the majority were pro-Pentagon Republicans. The report was issued on October 11, 2000.
23. The report states that "lifting this prohibition would allow for closer and more efficient security cooperation."
24. According to Gordon, "How Politics Sank Accord," A-8.
25. See Francis Fukuyama, "Re-envisioning Asia," *Foreign Affairs* 84 (January/February 2005): 75–87.
26. Quoted in Barbara Crossette, "Boutros-Ghali vs. 'Goliath': His Account," *New York Times,* November 20, 1998, A1 and A7, quote on A7.

CHAPTER 3

The Outlook for Economic Integration in East Asia

David Hale

ONE OF THE DISTINGUISHING FEATURES of the global trading system during the past two decades has been a proliferation of regional and bilateral free trade agreements. Since the establishment of the World Trade Organization (WTO) in the mid-1990s, more than a hundred free trade agreements (FTAs) have been launched by countries all over the world. Until recently, Asia's only experiment with regional trade liberalization was the attempt by the countries of the Association of Southeast Asian Nations (ASEAN) to reduce trade barriers among themselves.

Since 2000, there has been an increasing number of bilateral trade deals in the region. Japan has signed FTAs with Chile, Malaysia, the Philippines, and Singapore. It is now negotiating new ones with Chile, Korea, and Thailand. The Japan Federation of Economic Organizations (Nippon Keidanren) has called for the creation of an economic partnership agreement with the United States. Tokyo and Canberra are now seriously exploring the possibility of a Japan-Australia free trade agreement. China has proposed the creation of a regional free trade zone with ASEAN. Australia has negotiated an FTA with Singapore, Thailand, and the United States and is now seeking to create another with China. New Zealand has launched a bilateral trade agreement with Singapore and is also working on another with China. Singapore has signed FTAs with India, Japan, and the United States as well as with Australia and New Zealand. The United States has been negotiating an FTA with Thailand, has announced plans to pursue an agreement with Malaysia, and recently concluded negotiations on an FTA with South Korea. Additionally, there is recurring discussion about creating a free trade zone for the countries of the Asia-Pacific Economic Cooperation (APEC).

Several factors explain the new enthusiasm for bilateral and regional FTAs in East Asia. First, the great Asian financial crisis of 1997–98 has encouraged Asian countries to explore new forms of economic cooperation. They have launched a framework under ASEAN Plus Three for regular discussions among central bankers and finance ministers. In December 2005, the countries of the region held a conference of their heads of government in Kuala Lumpur for the first time, and they have been continuing it annually since then. The group also included Australia, India, and New Zealand.

Second, there is great concern about whether the WTO Doha Round of global trade negotiations will be able to produce a successful outcome. The major disputes in the Doha Round center on issues that Asia cannot directly control, such as agricultural trade. But the inability of the developing countries to resolve disputes with the old industrial countries is a further incentive to pursue alternative strategies for trade liberalization.

Third, the rise of China as a great economic power is producing major changes in both regional and global trade flows. Beijing is trying to reassure other Asian countries that it will not be a threat to their economies. Most Asian countries currently have trade surpluses with China and are anxious to enhance their access to the Chinese market.

Fourth, Japan is concerned that China will displace it as the leading regional economic power and is trying to use trade diplomacy to enhance its relationship with other countries in the region.

Fifth, small countries such as Singapore are attempting to promote both trade and investment in the region through the FTAs. Singapore's state companies, such as Temesek, also have become major investors all over the region.

Sixth, East Asia has a high level of trade integration without any FTAs. According to the World Bank, intraregional trade in East Asia represented 26.5 percent of the region's GDP in 2002, which is more than in any other developing region. As a result, there is natural support for promoting further economic integration in Asia.

As Asia moves toward greater economic integration, it is tempting to make comparisons with Europe or North America, but such comparisons are of limited value because of profound historical differences. On the eve of World War II, there were only three independent nation-states in East Asia: China, Japan, and Thailand. All other countries were either European or Japanese colonies. The nation-states of Europe have been independent for many centuries. Germany and France fought three wars, in 1871, 1914, and 1939, before they were ready to pursue a high level of economic integration. Japan invaded China and many European colonies during the 1930s and early 1940s. It has apologized for its acts of aggression but has never been able to pursue a policy of accommodation as far-reaching as Germany's after 1945. On the contrary, Prime Minister Junichiro Koizumi provoked other Asian countries by visiting the Yasukuni Shrine, which entombs war criminals. The process of economic integration in East Asia is therefore going to proceed along a very different path than did that of Europe starting in the 1950s. There will be new bilateral and multilateral trade agreements. There will be more cooperation on issues such as financial regulation and managing foreign exchange reserves. But there is not going to be any discussion of a political union or of establishing a common currency comparable to the Euro.

Until recently, the United States played a dominant role in shaping East Asia's trade and international economic policies because it was the leading export market for most countries in the region. The United States is still a very important market for the region but is increasingly being eclipsed by China, which has displaced the United States as the leading trade partner of Japan, Korea, and Taiwan. But, ironically, the United States remains critical because it has become the market for 20 percent of China's exports. If the United States were to experience a recession with falling imports, China's growth rate would drop at least 2–3 percent. Two-thirds of the value added to Chinese exports also accrues to other Asian countries because China depends heavily on them for components used in its assembly operations.

There is little doubt that the rise of China as a great trading nation will play a decisive role in shaping both regional and global trade policy during the next few decades. China's trade achievements since the 1980s have been daunting. The country has enjoyed nearly 14 years of 18 percent export growth. Its exports now exceed U.S.$1 trillion, and China will overtake Germany as the world's leading export nation during 2008. As a result of prodigious growth in export industries, Beijing's trade surplus exceeded $150 billion during 2006 and its ratio of exports to GDP was around 36 percent, compared to only 10–12 percent for Europe, Japan, and the United States. China has achieved this success because its economy today is far more open than were the economies of Japan and Korea during the decades after World War II. During the past dozen years, China has attracted well over U.S.$600 billion of foreign direct investment. Foreign firms went to China both to penetrate the local market and to use China as an export base for the rest of the world. They now produce over 57 percent of China's exports and account for many of the country's top exporters. The trade balance of multinational firms operating in China swung from a deficit of U.S.$14.1 billion in 1996 to a surplus of $14.6 billion during 2004. China's total trade surplus during 2004 was only $32.8 billion.

Foreign firms have also increased China's integration with other Asian countries by importing two-thirds of their components from Korea, Malaysia, Taiwan, and other Asian countries in order to produce goods for reexport to Europe and North America. Some economists contend that China's true ratio of exports to GDP is only 18 percent because such a large share of the value added to China's foreign trade is sourced in other countries, especially East Asia. Taiwan alone accounts for 19 of China's top 100 exporters, compared to 8 each from Japan and Korea. As a result, it is not surprising that two-thirds of China's foreign investment comes from other Asian countries, especially Hong Kong, Japan, Korea, Singapore, and Taiwan. Japan and Korea never allowed foreign direct investment (FDI) to occur on such a large scale. They wanted to protect local companies from foreign competition until they were ready to become global players. On the eve of the East Asian financial crisis in 1997, Japan had only U.S.$17 billion of FDI, while Korea had $12 billion.

China's trade relations with East Asia have been increasing steadily since the 1980s. China joined APEC in 1991. After joining APEC, Beijing unilaterally reduced its tariff barriers with the group from 44.1 percent in 1991 to 15.3 percent in 2001. At the Vancouver APEC summit in 1997, China's government promised to reduce customs duties on industrial goods to 10 percent by 2005. China also promised to gradually reduce all nontariff barriers and increase its regulatory transparency. This was followed by promises to open the service sector, increase the transparency of investment policies, and reinforce the protection of intellectual property rights. In April 2005, China joined the Bangkok Agreement, which was the first regional trade agreement with preferential arrangements for China. In 2001, China's prime minister proposed the creation of a regional free trade zone with ASEAN. In the first half of 2005, Chinese firms invested U.S.$1.9 billion, or 75 percent of the country's total outward investment, in other Asian countries.

As a result of its economic takeoff, China has developed an immense need for raw materials that is also influencing the continuing evolution of its trade policy. In 2003, China displaced the United States to become the world's leading consumer of most industrial raw materials and surpassed Japan as the world's second-largest oil consumer. China now consumes 22 percent of global copper output, compared to 16 percent for the United States, and China's steel production is now twice as great as that of Japan and the United States combined. The Chinese economy accounted for nearly 40 percent of the growth in global oil consumption during 2004, exerting strong upward pressure on petroleum prices. This need for commodities is encouraging China to pursue FTAs with resource-producing countries such as Australia, Chile, New Zealand, Saudi Arabia, and South Africa. China has also promised to make large infrastructure investments in Argentina and Brazil in order to facilitate their growing trade with China.

Because China will soon be the world's leading exporter, she has a great strategic interest in promoting an open multilateral trading system rather than a world characterized by regional trade agreements. But she has a limited capacity to resolve the issues that are now hampering the completion of the Doha Round. Those issues do not center on trade in manufactured goods. The great conflicts center on agriculture, especially American and European subsidies for farmers, as well as various aspects of service trade. China will therefore pursue a two-track policy: she will encourage an open global trading system but also pursue regional FTAs for both economic and geopolitical reasons.

Other East Asian countries will likely be happy to cooperate with China because they are concerned about competing with it and fear that China will consume too large a share of the region's FDI. After the East Asian financial crisis, China's share of FDI flows in the region rose from 50 percent in 1995 to 70 percent in 2002, while ASEAN's plunged from 40 percent to 20 percent in the same period. Asian economies are concerned that China will undermine their competitive position in sectors that depend on low wages. The countries that are most vulnerable to competition with China are Malaysia and Thailand. Their exports have a correlation of 58 percent and 64 percent, respectively, with China's mix of exports (see Table 3.1). Also, Malaysia has never fully recovered from the East Asian financial crisis. Its investment share of GDP is still only 14 percent, compared to 35 percent before 1997. Malaysia's problem is that it depends heavily on low-value-added electronic goods, which are competitive rather than complementary to China's output. Korea's and Taiwan's exports also have a high correlation with Chinese exports, but their firms have shifted a great deal of output to China, whereas Malaysian investment in China is very modest.

The differences in economic structure are apparent from trade flows. China now consumes 44 percent of Hong Kong's exports, 37 percent of Taiwan's, 22 percent of Korea's, 13 percent of Japan's, and 11 percent of the Philippines'. Its trade with ASEAN is more modest. It consumes only 8.6 percent of Singapore's exports, 7.5 percent of Indonesia's, 7.3 percent of Thailand's, and 6.7 percent of Malaysia's. The United States, by contrast, absorbs over 20 percent of Malaysia's exports.

The character of Asian intraregional trade has also been changing. Ten years ago, ASEAN relied heavily on exports of commodities, whereas it now

Table 3.1 Correlations of Asian Countries' Export Structures with China's Export Structure, 1990, 2000, and 2004

Correlations of three-digit SITC with China	1990	2000	2004
Indonesia	0.38	0.34	0.31
Korea	0.33	0.43	0.55
Malaysia	0.28	0.44	0.58
Philippines	0.19	0.33	0.37
Singapore	0.11	0.41	0.47
Taiwan	0.34	0.53	0.53
Thailand	0.31	0.51	0.64

Source: BNP Paribas statistical calculations, based on national trade statistics.
Note: SITC, standard international trade classification.

exports primarily intermediate manufactured goods. In 2000, electrical equipment represented 32 percent of ASEAN's exports to China, compared to 6 percent in 1990. Energy, by contrast, fell from 32 percent to 13 percent, while wood fell from 22.6 percent to 2.75 percent. In 2004, manufactured exports accounted for 55.5 percent of ASEAN's exports to China, compared to 34.9 percent in 1995 and 31.1 percent in 1990. The ratios of manufactured exports to total trade were 92.5 percent for the Philippines, 68.4 percent for Singapore, 59.7 percent for Thailand, 50.2 percent for Malaysia, and 22.3 percent for Indonesia.

ASEAN has been regaining its competitive position vis-à-vis China because of both rising costs in China and improved domestic policies. In 2005, FDI in ASEAN rose 48 percent, to U.S.$38 billion or a level $4 billion above the 1997 peak. It had dipped below $15 billion during 2002. Some analysts estimate that it could rise to $50 billion, or 5 percent of GDP, by 2007, a level not seen since 1997. ASEAN once had higher wage costs than China, but it no longer does. The minimum monthly salary in Guangdong is now U.S.$83, compared to $75 for Jakarta, $70 for the Philippines, $45 for Cambodia and Vietnam, and $32 for east Java. The annual wages of lower middle management employees are also higher in China than ASEAN. According to data from Mercer, the average monthly wage in China is U.S.$977, compared to $857 for Thailand, $761 for the Philippines, $702 for India, $655 for Indonesia, and $494 for Vietnam. Office rents in ASEAN capitals are one-half or one-third below those now being paid in Shanghai. The cost of a three-minute phone call to Japan is U.S.$3.00 in China, $1.50 in Thailand, $1.43 in Malaysia, and $1.20 in the Philippines. The cost of electricity per kilowatt-hour in China is 4–11 cents versus 4–6 cents in Thailand and Indonesia and 5 cents in Malaysia. Today China's major cost advantage is in shipping. The cost of shipping a container from China to the United States is U.S.$2,000–2,500, compared to $3,900 for Thailand, $3,200 for Malaysia, and $2,650 for the Philippines.

With China's rising regional profile have come increased opportunities for leadership. China demonstrated its capacity for regional cooperation during the East Asian financial crisis of 1997–98 by not devaluing its currency. The crisis was one of the most dramatic economic shocks to strike Asia since the Great Depression of the 1930s. It caused unemployment to rise threefold in Thailand, fourfold in Korea, and tenfold in Indonesia. Nearly 15 percent of all males lost their jobs in Indonesia during the first half of 1998, while poverty rates in the urban centers skyrocketed. As the exchange rates of Indonesia, Korea, Thailand, and other countries plummeted, China recognized that a devaluation of its currency would only magnify the financial contagion. As a result, it decided not to devalue and to instead stimulate its economy with a large infrastructure spending program. This fiscal stimulus helped to sustain output growth despite a 30 percent rise in the real exchange rate and a sharp slowing of export growth. World leaders were very supportive of China for holding its exchange rate steady. For instance, British Prime Minister Tony Blair and French President Jacques Chirac publicly applauded China for helping to slow the financial contagion gripping East Asia at the time.

Japan has been a regional leader for much longer than China because of overseas development assistance (ODA), FDI, and trade. Japan accounts for 13–14 percent of ASEAN's exports and 17–18 percent of its imports. ASEAN accounts for 11.8 trillion yen of Japanese FDI, or 9.9 percent of the total, while China accounts for 3.1 trillion yen, or 2.8 percent of the total. In 2003, Japan sent 67 percent of its ODA to Asian countries, with the largest beneficiaries Indonesia (19%), China (12.6%), the Philippines (8.8%), and Vietnam (8%). Japan's influence diminished during the 1990s because its domestic economy entered a prolonged period of stagnation, while Japanese banks helped to set the stage for the East Asian financial crisis by greatly curtailing their lending in the region. When Japan attempted to contain the crisis by proposing the creation of an East Asian monetary fund, the United States rejected the idea and China failed to support it. After the crisis, Japan offered a U.S.$30 billion aid program (the Miyazawa plan) while collaborating in the ASEAN Plus Three talks on regional financial cooperation.

In 2002, Prime Minister Koizumi proposed the creation of a Japan-ASEAN Comprehensive Economic Partnership. The Japanese proposal goes beyond free trade to encompass scientific, educational, and cultural cooperation. Japan also signed an FTA with Singapore in 2001 and completed one with Malaysia in 2006. It is also negotiating new FTAs with Korea, the Philippines, and Thailand. Japan has so far avoided discussion of an FTA with China. There has been a sharp increase in political tensions during recent years because of Prime Minister Koizumi's decision to visit the Yasukuni Shrine, in which convicted war criminals are enshrined (together with millions of common Japanese who died during Japan's wars), as well as a territorial dispute over maritime areas in the East China Sea thought to harbor substantial deposits of hydrocarbons. The Japanese government is also skeptical about the ability of China to negotiate a comprehensive FTA encompassing issues such as services and protection for investments. But the fact is that both sides could benefit from an FTA limited to manufactured goods. China still has high tariffs on important Japanese exports, such as automobiles, and China is concerned that Japan's FTAs with ASEAN will give the countries of that group an advantage in penetrating the Japanese market. The Japanese corporate sector has made a large investment in China, but it has not been able to overcome the political tensions separating the governments in Tokyo and Beijing. In 2005, Japanese firms invested U.S.$6.53 billion in China, 19.8 percent more than in 2004, despite the increase in political tensions during the spring. The biggest investors were auto and auto parts companies as well as electronics companies.

It is clear from recent events that Japan is very suspicious of China, while the Chinese continue to harbor powerful historical memories of World War II. There is no simple way to bridge these differences. The Japanese increasingly perceive that China could be both an economic and a military threat to their position in East Asia. They have enjoyed an export boom to China, which helped to revive the economy during 2004, but they are reluctant to accept the geopolitical consequences of China's economic takeoff. In a recent opinion poll, a record 63.4 percent of respondents did not feel friendly toward China; the percentage of those who did feel positive declined to a record low of only 33.4 percent. China has also been a vigorous opponent of Japan's attempts to gain a seat on the United Nations Security Council. It sent a delegation to Africa to lobby against Japan as well as to encourage other Asian countries to withhold support. Japan's effort faltered, in part because of its inability to develop any regional support. Offers to support Japan came from only three minor Asian countries: Afghanistan, Bhutan, and the Maldive Islands.

As a potential harbinger of change, Japan's new prime minister, Shinzo Abe, decided to visit China only a week after taking office. His decision to engage Beijing as well as South Korea suggested that he wanted to move decisively to repair the damage caused by Prime Minister Koizumi. When he took office, Abe had not publicly stated whether he would visit the

Yasukuni Shrine, and some suspected that he had given the Chinese private assurances that he would not. Despite the fact that Abe's repeated rhetorical gaffes and outrages surpassed any such offenses committed by his predecessor, Chinese President Hu Jintao did not cancel his visit to Japan in the spring of 2007, and the visit was widely heralded as a success. Abe has since been succeeded by Yasuo Fukuda, who has a reputation for being more conciliatory toward China.

The delicate rapprochement between Beijing and Tokyo could have important consequences for political relations all over East Asia. It could set the stage for more cooperation on issues of regional economic cooperation and increase the odds of the evolution of a regional free trade area that could include all the major countries of East Asia. Abe has also tried to calm Chinese concerns about a revival of Japanese militarism by stating that Japan will not pursue nuclear weapons despite the 2006 North Korean nuclear test; China has long feared that Japan would use North Korea as an excuse to develop nuclear weapons. But Japan's decision will continue to leave it heavily dependent on the United States for military security, even if Japan is able to repeal Article 9 of the Japanese constitution (which restricts the size and role of the Japanese military) in order to expand Japan's global military role.

Security Relations

The focal point for China's security relations with East Asia is the ASEAN Regional Forum (ARF). China joined this group when it was formed in 1994. The membership of the forum is extensive, bringing together 23 countries from both sides of the Pacific as well as Europe. The organization's primary mission is to promote dialogue, not to create formal alliances. It allows countries to discuss issues of common interest and share information. China has not attempted to use the organization to achieve particular goals, but it has helped to promote peaceful discussion about territorial disputes in the South China Sea. China claims a variety of islands in the region and has occasionally deployed military forces to promote its position. But after 1994 it used the ARF to make clear that it would use the United Nations Conventions on the Law of the Sea to resolve its claims rather than pursuing a unilateral solution. The ARF is still evolving, but China clearly views it as important for promoting good relations and checking any American attempt to create an anti-Chinese alliance in the region.

China has been projecting a great deal of soft power in Southeast Asia through the rapid growth of trade and investment. It has also tried to play a behind-the-scenes role in managing local tensions. In 2003, there were anti-Thai riots in Cambodia's capital because of comments from a Thai film star about the country. The demonstrators looted Thai property and blockaded the embassy. China's foreign minister spoke to both governments in order to encourage them to defuse tensions.

China has also helped to create a new organization in Central Asia called the Shanghai Cooperation Organization (SCO). The demise of the Soviet Union led to the creation of several new independent states in Central Asia adjoining China's western frontier. China has played a major leadership role in encouraging them to come together in an organization to promote both security and economic cooperation. In contrast to the ASEAN countries, all the Central Asian countries have authoritarian political regimes, many of which are holdovers from the communist era. They all share an interest in suppressing Islamic fundamentalists and allowed the United States to develop a military presence in the region to pursue its war against the Taliban in Afghanistan. The SCO is unique because it is the first organization in which China has played a founding leadership role, but it remains highly informal, without a precise agenda. It may also become more economic in character because of China's desire to purchase oil from the region.

Between 1997 and 2003, China announced U.S.$9 billion of investments in Kazakh oil deposits and proposed to construct a pipeline from Kazakhstan to western China. In September 2005, China's National Oil Company launched a $4.2 billion takeover bid for a Canadian oil company with large Kazakh deposits, and in January 2006 the Chinese National Offshore Oil Company announced a takeover bid for Nation's Energy, another Canadian-listed oil company with assets in Kazakhstan. Additionally, in 2000 China signed an agreement to help develop oil deposits in Turkmenistan and build a pipeline to China.

The SCO has generated friction between Chinese and American foreign policy goals in the region, in large part due to the two countries' different approaches to the authoritarian regime in Uzbekistan. The regime violently put down an uprising in May 2005, killing hundreds in the process. The uprising came only a few weeks after a sudden revolution in Kyrgyzstan, so all the regimes in the region were particularly sensitive to such demonstrations of opposition. The United States and other Western countries condemned the killings. China, by contrast, welcomed the leader of Uzbekistan to Beijing and announced support for him, as did the Russians.

There is little doubt that China will continue to support authoritarian regimes in central Asia, because they will both protect China's oil supplies and restrain Islamic fundamentalists who threaten its unity in the country's western Muslim regions. The United States will promote democracy, but it will also have to bear in mind that democracy could produce support for Islamic fundamentalist political movements. The Chinese are also likely to show sensitivity to Russian views on the region, because both countries have manifested an increased willingness to collaborate. China is a major customer for Russian arms, and the two countries have recently conducted joint military maneuvers. China also hopes to greatly increase its imports of oil from Russia. The Russians have supported the incumbent regimes in Central Asia because they have been long-standing allies. Moscow resents attempts by the United States to promote revolutions comparable to the ones that occurred in the Ukraine and Georgia, and as a result, the SCO is now encouraging the United States to withdraw its military forces from the region.

China's other great multilateral initiative has been encouraging regional talks to end North Korea's nuclear weapons program. China is North Korea's oldest ally, but the two countries now have little in common. While China enjoys growing trade and investment links to South Korea, the economy of North Korea is moribund. Trade between the two countries in 2005 was only U.S.$1.58 billion, a small fraction of China's trade with South Korea. China is acutely concerned that North Korea's nuclear weapons program could encourage Japan to become a nuclear power while provoking the Americans to play a more aggressive role in the region. On top of this, North Korea's decision to detonate a nuclear device in October 2006 was a profound embarrassment for China. The government in Beijing strongly condemned the test and offered to support UN sanctions against North Korea. But there is a limit to how far China will go in punishing the North because of concerns that regime collapse would provoke a large wave of refugees to flee to China.

South Korea's government has been pursuing a policy of cooperation with the North. It has helped to establish an industrial zone on the North-South border where South Korean companies can employ inexpensive North Korean labor. The Kaesong Industrial Park is host to scores of factories and employs over 15,000 workers. The zone's sponsors hope that in seven years it will be able to provide employment for 730,000 North Koreans, or 8 percent of the country's total labor force. South Korea has also been reluctant to join American condemnation of North Korean economic crimes, such as counterfeiting dollars and smuggling drugs. South Korean attitudes have probably reinforced China's reluctance to pursue a hard-line policy toward the North. There is growing excitement in South Korea about the economic opportunities offered by China. South Korean companies invested over U.S.$6 billion in China last year, and thousands of Korean companies have China operations. There are 29,000 university students from South Korea in China and thousands more studying in secondary schools. As Asian economic integration proceeds, the odds are high that South Korea will revert to its atavistic position as Chinese ally.

In addition to the familiar quorum of countries engaged in East Asian diplomacy, there is a new player debuting on the stage of regional diplomacy: India. In the first 40 years after it achieved independence, India had isolationist economic polices. It promoted neither trade nor investment. It also pursued regulatory policies that undermined its manufacturing competitiveness and limited employment in that sector to only six million jobs in the formal sector. But after a foreign exchange crisis in 1991, India embarked on a policy of market opening that has boosted the country's growth rate to the 7–8 percent range from 2–3 percent previously. As a result of this policy, India is now actively pursuing economic integration with both China and Southeast Asia. It has negotiated an FTA with Singapore, and there have been important dialogues between India's leaders and China's on economic cooperation. Japan and Singapore lobbied to have India included in the recent summit of East Asian heads of government in Kuala Lumpur. Additionally, President George W. Bush recently announced a nuclear cooperation agreement with India in order to bolster trade links and promote the emergence of India as an alternative power center to China. The Indians have been reluctant to embrace the cause of containing China, but there can be little doubt that other Asian countries perceive India as a potentially important player in creating a new regional balance of power.

The other new economic power emerging in the region is Vietnam. As a result of economic reforms that began during the late 1980s, Vietnam is now achieving real GDP growth of 7–8 percent annually, making it a growth leader in Asia. Like China's boom, Vietnam's is being driven in part by an influx of FDI from other Asian countries. Adjusting for population differences, Vietnam's annual FDI inflows are now larger than China's (U.S.$7.9 billion in 2006). The largest investors are Singapore and Taiwan ($8 billion each), followed by Japan ($7.1 billion), South Korea ($6.2 billion), and Hong Kong ($4.6 billion). The United States has invested only $2.2 billion in Vietnam, but U.S. companies are now flocking into the country, and Intel recently announced an investment of $1 billion in Ho Chi Minh City (Saigon). The boom in the economy is also very much centered in the country's south, in particular Ho Chi Minh City. Exports from Ho Chi Minh City will exceed $18 billion this year, nearly five times as much as from any other province. The south also now controls a majority of the seats on the politburo. In November 2006, Vietnam hosted the annual APEC summit and used the event to demonstrate its new success as a market economy. Vietnam is also slated to join the WTO in 2007.

Implications for U.S. Policy

The rise of China as a great economic power and the new experiments with multilateralism in East Asia will pose serious challenges for U.S. policy. The United States has to recognize that there are new forces at play in the region that will alter the traditional balance of power and that the East Asian financial crisis of 1997–98 profoundly altered Asian views of how the world works. There is now far more willingness to collaborate in the region than was the case before the crisis. The countries in the region now hold regular conferences on financial and economic issues. They also have U.S.$2.7 trillion of foreign exchange reserves, nearly two-thirds of the world total, in order to ensure that they will never again be vulnerable to sudden changes in global capital flows. China has over $1.4 trillion of foreign exchange reserves, while Japan has more than $900 billion. Korea and Taiwan have over $250 billion each, and Hong Kong and Singapore have over $120 billion each. Until the recent oil price shock, all the East Asian countries were also running current account surpluses.

The United States has criticized China for accumulating reserves rather than allowing its exchange rate to appreciate, but the fact is that China's intervention has helped finance the U.S. budget deficit and propel its housing boom. During George W. Bush's first term, there was a larger real increase in house prices than under any other American president. If China and Japan had not been larger buyers of U.S. government securities during 2003 and 2004, interest rates might have been higher and dampened the housing boom.

Since the attacks on New York and Washington on September 11, 2001, the United States has been preoccupied with the Middle East and downplayed its relationship with East Asia. At the 2002 and 2003 APEC summit conferences, President Bush gave speeches about the war against terrorism, not about economic cooperation. Secretary of State Condoleezza Rice failed to attend the ASEAN Post-Ministerial Conference as previous U.S. secretaries of state had done. But U.S. policy has not been totally static. The United States has signed FTAs with Australia and Singapore and has been negotiating an FTA with Thailand for over two years. The United States has also announced plans to pursue an FTA with Malaysia and concluded FTA negotiations with Korea, despite the fact that many Korean groups, such as farmers, will oppose the latter FTA.

The Bush administration has also significantly expanded foreign aid to the region. The White House greatly impressed the Indonesian public by providing significant emergency relief after the Tsunami struck Aceh in January 2004. The new threat to U.S.-Asian relations is the Democratic takeover of Congress in the November 2006 midterm elections. The Democratic Party has become increasingly protectionist during recent years. In 2006, some new Democratic members not only campaigned against China and the Doha Round, but also called for repeal of the North American Free Trade Agreement. Because President Bush's fast-track negotiating authority expired in July 2007, the risk is now high that it will be impossible for the United States to negotiate any more bilateral FTAs. The Democrats could also attempt to use their new majorities to promote new legislation restricting trade with China. The emergence of a protectionist Congress could inhibit the ability of the United States to use trade diplomacy in the new regional competition with China over the balance of power. It could also limit the ability of the United States to use trade as a lever for promoting democratic reform in the Middle East. In 2001, the United States signed an FTA with Jordan that has caused trade with that country to expand sixfold. It has also signed FTAs with Bahrain, Morocco, and Oman. There has been talk about an FTA with Egypt, but the Democratic takeover of Congress could now prevent any further trade negotiations.

There is a natural unease in Washington about the geopolitical and military consequences of China's new status as an economic superpower. Many fear that China will use its new wealth to develop sophisticated weapons and challenge America's traditional military dominance in the region. But China has become so engaged in the global economy that it now has a diminishing capacity for radical foreign policy action. China has the world's third largest stock of FDI: China's ratio of exports to GDP is three times higher than that of Europe, Japan, or the United States, and it could become the world's largest exporting nation within two years. As a result of these circumstances, China must be a good global citizen, because it now depends on other countries to absorb nearly half of its manufacturing output. If China did not have foreign markets, its economy would plunge into recession, unemployment would rise sharply, and there would be massive protests against the ruling Communist Party.

The United States has long wanted to promote democracy in China, but it is far from clear that a democratic regime in China would be benign for American interests. The current regime in Beijing is firmly committed to economic modernization and market opening, which will lead over time to the emergence of a large middle class. If China had a democratic regime, there would be a great risk that the increasing income inequality in the country could produce a populist regime that would suspend economic reform and plunge the country into the kind of inflationary crises that have characterized Latin America for much of the modern era. What China needs today is more freedom of the press, greater transparency, and other developments that would increase government accountability and allow more debate about policy choices. The Chinese government undermines its own reform program when it arrests journalists for publicizing corruption or other injustices. Its role model should not be the old Soviet Union but rather Mexico and Singapore, countries with a long tradition of one-party rule that have also tolerated dissent and political debate.

The United States should support the experiments in regional cooperation, such as the ASEAN Plus Three meetings on financial and economic policy. They do not threaten any American interests. Washington was naturally apprehensive about the recent summit of East Asian heads of government, but it promoted only dialogue, not any major policy breakthroughs. The talks were also impeded by the bad relationship between China, Japan, and Korea. East Asia is likely to make further progress on issues such as sharing foreign exchange reserves, improving financial regulation, and promoting trade, but none of these initiatives will jeopardize American interests. The policies that could be damaging would be a decision by the East Asian central banks to sell their dollar assets and more aggressively diversify into the Euro or the yen. Such a move could drive up U.S. bond yields. The United States would also be threatened by any movement toward an East Asian free trade zone that was highly discriminatory against other countries and would encouraged trade diversion rather than trade creation. But because the United States is still the dominant export market for the region, it can probably hold regional protectionist forces in check.

There are some in Washington who would like to create an organization in East Asia comparable to the North Atlantic Treaty Organization in order to challenge China. However, as a result of East Asia's rapidly growing trade with China, it is doubtful that any country in the region would support such an organization. Australian attitudes toward the issue of Taiwan demonstrate how economic forces are changing political relationships. In 1996, Australia publicly supported the U.S. decision to deploy naval forces near Taiwan because of Chinese threats to fire missiles at the island. In 2004, the foreign minister, Alexander Downer, said that Australia would not support the United States in a conflict over Taiwan. The Labor Party protested that such sentiments violated the Australia–New Zealand–United States Security Treaty, but Downer's message was clear: Australia does not want its traditional American alliance to jeopardize a rapidly growing economic relationship with China. This deepening China orientation was reinforced by the election in late 2007 of Kevin Rupp, a fluent Mandarin speaker who is also friendly with the United States, as prime minister. The United States has been engaging in a formal trilateral security dialogue with Australia and Japan for some time. Ten years ago, it might have been able to use the dialogue to launch a China containment policy, but today Australia would be reluctant to embrace any foreign policy initiative that targeted China as an enemy.

There is concern everywhere that a China-ASEAN free trade zone could become discriminatory against other countries and regions. But ASEAN has a tradition of encouraging openness rather than increased protectionism. The United States should lobby the ASEAN countries to continue this tradition. China also has little self-interest in highly discriminatory trade policies because of a heavy dependence on markets in Europe and North America. The fact is that China needs a successful global trading system more than do most other countries. It has to pursue any regional or bilateral trade deals with this larger goal in mind. If the Doha Round fails, it is possible that the countries of East Asia will attempt to use APEC to create a new free trade zone. The United States has recently supported the idea. It is also supported by Australia, which will chair the 2007 APEC summit. But an APEC free trade zone will encounter many of the same obstacles as the Doha Round. Japan and Korea are very protective of agriculture, and the U.S. Congress might oppose an agreement that led to de facto free trade with China. Vietnam has just joined the WTO, while Russia will not join until 2007.

The United States will continue to be a critical player in East Asian regional economic cooperation because of its role in providing an export market (see Table 3.2). The United States typically takes 10–20 percent of exports from most Asian countries. The ratio of U.S. exports to GDP is 27.0 percent in Hong Kong, 23.8 percent in Malaysia, 14.7 percent in Singapore, and 10.2 percent in Thailand. But the U.S. share of Asian trade has declined over time because of rising incomes in the region. Domestic demand in East Asian countries is now equal to 37 percent of U.S. domestic demand, compared to 25 percent during the early 1990s. But because growth rates in East Asia are much higher than in Europe or North America, the annual growth of East Asian domestic demand is now equal to 82 percent of U.S. demand, compared to 68 percent five years ago and 47 percent ten years ago. As a result of this trend, intraregional exports are now usually two or three times as great as exports to the United States.

There is always a risk that as China's economy grows larger, China will become more arrogant or nationalistic vis-à-vis other countries. As a result of the country's history, there is always a suspicion of foreigners and a natural desire to compensate for past failures and defeats. But however much the Chinese government might want to flirt with nationalism, the scope of China's successful engagement in the global economy will limit its freedom of action. China could pursue a reckless foreign policy only by jeopardizing its domestic political stability.

The United States has been critical of China for pursuing relationships with rogue states such as Iran, Sudan, and Venezuela in search of oil reserves, and the United States naturally fears that China might give these countries military supplies in return for preferential access to raw materi-

Table 3.2 Exposure of Asian Countries to U.S. Growth, 2005

	Exports/GDP	Share of exports to the United States	Share of exports to Asia	Share of exports to the United States and Asia	U.S. export share of GDP	United States and Asia export share of GDP
China	33.6	21.4	41.6	63.0	7.2	21.2
Hong Kong SAR	181.0	14.9	59.6	74.5	27.0	134.8
India	21.3	16.3	24.9	41.1	3.5	8.8
Indonesia	42.2	11.5	62.5	74.1	4.9	31.3
Japan	13.7	22.5	48.4	71.0	3.1	9.7
Korea	54.1	14.5	49.4	64.0	7.9	34.6
Malaysia	121.2	19.7	55.5	75.2	23.8	91.1
Philippines	46.3	18.0	59.5	77.5	8.3	35.8
Singapore	102.4	14.4	54.7	69.1	14.7	70.7
Taiwan	64.8	14.7	61.9	76.6	9.5	49.6
Thailand	66.6	15.4	50.8	66.2	10.2	44.0

Sources: CEIC Data Co. and HSBC calculations. Data sources include International Monetary Fund, *Direction of Trade Statistics,* and World Bank, *World Development Indicators.*

als. But the United States effectively encouraged China to cultivate such relationships when Congress attempted to veto the Chinese takeover bid for Unocal in 2006. The fact is that a Chinese takeover of Unocal would not have posed any threat to American security, but it would have given China access to new oil reserves off the coast of Thailand. The decision to block the bid revealed an extraordinary insecurity about China that can only undermine America's ability to pursue a constructive relationship with the country. Since the collapse of the Unocal bid, Chinese companies have announced over U.S.$11 billion of other energy investments in Ecuador, Kazakhstan, Nigeria, and Syria. China is not content merely to buy oil on the open market. It wants to maximize its future security by purchasing petroleum reserves.

After an initial period of hostility, the administration of President Bill Clinton came to speak of a partnership with China. The Bush administration regarded China as more of a rival and began to distance itself from Beijing until the events of September 11, 2001, forced it to rethink who its enemies really were. Since 2001, the Bush administration has attempted to pursue a more collaborative relationship while remaining apprehensive about the long-term implications of China's rise as an economic power. Treasury Secretary Henry Paulson knows China well from his experience at Goldman Sachs and has launched an entire round of summits to promote U.S.-China dialogue at the highest level.

China's rise is somewhat comparable to the rise of Germany and Japan during the early twentieth century, but it has the potential to be even more significant because of the sheer scope of China's population size and land mass. Germany and Japan aimed to be regional powers. China has the potential to be a global power.

Rather than reacting to China on the basis of insecurity and fear, the United States should seek to engage China as a partner in promoting common global objectives. Both countries want a stable, prosperous world economy with open markets. Both countries need access to raw materials and commodities from countries that are potentially unstable. Both countries have populations that want to travel and experience the world without encountering terrorists or other threats. It will be difficult for the United States, as the world's sole superpower, to regard another rapidly emerging country as a potential equal partner, but the fact is that the United States will have overwhelming economic and military advantages compared to China for at least another two or three generations. It can engage China without running the risk of any great economic or political losses. The challenge will be to seek out opportunities for cooperation while continuing to encourage the forces within China that will ultimately produce both a more prosperous and a more democratic country.

Conclusion: Dangers of U.S. Inattention

The economic and political scene in East Asia is evolving rapidly: China is emerging as a great power, India is now attempting to pursue far more economic integration with China and East Asia, Indonesia and Malaysia are attempting to compensate for the effects of the East Asian financial crisis by bolstering their infrastructure investment, Japan is experiencing an economic recovery after many years of stagnation, Vietnam is emerging as a major new growth center, and all the countries in the region are accumulating large foreign exchange reserves in order to restrain currency appreciation and lessen the risk of future exchange rate crises.

Meanwhile, the United States appears to be consumed by conflicts in the Middle East. But America will continue to be influential because it is Asia's leading export market and dominant military power. However, America will not be able to dictate its policy desires in as simple and clear-cut a fashion as in the past. It will have to be more sensitive to the views of China and recognize that traditional allies such Australia now regard China as critical to their economic future. The Democratic takeover of Congress could inhibit U.S. diplomacy by promoting protectionism, but the president still has the power to veto any dangerous trade bills. The new equilibrium of promoting cooperation through economic integration is likely to persist for several more years because the private sectors of all the leading countries are strengthening their trade and investment links every day. China needs the American export market, and the United States needs capital inflows from China to finance its budget and current account deficits. Other Asian countries now export to America through China as well as through direct foreign trade. There is no way to stop the integration process without trade policies so protectionist that they would destroy the global trading system and raise the specter of another Great Depression. Not even congressional Democrats would dare provoke such a crisis. The Doha Round may fail, but it will not prevent further attempts at regional and bilateral free trade deals in East Asia, if not for APEC as a whole.

The great risks to the region are American apprehensions about the Chinese economic takeoff and an upsurge of nationalism in China, which could undermine its current policy of pursuing a peaceful rise as a great power. The United States has found effective ways to interact with China since the years of Richard Nixon's presidency, so it is difficult to imagine any radically destructive policy aberrations from the United States. China's political system remains authoritarian and is thus likely to offer continuity as well, but China, by definition, presents greater risks of upheaval at some point simply because its political system remains so controlled.

The critical difference between integrationist trends in East Asia today and previous attempts at economic integration, such as those in Europe during the 1950s, is the overwhelming role of the private sector. Certainly politicians and government officials have a critical role to play in managing the side effects of globalization; countries need to enforce the rule of law for international trade and investment just as they do for domestic transactions. But politicians would play only a minor role if corporate leaders and executives were not so excited about the business opportunities offered by economic interaction in the Pacific region. As a result, it is business leaders who will have a crucial role to play in controlling government officials and preventing them from allowing political conflicts to disrupt the benefits of East Asia's economic integration and progress.

CHAPTER 4

The New Trade Bilateralism in East Asia

John Ravenhill

FOR MOST OF THE PERIOD SINCE 1945, East Asian countries stood alongside the United States as the principal champions of economic multi-lateralism. They were strong supporters of global economic institutions and equally strong adversaries of discriminatory trading arrangements.[1] The reasons are not difficult to discern. Most East Asian countries had un-usually diversified export markets (not least because the region's economic powerhouse, Japan, had little appetite for its neighbors' exports other than raw materials) and had most to lose from any breakup of the global trad-ing system into closed regional blocs. East Asian countries were most fre-quently the victims when trading partners departed from rules-based approaches, whether discrimination against Japanese exports following Japan's entry into the General Agreement on Tariffs and Trade (GATT) or U.S. and E.U. unilateralism against Japan and the newly industrializing economies of East Asia in the 1970s and 1980s.

Rather than seeking to weaken the global trading regime, East Asian countries saw virtue in its further institutionalization and legalization as a means of countering bilateral pressures from Washington or Brussels, but not in a rapid extension of the scope of trade liberalization if this was likely to undermine the domestic social compact, an attitude evident in their re-sistance to the Early Voluntary Sectoral Liberalization (EVSL) agenda of the

Asia-Pacific Economic Cooperation (APEC) grouping.[2] Moreover, had there been any attempts to construct East Asian "regional" economic institutions, they would have faced formidable difficulties. These included the "shadow of the past" (Cold War divisions and the inability of Japan to dispel resentments about its colonial and wartime behaviors), a far greater diversity of cultures and of economic size and structures than in Europe,[3] and the lack of any agreement about the composition of the region. Indeed, 25 years ago it was rare to find references to "East Asia" or an "East Asian region" except in the "Harvard" sense of countries that shared a Confucian heritage.[4]

To the extent that economic regionalism in this part of the world was discussed before the 1990s (other than in various Japanese government–inspired arrangements to provide development assistance), the focus was Southeast Asia, where the Association of Southeast Asian Nations (ASEAN) had chosen economic cooperation as the principal vehicle for confidence-building among its member states. Yet while ASEAN had frequently rejigged its preferential trading arrangements, moving at a sedate pace toward the eventual implementation of a (less than comprehensive) free trade area,[5] extraregional markets remained of far greater significance for all ASEAN states, a dependence that shaped their foreign economic policies.[6] From the mid-1980s onward, as ASEAN members lowered their tariffs on intraregional trade they simultaneously reduced their rates for most favored nations (MFNs) substantially (and the grouping's most developed economy, Singapore, has long since implemented zero tariffs on almost all imports).

East Asia's new enthusiasm for preferential trading agreements (PTAs) thus marked a radical disjuncture from its previous foreign economic priorities. At the turn of the new century, East Asia (and the Asia-Pacific region more broadly) was significantly underrepresented in the rush to regionalism (Figure 4.1). China, Japan, Korea, and Taiwan were alone among the world's large economies in not having negotiated a PTA. Subsequently, East Asian countries have been rapidly making up for lost time: more than 60 PTAs involving them are currently being implemented or negotiated, and a couple of dozen more are the subject of semiofficial study groups. East Asia is now the world's most active region for the negotiation of PTAs.

The remainder of this chapter explores the implications of the new bilateralism in East Asia for existing and potential multilateral economic groupings involving countries from this region. I begin by looking at the origins of the new bilateralism, because these provide important signposts to how East Asian countries may respond to any multilateral initiatives on economic matters.

Figure 4.1 Number and Type of Regional Trade Agreements in Force and under Negotiation in 2001, by Region

Number of FTAs

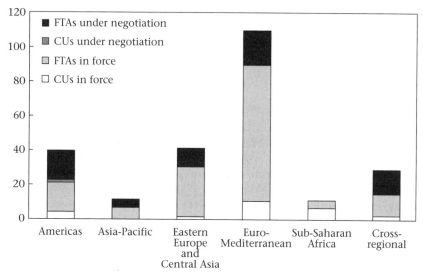

Source: World Trade Organization, "Regionalism: Facts and Figures" (2001), available at www.wto.org/english/tratop_e/region_e/regfac_e.htm (accessed April 4, 2001).
Note: FTAs, free trade agreements; CUs, customs unions.

The New Bilateralism

Like many developments in the international relations of the region, the variety of interests at play in the new bilateralism in East Asia is sufficiently complex that it would be naïve to attempt to explain it by pointing to a single factor.[7] For instance, contrast Taiwan's trade agreement with Panama with Singapore's PTA with the United States. For Taiwan, the principal motivation in signing the agreement with Panama was clearly the desire to find any partner willing to recognize its international standing by negotiating a trade treaty. Even after Taiwan's exports to Panama doubled in 2004, they constituted less than 0.2 percent of the total value of the country's exports: economic motivations are unlikely to have figured prominently in Taiwan's desire for the agreement, driven by its concern not to be completely excluded from the PTA bandwagon. In contrast, economic motivations were prominent in Singapore's negotiation of a PTA with the United States, which is the island state's largest single export market outside of ASEAN. But so, too, were strategic calculations; the govern-ment of Singapore has used free trade agreements (FTAs) as a means of at-tempting to secure the engagement of great powers in the region.

China's initiative in proposing a PTA with ASEAN, on the other hand, was arguably much more about regional politics—a brilliant diplomatic coup that placed Tokyo on the defensive—than about potential economic gains in the short or medium term. Other factors have motivated China's choice of other PTA partners, particularly its desire to attempt to ensure the security of supply of raw materials. Or take Korea, one of whose moti-vations in choosing Chile, again a very minor market and source of im-ports, as a partner for its first PTA was to gain experience in the negotia-tion of such treaties and to establish the precedent that its government would not allow its hands to be tied by protectionist interests in the do-mestic economy that were opposed to such arrangements. Even though PTAs are ostensibly "economic" agreements, motivations for their negoti-ation may owe as much to political or strategic considerations.

This stricture against seeking a single explanation for the new bilater-alism notwithstanding, some generalizations are possible about the con-text in which this major new development in foreign economic policies emerged in East Asia. I discuss these in the sections that follow.

The Growth of Preferential Trade Elsewhere

In the second half of the 1990s, East Asian governments were clearly concerned that they were missing out on a significant development in global trade relations as the wave of PTAs, particularly those that partnered industrialized with less developed economies, spread from Europe to em-brace the Americas. The reasoning behind the change in East Asian gov-ernments' views on PTAs is captured well by the evolution of Japan's offi-cial position. This rested on an analysis of the results of PTAs elsewhere that suggested they had positive effects on participants and no significant negative effects on other countries in the global economy, on political cal-culations that it was not in Japan's foreign policy interest to reject over-tures for PTAs from neighbors and significant partners, and on private sec-tor pressures that the government should act to level the playing field that Japanese companies faced overseas.

Despite the spread of regional arrangements throughout the global economy, particularly after the United States signed its first PTA in 1985 with Israel, the Japanese government had continued to criticize such arrangements within GATT working parties that scrutinized regional agreements.[8] Its fear of the potentially negative repercussions of discrim-inatory trading blocs had driven its commercial diplomacy in the Asia-

Pacific region. Increasingly, however, concerns were voiced within the Japanese government that the country was isolating itself through its refusal to enter PTAs. There were fears that preferential trade in the Asia-Pacific might become even more widespread, to Japan's disadvantage: one response of the U.S. government to the slow progress on trade liberalization within APEC had been to float a proposal in November 1997, through the Office of the U.S. Trade Representative, for a PTA with the four other APEC members perceived to be most enthusiastic about liberalization—Australia, Chile, New Zealand, and Singapore. The governments of Chile, New Zealand, and Singapore took up this proposal in 1999 after the failure of APEC's EVSL program—a failure that APEC's Western members blamed on Tokyo.[9]

In the second half of the 1990s, Japan's Ministry of International Trade and Industry (MITI) had begun to conduct studies of regionalism and of the potential costs and benefits to Japan of pursuing PTAs. The first public indication that the Japanese government was seriously reconsidering its stance on regional trade agreements came in MITI's "White Paper on International Trade 1999." Noting that Japan had traditionally stressed the negative impact of regional arrangements on third parties and thereby had distanced itself from the majority of countries in the international community that were now participating in such arrangements, the white paper asserted that evidence was now accumulating of the positive effects that regional arrangements were generating, not just for participating states but also for the global trading system as a whole. The white paper concluded that Japan should reconsider its policy on regionalism and use it as a supplement to the multilateral trading system.[10]

A report issued the following year by MITI, by then renamed the Ministry of Economy, Trade, and Industry (METI)—"The Economic Foundations of Japanese Trade Policy: Promoting a Multi-Layered Trade Policy"—articulated the new approach in more detail.[11] This report suggested that a broadening and deepening of regional integration had occurred in response to the growth of economic interdependence, reflected in increased flows of trade and foreign direct investment. The new regionalism had generated positive effects for participating economies, not just through conventional Vinerian trade creation and through enhancing the competitiveness of domestic industries but also by encouraging intraregional investment flows. METI noted that the new regionalism typically involved "deeper integration," with provisions relating not just to border barriers but also to investment and services and so on. Conventional economic models that focused only on the static effects of integration therefore tended to underestimate the gains from such arrangements. METI was particularly impressed with the benefits that the North American Free Trade Agreement (NAFTA) appeared to have delivered in the form of accelerated growth for its member economies. Moreover, various studies of the new regionalism seemed to suggest that it had relatively few negative consequences for nonparticipants.[12] METI also noted that by entering into regional arrangements, participants had strengthened their negotiating position in their talks with members of other regional groupings. Moreover, in a globalizing economy it was beneficial for a country if the technical standards used by its industries were adopted throughout the wider geographical area that a regional trading agreement might encompass.[13]

Calls for a reconsideration of Japan's policies toward PTAs also came from the private sector. In a statement on the agenda for the proposed "Millennium" round of WTO negotiations, Keidanren (the Japan Federation of Economic Organizations) asserted that Japan needed to give "concrete consideration" to pursuing WTO-consistent PTAs.[14] In July of the following year, Keidanren issued a more detailed call for the government to negotiate PTAs, noting that businesses were concerned that government action on this issue, despite business pressure, had been "lamentably slow."[15]

In pressing its case that the government should not confine its negotiation of PTAs to a specific region, Keidanren restated some of MITI's arguments about how such agreements might complement actions within the WTO and indeed facilitate multilateral negotiations. It also emphasized the beneficial effects such agreements might have in promoting Japan's own structural reform. However, Keidanren also added specific business concerns to the case for PTAs. Because the new regional agreements were typically "WTO Plus" in providing for investment protection and liberalization, harmonization and mutual recognition of standards, and liberalization of trade in services, they would offer expanded opportunities for Japanese business in the economies of partner states. Moreover, with European and North American countries aggressively expanding the number of PTAs to which they were party, Japanese companies would be at a disadvantage unless Japan's government negotiated similar arrangements. Keidanren pointed to the case of Mexico, where American firms enjoyed preferential access to the market through the NAFTA arrangements and European firms had similar access because the European Union had signed a bilateral PTA with Mexico. In contrast, Japanese companies faced Mexican tariffs of 10 to 20 percent on key exports, such as automobiles and household electrical appliances, and were excluded from bidding for government contracts. The intervention of Keidanren appeared to lend support to Baldwin's "domino" theory of regionalism, the argument that once momentum on PTAs gathers pace, the process becomes self-sustaining because export-oriented companies in countries that are nonparticipants will lobby their governments to take defensive action to negotiate equivalent concessions.[16]

The pressure from Keidanren marked a significant development in the evolution of the regionalism debate, not just in Japan but in the region more widely. Previously, regionalism in the Asia-Pacific had been largely a governmental affair. Although business had participated in the tripartite Pacific Economic Cooperation Council, governments had enjoyed little success in interesting large corporations in the activities of the principal regional arrangement, APEC. Indeed, the capacity of business to operate successfully across national boundaries in East Asia and its consequent lack of interest in regionalism was often held to be one of the most significant factors in the lack of institutionalization of intergovernmental collaboration in the Asia-Pacific.[17]

Japan, however, may be unusual in East Asia in the participation of its business community in active lobbying for PTAs.[18] The Korean equivalent of Keidanren, the Federation of Korean Industries, has largely abstained from public discussion of PTAs in Korea and has done little to offset the vocal opposition of domestic agricultural producers to these agreements. And in Southeast Asian economies, where export-oriented manufacturing is typically dominated by subsidiaries of multinational corporations, the key relationship in the domestic political economy between government and business is very different.

The Anticipated Slow Progress in Global Trade Talks

The move to negotiate preferential agreements in East Asia began before the 1999 Seattle WTO ministerial conference. Therefore, the failure of that meeting was not in itself a decisive factor in precipitating the new bilateralism, although it may certainly have accelerated the process. It did confirm the worst fears of some governments about the problems that a new round of global trade talks would likely encounter. Japan's MITI had noted that less developed economies were likely to be more active participants in the new round of global trade talks but that, because tariffs had been lowered worldwide, little was available to offer them by way of reciprocity for their participation in new WTO disciplines that industrialized economies were promoting. Stalemate or very slow progress at the global level was the prediction. And there were growing concerns among the more developed economies that the WTO was not well equipped to deal with "new" trade issues such as trade in services, competition policy, or the relationship between trade and the determination of environmental standards.

Financial Crises

The financial crises that wracked East Asia in 1997–98 were, in Calder and Ye's terminology, a "critical juncture" that caused East Asian elites to reconsider the merits of regional economic cooperation.[19] The resentment of East Asian governments toward the terms of the programs negotiated with the International Monetary Fund (IMF) can easily be overstated by failing to note the diversity of views represented in many governments and the capacity of pro-liberalization ministries to use the financial crises to pursue their preferred agendas.[20] Nonetheless, the crises did foster a new sense of regional identity and a determination to explore at the regional level means by which vulnerabilities generated by increased integration into the global financial system might be reduced. The crises thus helped pave the way for the negotiation of bilateral PTAs at the end of the decade. And, despite the emphasis on a regional (ASEAN Plus Three) financial response to the crises, protracted talks resulted in arrangements that were primarily bilateral in nature—a series of currency swap agreements known collectively as the Chiang Mai Initiative.[21]

The Weakness of Existing Regional Organizations

The ineffective response of existing regional institutions opened the way for the financial crises to prompt a search for new collaborative mechanisms. Neither APEC, whose leaders, meeting in Vancouver at the height of the crises in late November 1997, merely restated the desirability of further liberalization and endorsed the central role of the IMF in combating financial crises, nor ASEAN proved capable of putting forward a creative package in response to the crises. APEC's credibility was further damaged with the collapse of its EVSL initiative at its next leaders' meeting. ASEAN's own efforts to accelerate the pace of Southeast Asian economic integration in the wake of the crises were of limited effectiveness. Nonetheless, ASEAN's fortunes were revived when the ASEAN Plus Three proposals gave it a new centrality in negotiating broader East Asian regionalism. But ASEAN itself, given the relative weakness of its members, could at best be a moderately significant player in a broader region rather than an E.U.-like core whose membership could be expanded to embrace the whole region.[22]

Potential Effects of the New Bilateralism

The new bilateralism in East Asia could have three effects on the prospects for constructing a new economic multilateralism in the region:

- it could prove to be an obstruction in the road of such efforts,
- it could have no significant effect whatsoever, or
- it could play a positive role in laying the foundation for future collaboration on a broader geographical scale.

Within the final category, we can distinguish two possibilities: (1) the measures introduced through the new bilateralism could have positive consequences that would encourage countries to seek the extension of these agreements to other potential participants or, alternatively, (2) the new bilateralism could have negative and/or unintended consequences that would cause states to shift their preferences away from bilateral forms of cooperation toward multilateralism.

Economic Consequences of the New Bilateralism

The new bilateralism is relatively novel: few negotiations have been concluded to date, and only a handful of treaties are currently in force; of these, several have extended timetables before all their provisions will be implemented. This novelty renders any effort to speculate on the likely consequences of these agreements somewhat hazardous. Nonetheless, the content of the existing agreements and the circumstances in which they were negotiated allow several conclusions to be drawn that are relevant to the prospects for economic multilateralism.

Bilateralism as a Foundation for Multilateralism

The most optimistic scenario painted by proponents of multilateral liberalization was that the new bilateralism would produce agreements among like-minded states that would go beyond the current WTO agreements. They would thereby not just set a precedent for talks at the multilateral level but exert pressure on other countries to sign up for similar arrangements (in an ideal world, the bilateral agreements might be "open" in the sense of being able to be extended to additional partners). "Competitive liberalization" would inevitably accelerate the pace of global liberalization. Such arguments, for instance, characterize the position of the government of Singapore, the most active of the East Asian states in the negotiation of bilateral agreements.[23]

Experience to date provides little evidence to suggest that this most optimistic of scenarios will be realized. With the notable exception of agreements involving industrialized economies inside and outside East Asia (Australia, Japan, and the United States)—some of which do cover such "new" trade issues as competition policy, labor standards, and treatment of foreign investment and do go beyond current WTO commitments on intellectual property, trade in services, and so on—the treaties fail to move significantly beyond the current scope of global trade agreements. Indeed, in their selectivity of product coverage and their lack of specificity regarding what constitutes "free trade," some of the agreements are arguably "WTO minus" in the scope of their obligations. Besides, there is no evidence that even those agreements that go beyond WTO commitments (or PTAs elsewhere) have provided momentum for agreement at the multilateral level.[24]

Moreover, because each agreement has unique rules of origin, the proliferation of these agreements acts as an obstacle to collaboration on a wider geographical basis. An example is Singapore's negotiation of PTAs with Australia and New Zealand. Australia and New Zealand have a long-standing preferential trade treaty with one another, the Australia New Zealand Closer Economic Relations Trade Agreement (ANZCERTA), which has relatively simple rules of origin. The two countries nonetheless negotiated separate PTAs with Singapore; the latter two treaties have provisions for rules of origin that differ both from one another and from those contained in ANZCERTA. However, the rules in these agreements with Singapore, based on a simple value-added percentage, are straightforward compared with those of most of the new bilateral agreements (including, for instance, those involving Japan, Korea, and the United States), which usually specify product processing or transformation procedures that must be carried out locally for originating status to be achieved. These detailed product-specific rules frequently occupy several hundred pages of annexes to the treaties. In many instances, a principal objective underlying these complex rules appears to be to afford protection to sensitive domestic sectors.

Because these rules are specific to individual bilateral treaties, they serve as obstacles to rather than facilitators of the extension of the geographical coverage of the bilateral agreements to which they belong. None of the bilateral treaties negotiated to date makes any reference to the possibility of its extension to additional parties.[25] If the new bilateralism has not facilitated multilateralism by establishing precedents for deeper integration or producing agreements that can be easily extended to new participants, perhaps it has encouraged a renewed enthusiasm for multilateralism among East Asian states because they have become disillusioned with the results to date—an issue explored in the next section.

Bilateral Agreements as Positional Goods

The essence of bilateral trade agreements is that they are discriminatory. They are, in Fred Hirsch's terminology, "positional" goods whose value is maximized when others do not have access to them.[26] In the case of PTAs, the positional character may have either economic (privileged access to markets) and/or political or diplomatic benefits (the status of having negotiated an agreement so far denied to others). A proliferation of PTAs that leads to others' enjoying similar agreements and having access to the same markets on similar terms undermines the value of the original agreements to the participants. With all countries now seemingly engaged in an enthusiastic pursuit of PTAs with multiple partners, there is little opportunity for even the most powerful states to insist that they should receive exclusive privileged treatment from their partners (and any such demand would be entirely contrary to the spirit of the WTO's MFN principle and to the "open regionalism" principle of APEC). The "positional good" character of PTAs is increasingly being negotiated away. A similar argument applies to states' strategies of attempting to position themselves as "hubs" by negotiating multiple PTAs with regional partners. With several states attempting to establish themselves as hubs (Singapore and Thailand, for instance, in Southeast Asia), the effectiveness of any such strategy is likely to be quickly undermined.

Robbing PTAs of their positional good character might make states less enthusiastic about pursuing them. Moreover, any new reticence about the lack of opportunity to enjoy an exclusive arrangement might be reinforced by a desire on the part of the governments that are making market-opening "concessions" to minimize the risks of trade diversion by extending the agreements to all their significant trading partners. The logical—and most efficient—way for them to do so would be to lower their MFN tariffs either unilaterally or through a multilateral negotiation.

The logic of these arguments has yet to appear sufficiently compelling to effect a change in East Asian governments' behavior. One explanation may lie in domestic political economy considerations. While the advantages to any one economy and its domestic producers arising from an individual PTA may be diminished if its partner signs many such agreements, the *disadvantage* to nonmembers and their domestic economic interests will be compounded by a proliferation of discriminatory arrangements. Domestic interests may feel that the need for a solution is sufficiently urgent and the outcome of any negotiations at the multilateral level sufficiently uncertain that efforts must be concentrated on leveling the playing field by negotiating a bilateral agreement whose terms are similar to those enjoyed by principal competitors. The outcome will be a further proliferation of bilateral agreements and a possible diminution of attention to the multilateral level. This logic points to another possible effect of the new bilateralism, covered in the next section.

Removing Export-Oriented Interests from the
Domestic Political Economy Equation

Greater economic openness (measured as the ratio of trade to GDP) has accompanied the lowering of tariffs over the past half century. It is now well established in the literature of political economy that companies with significant interests in export markets have been the principal proponents of liberalization, not only of foreign markets but of the domestic market as well.[27] What impact will the proliferation of PTAs have on their behavior?

The optimistic scenario presented, for instance, in Baldwin's "domino" theory of regionalism suggests that export-oriented interests will be strengthened because of the access to new markets gained through bilateral agreements and therefore will have both the resources and the interest to lobby for further liberalization. However, the logic here may be overstated. An alternative scenario is equally credible: that export-oriented interests will achieve their objectives in securing access to major markets through bilateral PTAs and will therefore not have the incentive to invest resources in lobbying for liberalization at the multilateral level.[28] In countries with multiple agreements that cover the vast majority of their exports, such as Mexico, domestic interests may have little incentive to press for liberalization at the multilateral level (and even less if the FTAs to which they are party continue to enjoy the status of positional goods).

The Limited Economic Gains from East Asian PTAs

A striking characteristic of many of the early PTAs negotiated by East Asian governments is that they were undertaken with countries that were relatively insignificant trading partners. This argument applies not only to the agreement between Panama and Taiwan, whose government, as noted earlier, was desperate to sign an agreement with any state that would recognize its international standing, but also to many of the other trade relationships negotiated. An example is Korea's PTA with Chile, which took more than four years to negotiate. Chile accounts for less than 0.5 percent of Korea's current exports. Or Japan's agreement with Mexico, where each party accounts for less than 1 percent of its partner's exports.

In many instances, the transaction costs of negotiating these PTAs seem disproportionate to the potential benefits that they may generate, especially in an era of low tariffs and in a region where export-processing zones and duty drawback schemes facilitate the movement and assembly of components across national jurisdictions.[29] Not surprisingly, results from economic modeling of the predicted effects of trade liberalization in the region find that the benefits will be far greater if liberalization is undertaken on a regionwide (East Asia) basis, especially if APEC or the WTO is the organizing framework for liberalization.[30]

To the extent that governments become disappointed with the aggregate economic benefits of bilateral agreements, one might anticipate that they will be more sympathetic to efforts at multilateral liberalization. Against this, however, several counterarguments can be made. First, in several instances governments appeared to choose their partners for PTAs not on the basis of maximizing potential gains but of *minimizing potential losses,* particularly to sensitive domestic sectors (as I discuss further later). Governments may therefore continue to prefer to pursue PTAs rather than negotiations at the global level because they will likely incur fewer political costs in doing so.

Second, while the overall economic gains from the new PTAs might be relatively small, they may nonetheless be significant for particular domestic constituencies. For instance, the Japanese auto industry was concerned about being shut out of the Mexican market and lobbied vigorously for Tokyo to level the playing field for it against its American and European competitors by negotiating a PTA. Third, potential economic benefits provided only one of the motivations for PTAs. To the extent that economic factors were a relatively minor consideration on the part of some governments, the small gains may not precipitate a re-orientation of trade policy.

PTAs and Domestic Structural Reform

Some governments in the region perceived PTAs as instruments that could be used to leverage domestic economic reform, and regarded them as particularly important when progress in the WTO talks was seen as unlikely to bring about the desired pressure on protectionist domestic constituencies. Governments wished to begin their experimentation with bilateralism with relationships that would be relatively uncontroversial in order to establish a precedent with domestic constituencies that PTAs were sufficiently important instruments of national commercial diplomacy that protectionist forces should not be permitted to obstruct them. Once the principle of entering into PTAs was established, governments would be able to negotiate more controversial arrangements that would require more substantial concessions by domestic constituencies.[31] Although the new bilateral agreements have established the principle that governments will not allow protectionist interests to prevent their use of these new instruments of commercial diplomacy, the actual impact of the agreements in promoting domestic economic restructuring is questionable.

Two factors are particularly relevant to this issue. First, the negotiations for PTAs have succeeded in mobilizing protectionist forces opposed to governments' making any concessions on issues of interest to them.

Some governments, such as that of Korea, appear to have been taken by surprise by the vehemence of domestic opposition to the agreements.[32] Whether such opposition is greater than would have been experienced if the issue had been subject to negotiation at the WTO is debatable; PTAs, because of their novelty, their single-country coverage, and their limited possibilities for trade-offs, arguably may have generated more attention and opposition than negotiations conducted in Geneva. To some degree, pressures from protectionist interests have been offset by those from export-oriented interests that will benefit from improved market access, but whether the pro-liberalization coalition is as broad as would be achieved through multilateral liberalization is questionable. Moreover, in some countries it seems that pro-liberalization forces have backed down from voicing their support for PTAs when they have been threatened with retaliation (e.g., a boycott of their products) by nongovernmental organizations and the agricultural lobby (as has happened in Korea). And in countries where export-oriented manufacturing is dominated by the subsidiaries of multinational corporations, which might be expected to be the principal beneficiaries of PTAs, the domestic political equation for PTAs is very different to that in, say, Japan or the United States.

Second, the effectiveness of PTAs as instruments of domestic economic restructuring is hampered by the imprecision of the WTO conditions that such agreements must satisfy to qualify for exemption from Article I.1, which enunciates the MFN principle. Article XXIV.8 of the GATT allows for closer integration of economies that choose to implement free trade areas or customs unions provided that the customs duties under any new agreement are not higher or more restrictive than the individual countries had previously imposed, and that the new preferential agreement eliminates duties and other restrictions on "substantially all the trade" between the participants. The wording of this article has generated enormous controversy over the years, because members have failed to reach agreement on defining and operationalizing the clause that refers to "substantially all the trade." The WTO itself has noted that "there exists neither an agreed definition of the percentage of trade to be covered by a WTO-consistent agreement nor common criteria against which the exclusion of a particular sector from the agreement could be assessed."[33] The European Union, the pioneer in negotiating PTAs, has argued that the requirement of Article XXIV.8 has both a quantitative and a qualitative element, with at least 90 percent of the trade between parties covered and no major sector excluded.[34] But other members have contested this interpretation, which in any event raises its own problems of definition: how is the stipulated 90 percent of trade to be measured (does it refer just to current volumes of trade or to that which might take place should restrictions be removed, and how does one define a "major" sector?[35]

The lack of agreement on Article XXIV.8 has stymied the work of the WTO's Committee on Regional Trade Agreements, created in February 1996 to examine PTAs and their implications for the multilateral trading system. Members have simply failed to determine whether the large number of PTAs notified to the committee is fully compatible with the relevant rules. Meanwhile, member states have exploited the lack of specificity of Article XXIV.8 to reduce the domestic political costs of entering PTAs. Here the European Union has again led the way. It set a precedent for excluding sensitive sectors from bilateral agreements by excluding most agricultural products from its PTAs with Mexico and South Africa. These precedents were seized on by Keidanren in its lobbying in favor of Japanese negotiation of PTAs. In a paper on the subject, the Federation argued that, although it was desirable "to liberalize as much trade as possible" in the agreements, the WTO requirement that they cover "substantially all trade" among the participants provided an opening to omit "sensitive" items from the liberalization schedule, thereby minimizing the domestic political costs of the new regionalism: "as is evident looking at other PTAs, some items of the industry in question which simply cannot be liberalized because of the serious impact by the free trade agreement may result in being removed from the list." The paper then cited the example of products exempted from tariff liberalization in the E.U.-Mexico trade agreement, noting that "such examples should prove a useful reference in Japan's considering FTAs."[36]

This was precisely the case in the Japanese government's negotiation of the Japan-Singapore Economic Partnership Agreement (JSEPA): the few products in the ultrasensitive agricultural sector that Singapore exported to Japan, principally cut flowers and goldfish, were excluded from the liberalization provisions. Zero tariffs apply to less than 10 percent of the volume of agricultural products exported from Singapore to Japan: the JSEPA created no new preferences in the agricultural sector and excluded 90 percent of the (very modest) value of Singapore's exports of agricultural products to Japan. In a similar manner, Japan made very few concessions in its bilateral trade agreement with Mexico—to the extent that less than 90 percent of Mexico's total volume of exports to Japan are included in the agreement.[37] Other East Asian countries quickly signaled that they intended to follow Japan's precedent. The Korean government indicated that it would not expose its agricultural sector to additional competition from Chile and Mexico by lowering barriers as part of PTAs. And the Taiwanese government is reported to have sought to exclude 800 products, mainly textiles and clothing, from a proposed PTA with Singapore (an agreement that ultimately was not negotiated, largely because of Beijing's objections).[38]

The ambiguities of Article XXIV.8 provide a means by which the circle can be squared: a means of creating a pro-liberalization agreement that avoids imposing adjustment costs on the least efficient domestic sectors, a liberalization without political pain.[39] The new bilateralism might be seen as an exercise in negotiated protectionism as much as in negotiated liberalization. Such an approach essentially returns to the logic underlying APEC's original modus operandi: that governments should voluntarily and unilaterally choose which sectors they wish to expose to international competition and not be coerced by their partners to undertake liberalization that imposes domestic political costs.

For ministries in East Asian states that are intent on using external pressures to promote domestic economic restructuring, the experience of negotiating PTAs to date has been unpromising. Their disappointment could lead them to turn their attention once again to multilateral forums, especially if they take seriously the prospect, outlined earlier, that PTAs could have the unintended consequence of taking pro-liberalization export-oriented interests out of the domestic political economy equation.

Political Consequences of the New Bilateralism

Despite all the hype about the new East Asian regionalism and the attention given to the ASEAN Plus Three grouping, the actions of East Asian governments since the financial crises suggest that they have no desire to create exclusive East Asian regional institutions. The majority of the bilateral PTAs involving East Asian countries listed in Table 4.1 that are currently being implemented or negotiated or are under study involve one or more countries from outside East Asia itself. And there is no evidence from the spheres of monetary and financial cooperation that East Asian governments have any desire to create exclusive regional institutions.[40] As an additional signal of this nonexclusivity, one that surprised many observers, East Asian foreign ministers opened up the first East Asia Summit in November 2005 to extraregional governments—those of Australia, India, and New Zealand.

From the standpoint of access to markets, nonexclusivity is an entirely rational approach. Despite the rapid growth in intraregional East Asian trade since the financial crises, largely driven by China's emergence as the workshop of the world, East Asia still depends overwhelmingly on extraregional markets for its exports. The United States is still a substantially larger export market for Japan than is China (accounting for 22 percent of Japanese exports in 2005, compared with China's 13 percent).[41] The United

Table 4.1 Bilateral and Minilateral PTAs Involving East Asian Economies, June 2007

Country/grouping	Implementing/signed	Negotiating	Study group
ASEAN	AFTA, China, Korea	Australia–New Zealand, India, Japan	European Union, United States
Brunei	AFTA, Chile–New Zealand–Singapore[a]	Japan	United States
Cambodia	AFTA		
China	ASEAN, Chile, Hong Kong, Macau, Pakistan	Thailand, Australia, Gulf Cooperation Council, Iceland, New Zealand, SACU, Singapore	India, Japan-Korea, Korea, Peru, South Africa
Hong Kong	China	New Zealand	
Indonesia	AFTA	Japan, Pakistan	EFTA, India, United States
Japan	Malaysia, Mexico, Philippines, Singapore, Thailand	Australia, ASEAN, Brunei, Chile, Gulf Cooperation Council, Indonesia, Korea, Vietnam	Canada, India, South Africa, Switzerland
Korea	ASEAN[b], Chile, EFTA, Singapore, United States	Canada, India, Japan	Australia, China, E.U., India, China-Japan, Malaysia, MERCOSUR, Mexico[c], New Zealand, South Africa, Thailand
Lao, PDR	AFTA	Thailand	

Malaysia	AFTA, Japan	Australia, New Zealand, Pakistan, United States	Chile, India, Korea
Myanmar	AFTA, BIMSTEC		
Philippines	AFTA, Japan		Pakistan, United States
Singapore	AFTA, Australia, EFTA, India, Japan, Jordan, Korea, New Zealand, United States, Brunei–Chile–New Zealand[a]	Bahrain, Canada, China, Egypt, Kuwait, Mexico, Panama, Peru, Qatar	Pakistan, Sri Lanka, United Arab Emirates
Taiwan	Guatemala, Nicaragua, Panama	Dominican Republic, El Salvador, Honduras, Paraguay	
Thailand	AFTA, Australia, China, India, New Zealand, BIMSTEC	Bahrain, EFTA, India, Peru, United States	MERCOSUR

Notes: AFTA, ASEAN Free Trade Agreement; BIMSTEC, Bay of Bengal Initiative for MultiSectoral Technical and Economic Cooperation (Bangladesh, Bhutan, India, Myanmar, Nepal, Sri Lanka, Thailand); EFTA, European Free Trade Area; E.U., European Union; MERCOSUR, Southern Common Market; SACU, Southern African Customs Union.

[a] After the Clinton administration's proposal for an FTA among the United States, Australia, Chile, New Zealand, and Singapore lapsed, Chile, New Zealand, and Singapore signed the "Pacific-Three FTA" in October 2002. On June 3, 2005, with Brunei's accession to the agreement, it was renamed the Trans-Pacific Strategic Economic Partnership.

[b] Excludes Thailand, which refused to sign after Korea excluded rice and 200 other agricultural products from the agreement.

[c] After failing to reach agreement on negotiation of an FTA, Korea and Mexico agreed in September 2005 to negotiate a more limited economic cooperation agreement.

States continues to be the largest market outside ASEAN for Singapore. And it is by far the largest export market for China. The refashioned trade triangles that now link other East Asian countries as suppliers of components to China and then to the U.S. market for products assembled in China arguably provide a foundation for building an economic community that stretches beyond East Asia.

The new bilateralism in East Asia has as much to do with diplomacy and political positioning as with economics. A desire to reassure ASEAN states nervous about the economic consequences of China's accession to the WTO and about the potential consequences for the regional balance of power of China's rapid economic growth underlay the "charm offensive" that led to Beijing's proposal for a China-ASEAN PTA—as did the desire to score political points against Tokyo. Like the economic dimensions of the new bilateralism, the political advantages that accrue to individual governments rest significantly on the "positional good" character of the relationship. China may have secured a temporary advantage over Japan through its offer of a PTA, but Japan's decision to launch its own negotiations with ASEAN as a whole and with individual ASEAN states has gone a considerable way toward nullifying this advantage.

The failure of the ASEAN Plus Three grouping to move forward on proposals for an East Asian free trade area also attests to the positional character of the current bilateralism in trade. This stands in direct contrast to the regional character of the two principal initiatives on finance, the Chiang Mai Initiative and the Asian Bond Market Initiative, both of which have been supported by meetings at the ASEAN Plus Three level. Whereas ASEAN Plus Three initiatives include meetings of finance ministers and central bank officials, trade ministers do not participate in these meetings. Trade issues currently are simply not on the agenda at the East Asian regional level.[42] Barring the emergence of forces that produce a new critical juncture in East Asian economic relations, the safest prediction for the coming years is that the current wave of trade bilateralism rather than a truly East Asian trade regionalism is likely to continue.[43]

The positional maneuvering of East Asian states in their negotiation of PTAs suggests that there is considerable fluidity in their current definition of the "region." The choice of negotiating partners and forums rests as much on political considerations as on economic ones. The current behavior of some ASEAN states (particularly Indonesia and Singapore) and of Japan suggests that they are concerned about potential Chinese domination of the ASEAN Plus Three grouping, and hence are willing to open East Asian "regional" meetings to countries besides the ASEAN Plus Three members, bringing in India and possibly Australia and New Zealand to balance China's influence. (These states may also be following the Malaysian ploy used under Prime Minister Mohamad Mahathir in APEC of expanding the number and diversity of members to weaken the institution.) If an exclusive East Asian regionalism on trade is not on the agenda, does this open the way for other multilateral trade institutions?

The APEC Problem in Trans-Pacific Economic Multilateralism

The early experience of East Asia's experiment with bilateralism suggests a number of conclusions. East Asian governments are not seeking to construct arrangements that exclude Western industrialized economies. Many of the arrangements that they have negotiated with one another to date are of limited economic consequence (especially in comparison with the agreement that Singapore has negotiated with the United States).[44] The proliferation of agreements is quickly eroding the economic and political advantages derived from any "positional good" characteristics of the new bilateralism. They have not produced the stimulus for domestic structural reform that pro-liberalization elements had hoped for. Disappointment with the results of the new bilateralism and concern about China's potential dominance of any region defined as exclusively East Asian has caused governments to look outside the region to South Asia and to Oceania for other partners that might balance China's influence.

This willingness to open up the "region" appears to afford an opportunity to the United States to seize the initiative and propose a broader "regional" trade grouping. The problem here is that such an organization is already in existence—APEC—but it is one whose efforts at trade liberalization have largely lost credibility. While APEC arguably has been revitalized since September 11, 2001, its success in its new role rests on its suitability as an organization for promoting the securitization of trade (an extension of its long-standing trade facilitation agenda) and to its provision of the only current forum that brings together leaders from both sides of the Pacific.[45] Trade liberalization disappeared from APEC's agenda (other than its ritualistic endorsements of the desirability for progress in the WTO negotiations) after the EVSL debacle in Kuala Lumpur in 1998.

Part of the explanation for APEC's loss of any significant role in regional trade negotiations lies in the unwillingness of governments to invest resources in attempting to provide leadership on this issue since 1998. APEC's momentum had depended heavily on the readiness of groups (e.g., the Pacific Trade and Development Forum, or PAFTAD, and the Pacific Economic Cooperation Council, or PECC) or governments (and individuals within them, e.g., U.S. President Bill Clinton, Australian Prime Minister Paul Keating, and Indonesian President Suharto) to push forward initiatives. None of the successors to Clinton, Keating, or Suharto has shared their enthusiasm for the institution as an instrument for trade negotiations. The attempt by APEC's Western industrialized economies to promote sectoral liberalization through APEC alienated the Japanese government, which together with that of Australia had previously been APEC's most consistent champion. And PAFTAD and PECC, which together had provided much of the intellectual stimulus for APEC, like the governments of the region, largely turned their attention to the new bilateralism and away from trade liberalization on an Asia-Pacific basis.

But lack of leadership was only one of the problems that bedeviled APEC's efforts at promoting trade liberalization in the second half of the 1990s. The institution was split between nations that took seriously its early commitment to the "ASEAN way" of handling trade issues—leaving it to individual governments to determine on a unilateral and voluntary basis the pace and extent of liberalization—and those (mainly its Western industrialized economy members, but also Hong Kong and Singapore) that wanted APEC to engage in WTO-like negotiations that would produce legally binding outcomes. The collapse of the EVSL talks marked the decisive victory within APEC of the unilateral and voluntaristic approach over Western preferences that APEC develop a legally binding framework.

The experience with bilateralism suggests that no significant change has occurred in the attitude of East Asian governments toward trade liberalization. The desire to exclude sensitive domestic sectors has been prominent in the negotiations, whether within ASEAN or in the negotiations that the Japanese and Korean governments have had with countries both within and outside East Asia. The minimal concessions that have been made on issues such as agricultural trade and cross-border movement of workers suggest that protectionist forces are still ascendant. Agricultural interests remain a potent domestic interest group in Japan and Korea and, when it comes to negotiating PTAs with efficient Western agricultural producers, in China also (where it has been reported that there is significant domestic opposition to including the agricultural sector in the PTA currently being negotiated with Australia).[46] The bilateral agreements reflect a desire for unilateral and voluntary reductions in trade barriers, that is, a continued preference to minimize domestic political costs rather than to maximize potential economic gains.

Conclusion: A Return to Multilateralism?

Any effort to promote a new multilateral economic institution would face formidable challenges. The first would be to determine what geographical scope it will have. If the desire is to link East Asia with North America, how would the institution differ from APEC? Although APEC also includes Chile, Mexico, Papua New Guinea, Peru, and Russia, none of these countries has ever been a significant player in the institution, and their exclusion, while giving an Asia-Pacific grouping a little more geographical coherence, would not change its fundamental dynamics. For the United States to exclude Oceania would alienate like-minded governments in Australia and (at least on trade issues) in New Zealand. And any effort to include only some parts of East Asia would be tactically unwise; the divisions among members of the ASEAN Plus Three grouping notwithstanding, "East Asia" currently continues to enjoy great symbolic significance for governments in the region.

The second challenge would be to determine rules and procedures that would be acceptable to countries on both sides of the Pacific. Most East Asian governments became disillusioned with APEC when its Western members attempted to use it to push forward liberalization in sensitive sectors at a pace more rapid than that they had accepted within the WTO. On the other hand, the failure of APEC to move beyond vague commitments to "free trade" at some distant point in time ensured that it generated little enthusiasm among business constituencies in its Western members and ultimately caused disillusionment in the United States on the part of Congress and the executive branch.

Is there any basis for a new multilateral agreement involving East Asia? Whatever the pro-liberalization noises coming from ministries of trade in Japan and Korea (and, in the latter's case, whatever the enthusiasm within some government as well as business and academic circles for an FTA with the United States),[47] the pro-liberalization forces have yet to fully establish their ascendancy. Of course, East Asia is not alone in continuing to protect sensitive domestic sectors, particularly in agriculture; consider the exemptions for sugar, beef, and dairy products that the United States insisted on in its PTA with Australia. But what is good politics in the United States does not make for good domestic politics in Congress when potential partners try to do the same.

Washington is unlikely to tolerate any agreement in which Northeast Asian partners attempt to exclude those major sectors in which trade barriers are currently highest. It is difficult to envision that domestic interests in the United States will be willing to sign up for a trade agreement with East Asia that permits the type of exceptions to trade liberalization that these governments continue to seek in their bilateral agreements. And, looking at matters from the other side of the equation, recent U.S. bilateral agreements (with Australia, Singapore, etc.) have been characterized by an asymmetry in obligations that favors the United States—a simple reflection of power realities—that is unlikely to encourage Northeast Asian governments to seek trade agreements with the United States on either a bilateral or a trans-Pacific regional basis. Attempts by Congress to incorporate labor and environmental standards are likely to further alienate East Asian partners.

The difficulties in designing a new multilateral trade institution for the Asia-Pacific point to the desirability of Washington's working energetically with like-minded governments to bring the current round of WTO negotiations to a successful conclusion. These offer the best hope for extracting significant concessions from recalcitrant East Asian governments on sensitive sectors. There is also a modest but constructive and positive role for APEC to play in working for progress on trade facilitation issues.[48] But it is at the global level that the most significant gains can be made.

Notes

1. By *East Asia* I mean the 10 member states of the Association of Southeast Asian Nations (Brunei, Cambodia, Indonesia, Laos, Malaysia, Myanmar, the Philippines, Singapore, Thailand, Vietnam) plus China, Hong Kong, Japan, Korea, and Taiwan.
2. For discussion of how the Japanese government has very effectively used the greater legalization afforded by the World Trade Organization's (WTO's) dispute settlement mechanisms (DSMs), see Saadia M. Pekkanen, "Aggressive Legalism: The Rules of the WTO and Japan's Emerging Trade Strategy," *World Economy* 24 (2001): 707–37, and "At Play in the Legal Realm: The WTO and the Changing Nature of U.S.-Japan Antidumping Disputes," in E. S. Krauss and T. J. Pempel, eds., *Beyond Bilateralism: U.S.-Japan Relations in the New Asia-Pacific* (Stanford, Calif.: Stanford University Press, 2004), 221–47. China has also begun to make use of the DSMs; its first action was against U.S. safeguard measures to restrict steel imports (WTO case number WT/DS252).
3. See, for instance, Edward J. Lincoln, *East Asian Economic Regionalism* (New York and Washington, D.C.: Council on Foreign Relations and Brookings Institution Press, 2004), and Joseph M. Grieco, "Systemic Sources of Variation in Regional Institutionalization in Western Europe, East Asia, and the Americas," in E. D. Mansfield and H. V. Milner, eds., *The Political Economy of Regionalism* (New York: Columbia University Press, 1997), 164–87.
4. Paul Evans, "The Concept of Eastern Asia," in C. Mackerras, ed., *Eastern Asia: An Introductory History,* 3rd ed. (Melbourne: Longman Australia, 2000), 7–14.
5. John Ravenhill, "Economic Cooperation in Southeast Asia: Changing Incentives," *Asian Survey* 35, no. 9 (1995): 850–66.
6. Over more than three decades of economic cooperation, the share of intra-ASEAN trade in the overall exports of member economies has been largely

unchanged, around 20 percent. And Singapore accounts for the bulk of this intraregional trade.

7. Francis Fukuyama, "All Quiet on the Western Front?" *Wall Street Journal,* March 1, 2005, online edition.

8. Eguchi Masato, "JSEPA (Japan-Singapore Economic Partnership Agreement) and Future Trade Policy," *Journal of Japanese Trade and Industry,* 2001, available at www.jef.or.jp/en/jti/200101_001.html (accessed February 27, 2002).

9. Krauss makes a compelling argument that the blame for the EVSL debacle extends beyond the Japanese government. See Ellis S. Krauss, "The United States and Japan in APEC's EVSL Negotiations: Regional Multilateralism and Trade," in E. S. Krauss and T. J. Pempel, eds., *Beyond Bilateralism: U.S.-Japan Relations in the New Asia-Pacific* (Stanford, Calif.: Stanford University Press, 2004), 272–95.

10. Ministry of International Trade and Industry, "White Paper on International Trade 1999" (Tokyo: Government of Japan, Ministry of Economy, Trade, and Industry, 1999), available at www.meti.go.jp/english/report/data/gWP1999e.html (accessed February 24, 2002).

11. Ministry of Economy, Trade, and Industry, "The Economic Foundations of Japanese Trade Policy—Promoting a Multi-Layered Trade Policy" (Tokyo: Government of Japan, Ministry of Economy, Trade and Industry, 2000), available at www.meti.go.jp/english/report/data/g00Wconte.html (accessed February 24, 2002).

12. This reasoning, however, contradicted the argument that an active FTA policy was needed for "defensive" reasons—to level the playing field for domestic exporters in markets where competitors benefited from FTAs. Contrast this with Wall, who estimated that Japan's exports might be as much as 19 percent lower than they would otherwise have been because of the negative effects of NAFTA and the European Union. Howard J. Wall, "Has Japan Been Left Out in the Cold by Regional Integration?" Institute for Monetary and Economic Studies Discussion Paper 2001-E-15 (Tokyo: Bank of Japan, 2001).

13. Ministry of Economy, Trade, and Industry, "The Economic Foundations of Japanese Trade Policy—Promoting a Multi-Layered Trade Policy" (Tokyo: Government of Japan, Ministry of Economy, Trade, and Industry, 2000), available at www.meti.go.jp/english/report/data/g00Wconte.html (accessed February 24, 2002).

14. Keidanren, "Challenges for the Upcoming WTO Negotiations and Agendas for Future Japanese Trade Policy" (Tokyo: Keidanren, 1999), available at www.keidanren.or.jp/english/policy/pol102/proposal.html (accessed November 5, 2001).

15. Keidanren, "Urgent Call for Active Promotion of Free Trade Agreements—Toward a New Dimension in Trade Policy" (Tokyo: Keidanren, 2000), avail-

able at www.keidanren.or.jp/english/policy/2000/033/proposal.html (accessed November 5, 2001).

16. Richard E. Baldwin, "The Causes of Regionalism," *World Economy* 20, no. 7 (1997): 865–88.

17. For further elaboration, see John Ravenhill, *APEC and the Construction of Asia-Pacific Regionalism*, Cambridge Asia-Pacific Studies (Cambridge: Cambridge University Press, 2001).

18. In private comments, Kent Calder pointed out that Keidanren's activism may have reflected the fact that the organization has recently been dominated by Toyota, which supplied two of its past three chairmen. For further discussion of Keidanren's role in the FTA debate in Japan, see Hidetaka Yoshimatsu, "Japan's Keidanren and Free Trade Agreements: Societal Interests and Trade Policy," *Asian Survey* 45 (2005): 258–78, and Mark Manger, "Competition and Bilateralism in Trade Policy: The Case of Japan's Free Trade Agreements," *Review of International Political Economy* 12 (2005): 804–28.

19. Kent Calder and Min Ye, "Regionalism and Critical Junctures: Explaining the 'Organization Gap' in Northeast Asia," *Journal of East Asian Studies* 4, no. 2 (2004): 191–226.

20. Mo and Moon discuss the interaction of domestic and external actors in the Korean context. See Jongryn Mo and Chung-in Moon, "Business-Government Relations under Kim Dae-Jung," in S. Haggard, W. Lim, and E. Kim, eds., *Economic Crisis and Corporate Restructuring in Korea: Reforming the Chaebol* (New York: Cambridge University Press, 2003), 127–49.

21. Jennifer Amyx, "Regional Financial Cooperation," in Andrew J. MacIntyre, T. J. Pempel, and John Ravenhill, eds., *After the Crisis: East Asia's Changing Political Economy* (Ithaca, N.Y.: Cornell University Press, 2008), chap. 4.

22. On ASEAN's continuing ineffectiveness in promoting regional economic cooperation, see John Ravenhill, "Fighting Irrelevance: An Economic Community with 'ASEAN' Characteristics," *Pacific Review* (forthcoming).

23. See, for instance, Berry Desker, "In Defence of FTAs: From Purity to Pragmatism in East Asia," *Pacific Review* 17 (2004): 3–26.

24. The Organisation for Economic Co-operation and Development (OECD) reports a lack of relationship between bilateralism and progress at the multilateral level for a much larger and more geographically diverse sample of agreements. See OECD, "Regional Trade Agreements and the Multilateral Trading System: Consolidated Report," 2002, available at www.olis.oecd.org/olis/2002doc.nsf/43bb6130e5e86e5fc12569fa005d004c/db1bbc3ddbadceeec1256c770042bc1b/$FILE/JT00135547.PDF (accessed August 18, 2003).

25. The only exception to this argument is the trilateral agreement between Chile, New Zealand, and Singapore, which is open to other states for accession. Brunei has signed on to this agreement.

26. Fred Hirsch, *Social Limits to Growth* (Cambridge, Mass.: Harvard University Press, 1976).
27. Gerald K. Helleiner, *Intra-Firm Trade and the Developing Countries* (London: Macmillan, 1981); Helen Milner, *Resisting Protectionism: Global Industries and the Politics of International Trade* (Princeton, N.J.: Princeton University Press, 1988).
28. This argument is a variant of that put forward by Aggarwal and Ravenhill on the potential dangers of sectoral agreements in the WTO. See Vinod K. Aggarwal and John Ravenhill, "Undermining the WTO: The Case against 'Open Sectoralism,'" *AsiaPacific Issues* 50 (2001). For further discussion, see John Ravenhill, "The Political Economy of the New Asia-Pacific Bilateralism: Benign, Banal or Simply Bad?" in Vinod K. Aggarwal and Shujiro Urata, eds., *Bilateral Trade Agreements in the Asia-Pacific: Origins, Evolution and Implications* (London: Routledge, 2006), 27–49.
29. Even among the 13 countries of ASEAN Plus Three, the transaction costs of negotiating complete coverage through a network of bilateral treaties would be substantial, because a total of 78 bilateral relationships are involved (81 if China, Japan, and Korea also negotiate an arrangement with ASEAN as a whole as well as with individual ASEAN states, as China and Japan are currently doing).
30. See, most notably, Robert Scollay and John Gilbert, *New Regional Trading Arrangements in the Asia Pacific?* (Washington, D.C.: Institute for International Economics, 2001), and, for East Asia, Yung Chul Park, Shujiro Urata, and Inkyo Cheong, "The Political Economy of the Proliferation of FTAs," paper presented at the conference PAFTAD 30, Honolulu, February 19–21, 2005.
31. On the Japanese strategy, see Naoko Munakata, "Evolution of Japan's Policy toward Economic Integration" (Washington, D.C.: Brookings Institution, 2001), and "How Trade Agreements Can Reform Japan," *The Globalist* (Washington, D.C.: Brookings Institution, 2002), available at www.theglobalist.com/dbweb/StoryId.aspx?StoryId=2560 (accessed August 18, 2003).
32. Author interviews of government officials and private sector representatives, Seoul, September 2005.
33. World Trade Organization (WTO), "Regionalism: Article XXIV of GATT 1994 (2)," training package (Geneva: WTO, 1998).
34. Commission of the European Union, "Commission Staff Working Paper Concerning the Establishment of an Inter-Regional Association between the European Union and Mercosur," Commission of the European Union Directorate General Trade (Brussels: Commission of the European Union, n.d.).
35. In a paper on Japan's strategy on the negotiation of free trade areas, the Japanese Ministry of Foreign Affairs suggested that the "substantially all trade" criterion "implies that countries must achieve a standard of liberalization

that compares favorably to international standards in terms of trade volume" and notes that the NAFTA average is 99 percent, while the average for the FTA between the European Union and Mexico is 97 percent. The paper makes no reference to coverage of all sectors. Government of Japan, Ministry of Foreign Affairs, "Japan's FTA Strategy (Summary)" (Tokyo: Economic Affairs Bureau, Ministry of Foreign Affairs, 2002).

36. Keidanren, " 'Urgent Call for Active Promotion of Free Trade Agreements— Toward a New Dimension in Trade Policy" (Tokyo: Keidanren, 2000).

37. For further discussion, see Mireya Solis, "Japan's New Regionalism: The Politics of Free Trade Talks with Mexico," *Journal of East Asian Studies* 3 (2003): 377–404.

38. "Some 800 Items on Taiwan Protected List in FTA with Singapore: Report," Agence France-Presse, April 21, 2002, available at http://asia.news.yahoo.com/020421/afp/020421050556singapore.html.

39. John Ravenhill, "The New Bilateralism in the Asia-Pacific," *Third World Quarterly* 24 (2003): 299–317. The WTO's Article XXIV applies only to preferential trade agreements that involve at least one industrialized economy. Agreements among developing countries (all East Asian countries apart from Japan) are covered by the Enabling Clause, whose requirements are even less stringent than those of Article XXIV.

40. Jennifer Amyx, "What Motivates Regional Financial Cooperation in East Asia Today?" *Asia-Pacific Issues* 76 (2005), available at www.eastwestcenter.org/fileadmin/stored/pdfs/api076.pdf (accessed March 6, 2005).

41. The U.S. share of Japanese exports, however, is dwarfed by that of East Asia as a whole, which currently accounts for 47 percent of total Japanese exports. Data from the Web site of the Japan External Trade Organization (JETRO): www.jetro.go.jp/en/stats/statistics/.

42. Yung Chul Park, Shujiro Urata, and Inkyo Cheong, "The Political Economy of the Proliferation of FTAs," paper presented at the PAFTAD 30 conference, Honolulu, February 19–21, 2005.

43. For a similar conclusion, see Ellen L. Frost, "Implications of Regional Economic Integration," in R. J. Ellings, A. L. Friedberg, and M. Wills, eds., *Strategic Asia 2003–4: Fragility and Crisis* (Seattle: National Bureau of Asian Research, 2003). Ongoing bilateral tensions make the negotiation of a three-way PTA between China, Japan, and Korea highly unlikely.

44. The success of the United States in negotiating with Singapore a PTA that it intends to use as a template for other agreements in Southeast Asia (with negotiations having begun with Thailand and Malaysia) suggests that alarmist views about the marginalization of the United States in East Asia are incorrect —as does the conclusion of negotiations for an agreement with Korea. The PTAs that the United States has negotiated have several distinctive features: they are comprehensive in their coverage (most definitely WTO Plus), come

into effect immediately, and are closely monitored. They are therefore likely to have a more significant economic impact on partner countries in East Asia than the "woolly" agreements that the East Asian economies have negotiated among themselves.

45. John Ravenhill, "Mission Creep or Mission Impossible? APEC and Security," in Amitav Acharya and Evelyn Goh, eds., *Reassessing Security Cooperation in the Asia-Pacific: Competition, Congruence, and Transformation* (Cambridge, Mass.: MIT Press, 2007).

46. See, for instance, "Beijing Sends Warning over Farm Exports," *Australian Financial Review,* March 22, 2005, 3. Similarly, Japan's Ministry of Agriculture, Forestry, and Fisheries was reported by *Nihon Keizai Shimbun* to have blocked a proposal to conduct a preparatory study for negotiating an FTA with Australia. See "Japanese Farm Lobby Threatens Trade Pact," *Sydney Morning Herald,* April 18, 2005, available at www.smh.com.au (accessed April 18, 2005).

47. Inbom Choi and Jeffrey J. Schott, "Korea-US Free Trade Revisited," in J. J. Schott, ed., *Free Trade Agreements: US Strategies and Priorities* (Washington, D.C.: Institute for International Economics, 2004), 173–96.

48. Lincoln draws similar implications for U.S. policy of the new East Asian regionalism. See Lincoln, *East Asian Economic Regionalism.*

Part II · Country Perspectives

CHAPTER 5

China's Evolving Multilateralism in Asia

The *Aussenpolitik* and *Innenpolitik* Explanations

Cheng-Chwee Kuik

IF MULTILATERALISM IS DEFINED as a country's inclination to use multilateral diplomacy as an active means to advance its key policy ends,[1] China's multilateralism is a new phenomenon that emerged only toward the end of the 1990s. Prior to this period, the People's Republic of China (PRC) neither preferred nor relied on a multilateral approach as an active way of pursuing its core interests. Bilateral diplomacy and unilateral action remained the principal thrusts in handling major foreign relations issues, ranging from political and economic cooperation to strategic and security affairs. Certainly, China has been a member in a range of global organizations (mainly the United Nations and its specialized agencies) since the 1970s. Since the 1990s, it has also been a participant in various regional institutions, such as the Asia-Pacific Economic Cooperation (APEC) and the forums driven by the Association of Southeast Asian Nations (ASEAN). Nevertheless, mere participation in these multilateral processes did not signal the rise of China's multilateralism. The pattern of Chinese multilateral involvement during this period was largely passive and reactive, as evidenced by Beijing's record in responding to others' initiatives rather than proposing and promoting its own. Thus, multilateral diplomacy played a negligible role in the PRC's foreign policy throughout the first four decades of its existence.

A change in China's multilateral policy gradually took place only after the mid-1990s. This change was first manifested in Beijing's rising comfort and confidence with regard to the ASEAN Regional Forum (ARF). At first, China's participation in the security forum was marked by a watchful and at times suspicious attitude, partly due to Beijing's sensitivity to sovereignty issues (Taiwan and the Spratly Islands territorial disputes) and partly due to its lack of familiarity with multilateral practices.[2] A similarly cautious and tense atmosphere also surfaced in the annual ASEAN-China senior officials' political consultation.[3] After a period of participating and observing, however, the PRC slowly realized that these forums, which feature a consultative mode of interaction and are led by the ASEAN states rather than the United States and Japan, might not be harmful to its national interests.[4] Thus, Beijing judged that it could use these institutions as a platform to promote its own foreign policy objectives, including maintaining a stable external environment, marginalizing Taipei's diplomatic endeavors, and refuting the theory of the alleged "China threat" seen in the region.[5] Later, China's desire to hedge against a perceived U.S. encirclement campaign further increased its resolve to promote these policy goals.[6]

Such a reevaluation led to a shift in China's regional multilateral policy from passive involvement to active participation.[7] After the mid-1990s, China began to take part in an increasingly active manner. It offered to co-chair the 1997 ARF intersessional support group meeting; advocated the "new security concept [*xin anquan guan*]"; played a central role in the inception of the Shanghai Five; and has been actively involved in the ASEAN Plus Three (APT, i.e., ASEAN plus China, Japan, and Korea) ever since its inaugural summit in 1997. China's embrace of multilateral diplomacy reached a high point in 2000, when it proposed the establishment of the ASEAN-China Free Trade Area (ACFTA). This could be regarded as a watershed moment, for it signaled the PRC's entry into a new phase in which it has started to advance a series of important regional initiatives, such as the idea of the ASEAN-China Strategic Partnership and recommendations to broaden the purpose of the APT from mainly economic cooperation to political and security dialogue. I will discuss Beijing's motivation for these actions later. Here, suffice it to say that the *proactive* twist is a clear testimony to China's growing multilateralism. At the turn of the new century, multilateral diplomacy has emerged as an indispensable part of the conduct of China's foreign policy.

Much has been written on how China's evolving multilateralism or "new diplomacy" over the past decade has enabled Beijing to defuse regional apprehensions about its rapid rise, increased Chinese influence in Asia, and presented a political challenge to American and Japanese interests in the region.[8] Few studies, however, have attempted to take a longer evolutionary view by looking at China's changing attitudes toward multi-lateral institutions since 1949.[9] Such an approach is necessary because without a better understanding of the underlying forces that have driven the PRC's shifting multilateral policies at different historical junctures, chances are good that we will be unable to account for the current nature and future direction of China's multilateralism.

Specifically, this understanding will help us to address a central question regarding Chinese foreign policy: is China's present multilateralism the result of an externally calculated *tactical adaptation* designed to reassure other regional states while it is "still growing and relatively weak,"[10] or is it the product of an *internally driven necessity* in which Chinese leaders are recognizing that multilateral cooperation is a vital means of interacting with the outside world for the ultimate purpose of serving the regime interests at home?[11]

While these two perspectives are not entirely mutually exclusive, they are sufficiently distinct in their assumptions to offer competing interpretations and alternative propositions for explaining China's multilateralism. The first perspective, which is termed the *Aussenpolitik* perspective, highlights the primacy of "structural forces" in influencing a state's foreign policy. It owes its theoretical roots to structural realism or neorealism, which insists that all states are "functionally alike units" whose task is to seek security in an anarchic environment by responding to the changes in the distribution of global power, chiefly through forming military alliances and upgrading their armaments.[12] In contrast, the second perspective, termed the *Innenpolitik* perspective, stresses the centrality of domestic politics in foreign policy formation.[13] It is theoretically linked to neoclassical realism, which argues that structural pressures are important only if they are linked to unit-level variables such as domestic state structure.[14]

The *Aussenpolitik* perspective focuses on the question of *relative capabilities*. Its assumption is that a state's foreign policy behavior is externally motivated and constrained by the level of its material power vis-à-vis others within the international system. Accordingly, it contends that China's current position in upholding multilateralism is due to the country's lack of adequate capabilities to take coercive actions for imposing its international agenda. It envisages that once China grows stronger both economically and militarily, there will be a decreasing need for Beijing to employ multilateral diplomacy as a reassuring tool and therefore a greater possibility that it may turn to an aggressive approach to advance its interests.

The *Innenpolitik* perspective, on the other hand, looks at the issue of *domestic political necessity*. It postulates that a state's foreign policy choice is internally driven by the ruling elite's concern to justify its domestic authority and to enhance its governance capability.[15] From this perspective,

China's present multilateralism is viewed as a continuous part of the country's decades-long quest for greater integration into the international community, as required by the regime's ultimate goal of preserving its political relevance at home. It follows that whether Beijing will uphold multilateralism, and to what extent, depends on whether such an approach will consolidate or constrain the efforts of the Chinese Communist Party (CCP) to remain in power. It is true that China's multilateralism may move in either direction. However, considering that multilateral linkages are becoming a sine qua non of virtually every aspect of China's external interactions and that they are strengthening rather than hindering the party's grip on power, this perspective contends that China is likely to stay on the multilateral path in the decades to come. If this contention is valid, we should expect to observe that major shifts in China's multilateral policy at different junctures are consistently in line with the CCP's goal of strengthening its regime interests, which may or may not overlap with its task of maximizing its relative power. In instances in which regime preservation contradicts rather than coincides with power maximization, we should expect to see China choose the former over the latter.

The central argument of this chapter is that the shifts in the PRC's multilateral policy over the past few decades have been driven principally by the changes in the CCP's bases of regime justification. I contend that concern about relative power affects only the *pace* of Beijing's multilateral involvement; it does not determine the *direction* of China's policy. It was the CCP's changing bases of regime preservation that compelled China to evolve from an outsider and challenger to the world of multilateral organizations in the 1950s and 1960s to a pragmatic participant in the 1980s and, finally, to an active player in the regional multilateral game in the late 1990s.

The remainder of this chapter reviews the evolution of the PRC's multilateral involvement since 1949 in four phases, with a focus on its present multilateralism in East Asia.[16] I identify the features of and shifts in each phase before offering contending explanations to account for these changes.

China's Changing Policies toward Multilateral Institutions

China's attitude toward multilateral institutions, which can be seen as having evolved in four phases, has been a mirror image of its shifting foreign policy concerns since 1949.[17] The characteristics of China's multilateral policy in each phase of its evolution have been, for the most part, direct extensions of its key foreign relations strategy during that phase.

Phase I (1949–1970): China as an Outsider and Challenger

Throughout the first two decades of the PRC's existence, its multi-lateral policy was marked by its posture as an outsider and challenger to the world of international organizations.[18] From 1949 until the late 1950s, Mao Zedong pursued a "lean-to-one-side [*yibiandao*]" strategy, bringing the newly established nation into the socialist camp headed by the Union of Soviet Socialist Republics (USSR). Due to this strategy, China participated only in a handful of the Soviet-led organizations and vilified those headed by the Western camp. Such a posture was not surprising, given that China not only was excluded from the United Nations (UN) but also was a target of UN sanctions after it entered the Korean War (1950–53).[19] During the 1960s, as a result of the Sino-Soviet split, Mao replaced the lean-to-one-side policy with the "dual-adversary [*fanliangba*]" strategy, leading China to simultaneously confront the two superpowers in a bipolar world. The PRC labeled the United States "imperialist" and the Soviets "revisionists" and "social imperialists." Dismissing multilateral institutions as the "hegemonic tools" of the imperialist powers, it chose to exclude itself from both the Western and socialist international organizations.[20]

From the *Aussenpolitik* perspective, the pattern of China's shifting attitudes was a function of Beijing's response to the changing balance of power between Washington and Moscow. In this view, the ebb and flow of East-West confrontation resulted in the twists and turns in China's relations with the two superpowers, which in turn resulted in Beijing's changing policies toward multilateral organizations.

Accordingly, from this perspective it can be argued that China's leaning toward the socialist camp and joining Soviet-led organizations were principally driven by China's desire to seek security assurance. The direct confrontation between Chinese and American troops in the Korean War, together with the U.S. move to dispatch the Seventh Fleet into the Taiwan Straits, had the effects of justifying and prolonging the centrality of Mao's lean-to-one-side strategy.[21] As a result of these events, the United States was perceived as the greatest threat to the newly established PRC, and China's alliance with the USSR was viewed as the only viable option to deter "imperialist" aggression. Following the Sino-Soviet schism in the 1960s, Beijing switched to the dual-adversary strategy. In *Aussenpolitik* accounts, China's changing posture was primarily pushed by the perceived changes in the distribution of global power. As noted by H. Lyman Miller, the moment the USSR achieved strategic parity with the United States, China adjusted its strategy by backing away from Moscow and pursuing adversarial policies to confront both superpowers at once.[22]

This explanation, however, is not entirely convincing because it overlooks the crucial domestic determinants that underlined the Chinese leaders' decisions. From the vantage point of *Innenpolitik,* domestic factors were more important than structural factors in accounting for China's actions, particularly its decisions to refuse to join the Western camp and to ally itself with the Soviets throughout the first decade of CCP rule.

For *Innenpolitik* analysts, any attempt to explain a country's foreign policy choices must begin with a scrutiny of its ruling elite's political legitimacy. Viewed in this light, Mao's pronouncement on October 1, 1949, that "the Chinese people had finally stood up" was not simply rhetoric, but an expression that underscored the very sources of the new regime's legitimacy—that is, the liberation of the Chinese people from century-long foreign oppression as well as the restoration of China's autonomy in the modern world.[23] For Mao, who sought to justify and consolidate his authority to rule, these sources led him to pursue the following pathways for regime legitimation: enhancing China's international status on the grounds of proletarian internationalism, preserving the country's security; pursuing national reunification, safeguarding China's newly acquired autonomy, promoting economic reconstruction, and transforming the nation's "old" state and society through "continuous revolution."[24]

These pathways, in combination, constituted and guided the direction of Chinese foreign policy throughout the Maoist era. This can be seen with regard to the two issues at hand. First, the PRC's refusal to inherit the diplomatic heritage of the Kuomintang (KMT), most notably its political ties with Western capitalist countries and the China seat at the UN, was due to Mao's ideologically driven rationale of breaking from the old KMT order and making a fresh start for CCP rule.[25] Joining the Western camp would have undermined the CCP's ideological appeal on the grounds of proletarian internationalism and continuous revolution.

Second, China's decision to join the socialist camp and to participate in Soviet-led organizations was driven by Mao's identification with Moscow's international proletariat movement, his determination to create new momentum for the Chinese revolution, and the perceived security threat from the Western "imperialist" forces.[26] Allying with the Soviets was also a natural choice for the CCP, considering that the USSR was then the only source of the developmental aid and technical assistance China desperately needed to reconstruct its war-torn economy and to boost domestic confidence in the PRC's future.[27]

The Sino-Soviet alliance, however, did not last long. The divergent interests of Beijing and Moscow over a range of domestic and external issues —from de-Stalinization to China's commune and Great Leap Forward programs, from the Polish and Hungarian crises to the 1958 Taiwan Straits crisis—eventually led to the demise of the alliance in the 1960s.[28] After the Sino-Soviet border clashes in 1969, Mao reevaluated his policy of confronting the United States. This reevaluation converged with U.S. strategic readjustment under President Richard Nixon and Secretary of State Henry Kissinger, paving the way for the American-Chinese rapprochement.

Phase II (1971–1978): China as a Passive Actor

Thanks to the Sino-U.S. rapprochement, the PRC entered the United Nations and gained the China seat in October 1971. This was a watershed event for China's relations with multilateral institutions. It also set the stage for Mao's "one-front [yitiaoxian]" strategy, in which China tilted toward the United States in order to counterbalance the growing Soviet threat. Mao abandoned his earlier ideologically driven position of not joining Western-led institutions. In less than seven years, China's memberships in First World organizations increased from zero in the early 1970s to 21 in 1976.[29]

Why did China make a 180-degree turn in its foreign policy by choosing to ally with the United States and to join the UN system, whose legitimacy Beijing had once sought to challenge by advocating an "alternative UN"? The *Aussenpolitik* explanation is that China's move was made in response to the shift in the distribution of global power, which had become apparent by the late 1960s. The Soviet invasion of Czechoslovakia in 1968 and the subsequent proclamation of the Brezhnev Doctrine (which was aimed at justifying the Soviet military interventions in the socialist countries), along with American disengagement from Vietnam, led Chinese leaders to view "the Soviets on the offensive and American power waning."[30] For China, increasing Soviet power was a growing threat that had to be counterchecked, especially after the Sino-Soviet conflicts broke out in 1969 on Zhenbao Island. Although this border clash was limited in scope, its psychological impact on the Chinese leadership was profound. Mao began to worry about the possibility of a large-scale war with the Soviets, who were militarily superior and shared a long border with China. Allying his country with the United States was thus seen as an imperative move.

Unlike the *Aussenpolitik* model, the *Innenpolitik* perspective attempts to explain China's *passivity* in multilateral institutions during this period. Viewed from this perspective, the PRC's symbolic participation in the UN system was the result of Mao's insistence on "self-reliance [zili gengsheng]." This can be observed from the fact that despite China's entry into the various functional bodies under the UN system, it had chosen not to join the World Bank and the International Monetary Fund (IMF) to avoid dependence on the outside world. Any signs of becoming dependent on the West would have undermined Mao's very claim of restoring China's "autonomy."

Phase III (1979–1988): China as a Pragmatic Participant

The year 1978 was a turning point in the PRC's multilateral policy. That year, China began to pursue a pragmatic multilateral policy. This was best illustrated by the country's effort to seek technical aid under the UN Development Program in 1978 and its subsequent move to enter the World Bank and the IMF in May 1980, which effectively ended the Maoist practice of self-reliance.[31] The PRC's pragmatic turn was a direct result of the "reform and openness [*gaige kaifang*]" policy under Deng Xiaoping, who emerged as the paramount Chinese leader in the post-Mao era. Under Deng's direction, China joined international organizations that it regarded as instrumental in boosting its domestic development,[32] and, by extension, the CCP's regime preservation. Consequently, Beijing's multilateral involvement in this period was characterized by a concentration on economic and functional international institutions.

The *Aussenpolitik* explanation of China's change in policy focuses on Beijing's strategic decisions in 1979 and 1982. It points out that both decisions were driven by the changes in the distribution of global power. In the case of the former, the perceived expansion of Soviet power following the Soviet invasion of Afghanistan and the Vietnamese invasion of Cambodia further galvanized Deng's rationale for pushing for the normalization of Sino-U.S. relations.[33] In the case of the latter, China's 1982 decision to pursue an independent policy was partly attributed to its concern about systemic change, spawned by the perception that the two superpowers had reached a strategic parity following Reagan's military buildup.[34] Such a reassessment eventually led China to see a need to maintain a more balanced position between Washington and Moscow and to reemphasize its identification and cooperation with the Third World.[35]

One problem with this structural account is that it fails to explain the decisive shift in China's multilateral policy since 1978. This is where the *Innenpolitik* analysis comes in. It argues that Deng's reform as well as the resultant pragmatic turn in China's multilateral involvement was primarily propelled by the CCP's determination to restore its legitimacy, which had been substantially eroded by the turmoil and shocks of the 1966–76 Cultural Revolution. Deng and other CCP elites decided that pursuing economic construction and raising living standards represented the only pathway to regaining the party's authority.[36] Accordingly, they decided to adopt the "Four Modernizations"—of agriculture, industry, science and technology, and national defense—as the highest priority of the national agenda. This development unequivocally reflected the changing sources of the CCP's regime legitimacy, from revolution during the Mao years to economic performance in the reform era.[37]

Against this background of the shifting basis of regime legitimacy after 1978, foreign policy became even more intertwined with domestic politics than ever before. Because economic development requires a stable external environment and calls for closer interaction with the outside world, China saw better relationships with the United States and neighboring countries and the pursuit of membership in key international organizations as critical to its acquiring access to foreign capital, technology, and markets.[38] Therefore, it was not surprising that almost immediately after the conclusion of the Third Plenum of the Eleventh Central Committee, which formally launched the reform policy, Deng visited Washington and pushed for China's accession to the Bretton Woods institutions.

According to Zhang Baijia, a leading scholar of the CCP's Central Party School, Deng's determination to integrate China into the world was reinforced by his changing view in three respects. First, considering the key developments during the first half of the 1980s, Deng abandoned the long-held view that "world war is inevitable"; instead, he recognized that "peace and development [*heping yu fazhan*]" is the central theme of the contemporary world. Second, Deng acknowledged that the contemporary world is heterogeneous in nature, conflict coexists with cooperation, and competition lives side by side with interdependence. Relations between states, especially among great powers, can and must be based on cooperation for the sake of common interests. Third, Deng stressed that independence does not equate to isolation and self-reliance and does not mean blind rejection of all things foreign.[39]

Due to this new thinking, China marched toward greater integration into the international community. In 1986, China started its efforts to accede to the General Agreement on Tariffs and Trade (GATT), the predecessor to the World Trade Organization (WTO).[40] By then, it had become evident that Mao's ideology-driven foreign policy had been replaced by Deng's pragmatism and that the long-held "proletarian internationalism" had also been supplanted by an amalgamation of "patriotism and internationalism."[41] Beyond trade and the economic realm, since the 1980s China has also increased its involvement in the arms control processes by signing conventions and making commitments it had previously opposed.[42]

In short, the PRC's growing involvement in multilateral institutions throughout this third phase of its multilateral policy evolution was primarily a result of the CCP elite's pragmatic calculation of the need to restore its domestic legitimacy rather than a response to the changes in the distribution of global power.

Phase IV (1989–Present): China as a Proactive Player Instead of a Reluctant Participant

The Tiananmen tragedy on June 4, 1989, coupled with the collapse of the Soviet Union and the end of the Cold War, pushed Beijing's multilateral policy into a new phase. Two major features distinguish China's present multilateral participation from that of the earlier periods. The first feature of this period is the expanding multilateral involvement of the PRC at the regional level. As the direct result of the growing, albeit nascent, regionalism in the Asia-Pacific after the Cold War, China's new multilateral memberships during this period have been acquired mostly from regional and interregional groupings. These have included the APEC in 1991, the ARF in 1994, the ASEAN-China political consultation in 1995, the Asia-Europe Meeting in 1995, the Shanghai Five in 1996 (enlarged and renamed the Shanghai Cooperation Organization [SCO] in 2001), the Track II Council for Security Cooperation in the Asia Pacific in 1996, the ASEAN-China and the APT Summits in 1997, the China-E.U. Summit in 1998, the Forum on China-Africa Cooperation in 2000, the Boao Forum for Asia (BFA) in 2001, the Forum for East Asia–Latin America Cooperation in 2001, the Asia Cooperation Dialogue in 2002, the Six-Party Talks in 2003, and the East Asia Summit in 2005.[43]

This feature, in turn, has greatly contributed to another characteristic of China's multilateralism—a subtle but observable aspiration to shape the rules of the multilateral game. The rules of other global organizations were determined prior to Beijing's participation, but the PRC has had an unprecedented opportunity to influence the organizational designs and directions of the embryonic regional institutions, in which China has been one of the founding members.[44] This has especially been the case in institutions that China has played a central role in creating, most notably the multilevel, multisector SCO (with a permanent secretariat in Beijing), but also ACFTA and BFA.

This is not to say that China was determined to use multilateral diplomacy as a key foreign policy tool from the start. In fact, Beijing's multilateralism has come a long way. When the PRC first became involved in regional multilateral processes in the early 1990s, its participation was marked by suspicion and passivism, not enthusiasm.

In retrospect, China's multilateral journey in the Asia-Pacific began more by default than by design. Its decision to engage in the ASEAN activities in the early 1990s was chiefly motivated by its "good-neighbor [*mulin waijiao zhengce*]" policy, by which it aimed to break out of its diplomatic isolation in the wake of the 1989 Tiananmen crackdown.[45] There was no grand plan on the part of China to launch multilateral diplomacy in the region. As mentioned at the outset, China had viewed the idea of establishing a multilateral security forum in the Asia-Pacific with deep apprehension in the early 1990s for a range of reasons: its traditional uneasiness toward multilateral organizations, a lack of familiarity with multilateral matters, its trepidation over Washington's dominating role, and its sensitivity about sovereignty issues (Taiwan and the Spratly Islands territorial problems).[46]

For these reasons, China was not enthusiastic about multilateral arrangements. Rather, it was a reluctant actor who treaded "warily in the new Asia-Pacific multilateral water."[47] It cautiously guarded against any institutional development that might challenge its interests or constrain its capabilities. Consider, for example, its move in 1995 to oppose the idea of making "conflict resolution" the third and final stage of the ARF.[48] It was only toward the second half of the decade that China started to pursue a more active multilateral policy. A strict sense of multilateralism, however, emerged only at the beginning of the new century.

What explains the shift in China's attitude from that of a reluctant participant to that of an increasingly proactive multilateral player after the mid-1990s? The immediate reasons had to do with two realizations that Beijing experienced after a process of participation and interaction. The first of these concerned the institutional feature of the ASEAN-led forums. For instance, the ARF, an extended model of ASEAN, has been operated in the "ASEAN way," which emphasizes informal, incremental, widely consultative, and consensual approaches.[49] Rosemary Foot has observed that these features have enabled China to participate in the forum with confidence because there is less need for it to form coalitions of supporters to vote against any agenda that may harm its interests.[50]

The second realization that assuaged China's suspicion was related to ASEAN's unique role in maintaining roughly an equal distance among major powers.[51] For China, the fact that ARF is led by ASEAN and not other major powers such as the United States and Japan is politically acceptable and in fact preferable. Indeed, ASEAN's careful avoidance of taking a confrontational approach has been viewed by China as a gesture of engagement and not containment. Consequently, Beijing has been convinced that the forum is unlikely to develop into an anti-China coalition. This has enhanced China's confidence with regard to multilateral cooperation, paving the way for its higher level of participation over the years.

These organizational factors, however, explain only China's rising level of comfort with regional cooperation. They have not by themselves constituted a condition sufficient to *cause* China's growing enthusiasm for multilateral diplomacy. Other deeper political-strategic reasons have contributed to the shift in China's multilateral policy. The *Aussenpolitik* and *Innenpolitik* models provide two competing explanations.

The *Aussenpolitik* Explanation: A Function of Power Maximization

From the *Aussenpolitik* perspective, the PRC's shift to embracing multilateralism has essentially been a function of power maximization—that is, a desire to enhance China's relative power in an effort to mitigate the structural pressure of a changing security environment. The end of the Cold War and the demise of a bipolar order created mixed consequences for China. On the one hand, the fall of the Soviet Union significantly reduced the long-standing military threat along China's northern border, thus bringing an unprecedented level of security to Beijing.[52] On the other hand, the collapse of bipolarity ended China's strategic importance to the United States, which was now the only superpower in the world, effectively ending the Sino-U.S. "grand bargain" that had helped stabilize bilateral relations for almost two decades.[53] The net effect of the changing polarity, then, is that it altered the source and the form of the systemic pressures faced by China, but it did not eradicate them.

For China, the systemic pressures it experienced after the Cold War originated primarily in the unparalleled, unrivaled power enjoyed by the United States. Specifically, Beijing was worried that the superpower was determined to prevent it "from legitimately exercising international influence commensurate with its growing capabilities"[54] and from legitimately handling its sovereignty and domestic affairs.[55] This anxiety deepened after the 1995–96 Taiwan Straits crises as well as the strengthening of bilateral U.S. alliances in the region after the mid-1990s.[56] In order to check Washington's preponderance and to prevent a U.S.-led regional containment, the PRC has made promoting multipolarity the key goal of its foreign policy since the Cold War.[57]

Despite China's earlier assessment of the power structure after the Cold War as "one-superpower [the United States], many big powers [China, the European Union, Japan, and Russia] [*yichao duoqiang*]," since the mid-1990s Chinese leaders have realized that the march toward multipolarity has not been proceeding as quickly as they had hoped for.[58] Considering the repeated accurate projections of U.S. military superiority as well as a revitalized U.S. economy, Chinese elites have begun to recognize that multipolarity is "a distant goal" and that U.S.-dominated unipolarity will persist for the decades to come.[59] Accordingly, the Chinese have gradually accepted the enduring unipolar moment, "learning to live with the hegemon."[60]

Nevertheless, this adaptation process does not mean that China has called off its multipolarity goal. On the contrary, Beijing's desire to pursue this goal was further reinforced after the North Atlantic Treaty Organization's military intervention in Kosovo and the U.S. bombing of the Chinese embassy in Belgrade in March 1999.[61] These developments, along with the U.S. Theater Missile Defense program and the increased forward presence of America in the west Pacific, have deepened China's distrust of U.S. intentions. In the eyes of China, the U.S. "neointerventionist" strategy means that the hegemon is now using the notion of "human rights overriding sovereignty" to justify its interference in other countries' domestic affairs.[62] The perceived danger of an unrestrained hegemon sparked heated debate among Chinese elites over Deng's "peace and development" thesis, prompting China to reassess its foreign policy.[63] According to David M. Finkelstein, such a reassessment has called for a more *proactive* policy to shape China's immediate external environment, promoting closer ties with Russia, Western Europe, and countries on China's periphery.[64] It is against this backdrop that China has taken a proactive turn in its regional multilateral policy since 2000.

From the *Aussenpolitik* perspective, there are reasons to believe that Beijing is determined to pursue its multipolarity goal via *diplomatic and political* means and through *regional multilateral* platforms.[65] Partly due to the fact that Sino-U.S. relations are both cooperative and competitive in nature, and partly due to China's limited comprehensive national strength (*zonghe guoli*), Beijing considers a full-blown counterbalancing measure or a direct military confrontation as unnecessary, unfeasible, and unwise.[66] In contrast, participating in regional institutions and strengthening regional cooperation are viewed as a low-risk but potentially high-yield path to strengthening China's status as a major power and promoting multipolarity.[67] The *Asian* regional institutions, particularly the APT and the ASEAN-China consultation, but also possibly the ACD, are instrumental in this regard because they set their agendas largely independent of U.S. influence.[68] The SCO is also deemed important due to Central Asia's growing geostrategic value to China and the maturing Sino-Russian partnership.[69] The case of SCO illustrates that China's multilateral diplomacy has accompanied its efforts to cultivate so-called strategic partnerships with major powers. Beijing hoped that such partnerships would help to accelerate its transformation toward multipolarity over the long term.[70]

China's multipolarity goal has gone hand in hand with its move to foster regionalism. Specifically, through its efforts to promote East Asian regional cooperation, Beijing aims to hasten the emergence of a tripartite world divided among the countries of the North American Free Trade Agreement, the European Union, and East Asian groups.[71]

Empirically, there are signs that the PRC's multilateral policy has been driven by its concerns about relative power, as a calculation to maximize its own relative capabilities and, whenever possible, to limit others' influence and to ward off rivals' hostile moves. Some scholars observe that Beijing's shift toward embracing multilateral diplomacy after the mid-1990s was motivated by its decision to use regional institutions "as a hedge against U.S. power and the fear of encirclement by a coalition led by the United States."[72] Others point out that China has conspicuously used regional platforms to expand its own influence, sometimes at the expense of both Japan and the United States. For instance, during the Asian financial crisis (AFC), China vocally contrasted "its 'responsible' behavior with Tokyo's failure to provide regional and global leadership in managing the AFC,"[73] and allegedly cautioned some ASEAN countries "to guard against American 'hegemonic' ambitions" in using the IMF to demand greater economic and political liberalization.[74] At the ARF, China has sought to undermine the legitimacy of the U.S. security alliance structure in the region by describing the U.S.-Japan security pact as a reflection of the "Cold War mentality."[75] Although since 2001 Beijing has stopped its public criticism of U.S. hegemonic policy, some observers believe that China "continues to work over the longer term to weaken the predominance of the United States around China's periphery."[76]

In summary, the *Aussenpolitik* analysts generally see China's multilateral strategy following the Cold War as a zero-sum effort: it seeks to reduce its rivals' relative power, and to enhance its own.

The *Innenpolitik* Explanation: An Imperative of Regime Preservation

The *Innenpolitik* tradition, on the other hand, argues that China's emerging multilateralism is driven not so much by the country's concern about relative power as by the CCP regime's resolve to preserve its political relevance at home. This explanation is more convincing for one important reason. The very foundation that underlies and guides China's present multilateralism—that is, a persistent desire on the part of the CCP elites to develop close and comprehensive relations with neighboring countries as a hedge to offset the *domestic impact* of China's volatile relationship with the West—began to take shape immediately after 1989.[77] This was *well before* the Chinese elites began to worry about possible regional containment led by the United States, which prompted Beijing to pursue a more active and cooperative regional strategy after the mid-1990s. As I have already explained, China continued to rely on bilateral and not multilateral diplomacy in pursuing its good neighbor policy throughout the first half of the 1990s chiefly because of its habitual suspicion of and lack of familiarity with multilateral practice. But by 1996, once such psychological barriers had been removed after a learning process through which China got to know the multilateral game through direct participation, it became natural for Beijing to recognize and make use of the value of multilateral diplomacy as a complementary tool in pursuing its foreign policy for domestic ends.

This observation, of course, mainly reveals that there is a crucial *domestic* dimension that must not be overlooked in making sense of Beijing's current multilateral policy. It does not render the *Aussenpolitik* logic irrelevant, and certainly does not deny China's goal of maximizing its power. Nonetheless, it does underscore the fact that the CCP's regime interests (i.e., the party's overarching concern with restoring its domestic governance capacity in the wake of the Tiananmen upheaval) *preceded* Beijing's external calculation about relative power in China's decisive shift to pursuing an active and cooperative approach toward its neighbors. In other words, although the desire to maximize its power has indeed accelerated China's pace in pursuing multilateral diplomacy since the mid-1990s, it was the imperative of regime preservation that determined the *direction* of China's cooperative policy immediately after 1989, and this imperative, in turn, guided and sustained Beijing's growing multilateralism toward the end of the decade and beyond.

How Concerns for Regime Preservation Have Steered China's Good Neighbor Policy and Its Evolving Multilateralism

Following is a discussion of the ways in which China's determination to improve its ties with its neighboring countries was motivated by the CCP's concern for regime preservation after 1989 and the ways in which the CCP's regime preservation goal has steered China's regional multilateral involvement.

From the *Innenpolitik* perspective, the greatest challenge faced by the CCP-ruled China after the Cold War has been not American preponderance, but the enduring regime legitimation problem that was reflected, and aggravated, by the 1989 Tiananmen tragedy. Despite the fact that Deng's vibrant reform since 1978 has brought remarkable economic growth to China, this achievement has been accompanied by the painful dark side of socioeconomic transformation, ranging from intensified inflation and rampant corruption to widening social inequality and glaring regional disparity. The repression of student demonstrators on June 4, 1989, further deepened the mass alienations, leaving the CCP elite with its most serious legitimacy crisis since the Cultural Revolution.[78]

Legitimacy erosion and its corollaries—social unrest and political instability—were not the only problems faced by the CCP leadership after Tiananmen. Externally, China had to confront economic sanctions and political condemnation from around the world, particularly from the Western countries. The collapse of communist regimes in Eastern Europe and the Soviet Union further exacerbated the CCP's anxieties about the viability of its socialist system and the foundation of its political power. These developments led the Chinese communist leaders to fear that their regime survival "is now threatened by a combination of internal and external challenges," namely the Western-sponsored "peaceful evolution [*heping yanbian*]" (regime change in socialist countries that China believes is being perpetrated by "Western forces"), the influence of "bourgeois liberalism" within China, and social instability.[79]

Deng responded by proposing three principles: "carefully assessing the situation [*lengjing guancha*]; consolidating China's position [*wenzhu zhengjiao*]; and calmly coping with the challenges [*chenzhuo yingfu*]."[80] These principles, in turn, guided Chinese foreign policy after 1989 to focus on two major tasks: (1) stabilizing China's relations with the periphery countries by pursuing a good neighbor policy and (2) neutralizing sanctions imposed by the developed countries.[81] Together, these policy tasks were aimed at countering the West's political pressure and diplomatic isolation, as well as ensuring China's continuous access to markets and foreign investment in spite of the economic sanctions. Each of these tasks was considered essential to restore the CCP's political authority immediately after Tiananmen.

It was against this background that China was determined to cultivate a better relationship with its neighbors in the new era.[82] From 1990 to 1992, Beijing moved to strengthen its relations with Japan while establishing and normalizing its diplomatic ties with South Korea and several Southeast Asian states. The ASEAN states, in particular, have been the focus of the PRC's good neighbor policy.[83] As Chen Jie has observed, Chinese leaders have been greatly encouraged that Sino-ASEAN political and business ties have not been affected by the Tiananmen incident. Southeast Asian governments, with the partial exception of Singapore, not only did not condemn the CCP's suppression, but also continued to engage in reciprocal state visits by high-level leaders and officials. This stance was highly appreciated and much needed by the Chinese communist regime, because the trips "showed to the world that China was not isolated, at least in its own backyard."[84]

It is important not to view the good neighbor policy as simply a "regional" strategy. Rather, the policy must be understood as *an integral part of China's grand strategy* to hedge against political shocks produced by the cyclical ups and downs in Beijing's relations with the United States, for the ultimate purpose of offsetting the undesirable impact of such volatility on the CCP's domestic functions. As two Chinese analysts have noted, Beijing hopes that sound and stable ties with regional countries will help it to "hedge against downturns in Sino-U.S. relations."[85]

Significantly, China's good neighbor agenda converged with the common goal of the ASEAN states, which aspired to engage the rising power amid the strategic uncertainty since the end of the Cold War.[86] This convergence set the stage for China's involvement in the ASEAN meetings, in addition to its bilateral interactions with individual Southeast Asian countries.[87] China's first multilateral encounter with ASEAN took place in July 1991, when Foreign Minister Qian Qichen attended the opening session of the ASEAN ministerial meeting in Kuala Lumpur as a guest of Malaysia. Since then, the Chinese foreign minister has been able to meet with his ASEAN counterparts at the annual ASEAN meetings.[88] These developments planted the seeds for China's future involvement in the ARF and other ASEAN-led institutions. In retrospect, it was therefore no coincidence that China's enthusiasm for multilateralism was first developed and matured in its social interactions with Southeast Asia, and gradually expanded to the larger Asian region.

The CCP elite's resolve to develop closer Sino-ASEAN ties, together with its parallel efforts to maintain cordial relationships with its neighbors in Northeast Asia and Eurasia, is testament to the fact that, while relations with major powers remain crucial for China, the significance of "periphery countries [*zhoubian guojia*]" has increased considerably in Beijing's foreign policy calculations since the Cold War.

Even after Beijing had succeeded in breaking out of the diplomatic isolation and economic sanctions that had followed Tiananmen, the importance of regional countries to China did not fade away. In 2002, the Sixteenth Party Congress Report announced that the notion of "friendship and partnership with neighboring countries [*yulin weishan, yulin weiban*]" would be the guiding principle for China's "periphery diplomacy [*zhoubian waijiao*]."[89] Later, Chinese leaders elaborated this principle by introducing the policy of "reassuring, enriching, and befriending neighbors [*anlin, fulin, mulin*]."[90] Taken together, these policy guidelines indicate that China's strategy of using amicable ties with neighbors to hedge against the potential risks of its volatile relations with the West has remained unchanged, and in fact has been strengthened.

From the *Innenpolitik* point of view, the rising importance of regional states to China can be attributed to a wide range of factors, but four are the most critical. These factors constitute the key pathways to preservation of the CCP's regime, and all of them prompt China to increasingly *complement* its traditional bilateral approach with multilateral diplomacy.

1. *Ensuring uninterrupted economic growth.* The causes and the aftermath of the Tiananmen incident indicate that "economic performance"—the very source of the CCP's legitimacy since Mao—could no longer solely justify the party's power to rule.[91] Since the 1990s, while the CCP has continued to rely on economic development as the core basis for its political legitimacy, it has used this approach *in tandem with* other sources of inner justification. These include seeking the status of a great power, reviving nationalism, preserving national unity, promoting sustainable development, and promising to push for more equal income distribution between different social groups and between rural and urban areas.[92]

Each of these sources of legitimacy requires uninterrupted economic growth. CCP elites believe that the pursuit of continuous development is critical not only for its own sake, but also for their political survival. This was underscored most forcefully by Deng when he proclaimed during his 1992 southern tour that "development is an absolute necessity [*fazhan shi ying daoli*]." He elaborated: "If we don't develop the economy and don't improve people's living, there will be no future for the party."[93] Deng's successor, Jiang Zemin, stressed a similar point by warning his CCP comrades, "If we fail to develop our economy rapidly, it will be very difficult for us to consolidate the Socialist system and maintain long-term social stability."[94]

In what ways are East Asian countries and regional multilateral cooperation important for the CCP's goal of ensuring China's continuous economic growth? East Asia is economically critical for China in at least three major ways:

- *Trade and investment.* Largely due to economic compatibility, geographic proximity, and Beijing's diversification efforts, the volumes of China's trade and investment with the rest of the East Asian region have increased steadily over the past decade. In 2005, the region contributed as much as 30 percent of China's total trade.[95] This trend has served to reduce China's economic dependence on Europe and the United States, thus reducing the risks of cyclical economic recessions in the global market.
- *Financial interdependence.* China learned from the 1997 Asian financial crisis that, given the high level of interdependency among the East Asian economies, financial problems in one country would inevitably produce negative repercussions in other countries in the region, including China.[96]

- *Natural resources.* China realizes that its long-term growth is dependent on an uninterrupted supply of energy resources and raw materials. This factor has pushed China's interaction with the outside world into a new stage in which its target is access not only to international capital, technology, and markets, but also to resources. Indeed, China's energy security concerns have been the driving force behind its increasingly high-profile diplomacy in every region of the globe, including Southeast Asia.

In combination, these economic imperatives mean that China's economic future—and, by extension, the CCP's political relevance—is inextricably linked to both regional economic performance and China's cooperative relations with the regional countries. Chinese leaders recognize that the wave of globalization has become irreversible and that regional cooperation is an essential means to protect the national interest from the onslaught of globalization.[97] This recognition compels China to complement its traditional bilateral approach with multilateral cooperation. Accordingly, Beijing has taken an active role in various APT efforts, such as the Chiang Mai Initiative, and has sought to vigorously promote the ACFTA. Through APT, China hopes to further enhance East Asian intraregional trade and to prevent a recurrence of a regional financial crisis. Through ACFTA, China aims to strengthen the Sino-ASEAN trade and investment links, to facilitate and accelerate the acquisition of resources from its southern neighbors, and to boost economic growth in its underdeveloped southwestern region.

2. *Preserving the stability of the external environment.* The CCP elites regard a stable and peaceful regional environment as the sine qua non for China's continuing domestic construction.[98] They view territorial disputes in the South China Sea (involving China, Taiwan, and the four ASEAN states of Brunei, Malaysia, the Philippines, and Vietnam) and the uncertainty over the Korean peninsula as among the potential flashpoints that might create regional instability and, worse, invite foreign interference on China's periphery.[99] China seeks to avert the potential conflict, and multilateral platforms—namely the ASEAN-China dialogue mechanism and the Six-Party Talks—are essential means to this end.

3. *Defending sovereignty and territorial integrity.* China considers Taiwan, Xinjiang, and Tibet matters of its sovereignty and territorial integrity. Given the Chinese people's memory of the "century of humiliation" as well as its rising nationalist tide, any Chinese leadership would view its legitimacy as at stake should any of these sovereignty issues be compromised.[100] For this reason, Chinese leaders have unremittingly sought to prevent Taiwanese independence and marginalize Taipei's diplomatic endeavors in virtually

every part of the world, including Southeast Asia. Similarly, they have attempted to prevent the Uighur minorities in Central Asia from helping the Uighur separatists in Xinjiang.[101] In this regard, Beijing sees multilateral institutions such as the China-ASEAN meetings, the ARF, and the SCO as essential and useful platforms to underscore its sovereignty issues.

4. *Pursuing status as a great power.* China's aspiration to status as a great power is not new, but it was not until the beginning of the twenty-first century that such a goal was expressed as a national agenda and in a self-assured way.[102] The notion of "peaceful rise [*heping jueqi*]" (and later, "peaceful development [*heping fazhan*]"), which is intended to stress to the outside world the peaceful nature of the PRC's growth, subtly mirrors Chinese elites' newfound confidence in their country's inevitable reemergence in the new century.[103] Such confidence is rooted partially in China's growing wealth and power, partially in its rising nationalism.[104]

In the eyes of the *Innenpolitik* analysts, China's quest for status as a great power is not an end in itself, but a means to attain its ultimate goal of regime legitimation. It is an additional source of the CCP's moral authority that supplements economic performance in justifying and strengthening the party's grip on power. Given China's regional reach, East Asia is seen as the principal ground for China's pursuit of status as a great power, and regional institutions are regarded as the main platform for attaining this goal.[105]

From the *Innenpolitik* viewpoint, these four internally driven factors—the pathways to regime legitimacy—have collectively motivated China's increasingly active involvement in the Asian multilateral institutions over the past decade. Given that none of these concerns could be effectively addressed by bilateral diplomacy alone, the multilateral approach is deemed essential. This is not to argue that multilateralism has replaced bilateralism as the principal thrust of Chinese foreign policy. Rather, the point is that multilateral diplomacy has begun to play a complementary, in some cases an indispensable, role in promoting the CCP's external objectives.

In short, the *Innenpolitik* explanation contends that Beijing's multilateral diplomacy since the Cold War has been motivated by the CCP elites' desire to ensure China's continuous economic growth, to preserve its stable external environment, to defend its sovereignty, and to promote the country's growing interests and stature abroad, for the ultimate objective of preserving and consolidating the party's grip on power at home.

Why Stable U.S.-China Relations Are Central to the CCP's Current Regime Legitimation Efforts

The preceding analysis by no means implies that China now regards its relations with regional states as more important than its relations with major powers. As noted earlier, relations with the major powers, especially the United States, remain vital for China's foreign relations. Indeed, no analysts would dispute that the Sino-U.S. relationship is the most important bilateral tie for China. It is significant not simply because America is the key source of capital and technology as well as a crucial market for China's continuing growth, but because the United States, as the only superpower since the Cold War, "can do more to facilitate or hinder the attainment of vital Chinese foreign policy objectives than any other foreign country."[106] These objectives are, inter alia, the resolution of the Taiwan and other sovereignty issues, China's quest for status as a great power, the prospect of its energy security, and the future of its relations with almost all of the regional countries around its periphery.

Each of these issues affects, either directly or indirectly, the CCP's capacity to preserve its authority at home. The need for regime preservation thus demands that Beijing seek greater cooperation, not competition or conflict, in its relations with Washington. This represents a major contrast with the way things were in the days when the CCP elite, concerned with regime consolidation, made use of China's *adversarial relations* with other powers to strengthen its ideological appeal and mobilize the populace, as in the case of Sino-U.S. relations in the 1950s and Sino-Soviet relations in the 1960s.[107] Regime preservation explains why the CCP leadership attempted to limit rather than inflame the massive anti-U.S. demonstrations that erupted in China after the U.S. bombing of the Chinese embassy in Belgrade in May 1999 and after the EP-3 incident in April 2001.[108] It also explains why Beijing has chosen to cooperate closely with Washington on issues ranging from counterterrorism to the North Korean nuclear crisis. Such a change in China's attitude has occurred not because China has become kinder or gentler, but simply because the changing bases of the CCP's legitimacy have dictated it. Unless China's sovereignty is directly challenged, a confrontation with the United States is highly unlikely, because it would only disrupt China's economic performance. This, in turn, would precipitate domestic instability and erode the CCP's domination.

Conclusion: Regime Legitimation at Work

China's evolving multilateralism in Asia is a phenomenon that must be explained by *both* the *Aussenpolitik* and the *Innenpolitik* models. Neither can account for the evolution of China's multilateral policy independently. The *Aussenpolitik* model's emphasis on the changes in the distribution of global power leads us to see that structural factors constitute the contextual forces to which China must react in order to safeguard its security interests. This model, however, often overlooks the domestic sources of China's external policy. In particular, it says nothing about the internal factors that contributed to China's pragmatic turn in 1978, which marked the major shift in Beijing's policy toward the world of multilateral institutions. This is an area in which the *Innenpolitik* account is found to be more useful. By highlighting the changing domestic political foundations, this model demonstrates how the prevailing regime concerns of the day affect China's multilateral policy.

This finding, in turn, allows us to address the question of whether China's present multilateralism is an issue of relative capability or a product of domestic political necessity. It is true that capability maximization has been an important variable in accounting for Beijing's multilateral behavior, as underscored by the *Aussenpolitik* argument. For instance, China's long march since 1978 to integrate itself into the world has clearly been motivated by its desire to acquire greater capability, as is unequivocally reflected by its long-held goal of *fuguo qiangbing* (i.e., upgrading the country's economic and military power). It is also true that as China acquires more capability—in both absolute and relative terms—it is likely to have more policy options, encompassing both persuasive and coercive statecraft, in promoting its interests.

These observations, however, do not necessarily suggest that China's current multilateralism is caused or constrained by its lack of coercive capability to advance its interests. Such an argument essentially depicts a negative relationship between a state's coercive capability and its commitment to multilateral diplomacy or, for that matter, all forms of persuasive statecraft. That is, the lower a state's coercive capability, the greater the likelihood of its willingness to embrace multilateralism; conversely, the higher a state's coercive capability, the lower its tendency to commit to multilateralism. Empirically, however, China's inclination to pursue multilateral diplomacy over the past decade has grown at a time when China's military power is experiencing a steady rise, not a decline.

Two inferences can be made here. First, there are factors other than the level of coercive capability that may affect a state's multilateral policy. Second, while a major power's growing capability is likely to produce a growing appetite for greater space and resources, it does not necessarily make multilateral diplomacy irrelevant or coercive means a preferred option. In other words, greater capability might induce China to "want more," but it would not determine "what China wants" and "how China chooses to get what it wants."

Instead, as the preceding discussion made clear, China's policy goals as well as its chosen strategies are shaped principally by the domestic political necessities faced by its ruling regime in enhancing its governance capacity and by the availability of external options that help to serve those necessities. To the extent that the ruling elite's domestic needs are matched by its access to productive and diverse options from the outside world, the state would opt for high-yield multilateral cooperation rather than high-cost coercive means. Indeed, China's progressive integration into the international community since 1978 not only has increased its incentives to adopt a more cooperative approach, but also has raised the costs of Maoist-style confrontational action. In this regard, Beijing's expanding economic and institutional linkages have contributed to China's increasing tendency to treat multilateral cooperation as a more attractive and rewarding option for pursuing its goals.

This is especially true given that coercive approaches might not be as effectual as multilateral diplomacy in *simultaneously* achieving the regime's *multiple* goals, outlined earlier. To begin with, CCP elites realize that the use of military force would only jeopardize regional stability and devastate economic growth. They also recognize that military power alone would not grant China status as a great power. Based on past interactions between Imperial China and regional states, they view nonviolent means such as economic influence, cultural attractiveness, and diplomatic cleverness as equally or more valuable in inducing other countries' respect and deference.[109] Finally, while the CCP elites see military might as a necessary means to protect Chinese sovereignty, they realize that an offensive strategy is a counterproductive way of ameliorating China's security dilemma. As Zhang and Tang have noted, "With more than fifteen countries bordering China, an aggressive posture is simply not in China's interests, *no matter how powerful China becomes,* because aggression would lead to a counterbalancing alliance of China's neighbors and a distant power [the United States]."[110] Hence, multilateral diplomacy is likely to remain relevant and essential to China even as its coercive capabilities grow.

This is not to say that the CCP elites now regard military power as unimportant. In fact, China's military modernization effort indicates that its leaders have continued to take coercive capability seriously. But developments since 1979 also suggest that the use of Chinese military power has been limited to deterrence, not offensive purposes. Moreover, despite China's uneasiness about U.S. unilateralism, there is little behavioral evidence that China is making a concerted military effort or taking a revisionist approach to achieve a balance of power with America.[111] Given the enduring importance of economic growth and regional stability, it is highly unlikely that the confrontational approach will rise to the fore in China's external policy—unless, of course, China's sovereignty and security were directly challenged in the event of Taiwanese independence or external aggression. In these scenarios, popular pressure would compel the CCP leadership to resort to the aggressive nationalist route to legitimacy, even if such acts would result in economic stagnation and regional instability.

As long as Chinese sovereignty is not directly at stake, the performance route to regime legitimation is expected to prevail and drive Beijing toward more cooperative behavior, sometimes even at the cost of compromising its material interests. This can be observed from the pattern of China's territorial negotiations behavior. An empirical study conducted by Taylor Fravel reveals that, chiefly due to the regime's concerns over internal threats, Beijing has offered substantial concessions in most of the territorial settlements with its neighbors, "usually receiving less than 50 percent of the contested land."[112] Another example is Beijing's decision in 1994 to agree to ASEAN's suggestion that an annual political consultation be established, even though China was well aware that such a mechanism was likely to reduce its maneuverability in handling the disputes over the Spratly Islands. Chinese behavior in these instances apparently contradicted the *Aussenpolitik* model's reasoning on power maximization, but was consistent with the *Innenpolitik* model's claim: the state has persistently sought to create favorable external conditions for the ultimate goal of enhancing the regime's domestic authority, even at the price of limiting the state's interests and capability.

What does China's evolving multilateralism mean for China-U.S. relations? While the *Aussenpolitik* model paints a more alarming picture of China's policy, the *Innenpolitik* explanation leads us to believe that China's multilateralism is largely internally driven and that it may provide an avenue for cooperation, rather than a source of zero-sum competition or "inevitable" structural conflict, in future Sino-U.S. relations.

From the *Innenpolitik* viewpoint, China's multilateral diplomacy might not be an entirely zero-sum development in terms of U.S. interests in the region. For instance, consider Beijing's mediating roles in the Six-Party Talks, as well as its constructive involvements in the ARF confidence-building measures, which have contributed to the growing regional trust and stability over the past decade. Similarly, China requires U.S. cooperation at both bilateral and multilateral levels in order to promote its policy interests. For example, without Washington's involvement, Beijing clearly will not be able to push forward the idea of turning the Six-Party Talks into an institutionalized, permanent regional security mechanism in Northeast Asia, which could help ensure regional peace and stability.

In the *Innenpolitik* account, while China's multipolarity goal should not be ruled out, it should not be overstated either. This is because the prime concern of the CCP regime is preservation of its domestic domination rather than maximization of its external power. China is not directly threatened by the American preponderance. In fact, it benefits from the existing U.S.-dominated system in a variety of ways, ranging from the availability of capital, technology, market access, and resource flows to the supply of international public goods such as the maintenance of regional peace and the safety of sea lanes. The fact that Beijing has recently toned down its multipolarity rhetoric and expressed support for inclusiveness in East Asian cooperation may well be a reflection of China's growing willingness to employ multilateral institutions as platforms for facilitating greater cooperation with the superpower. Viewed in this light, the current U.S. policy of encouraging Beijing to be a "responsible stakeholder" in the international community would help China's multilateralism to evolve into a positive force for regional peace and prosperity over the long run.

Acknowledgments

I acknowledge the support of a Fulbright Scholarship and a Universiti Kebangsaan Malaysia Faculty Development Award in enabling me to pursue my doctoral studies at the Johns Hopkins University Paul H. Nitze School of Advanced International Studies (SAIS) and to conduct fieldwork for this chapter. I am thankful for the helpful feedback of Kent E. Calder, Laura Jones, Margaret Pinard, Ellen Psychas, and Qi Zhou. I am especially grateful to Francis Fukuyama, David M. Lampton, Serene Hung, and Bo Kong for their very detailed comments and constructive suggestions. All shortcomings of the chapter are entirely my own.

Notes

1. This definition is different from the one offered by John Gerard Ruggie in his 1993 work, in which he defines *multilateralism* as "coordinating relations among three or more states in accordance with certain principles" that entail "an indivisibility among the members of a collectivity" and "expectations of diffuse reciprocity." The distinction between these definitions is due to the adoption of different levels of analysis. This chapter focuses on a country's *foreign policy*, whereas Ruggie was concerned about *interactions* among three or more states. See John Gerard Ruggie, ed., *Multilateralism Matters: The Theory and Praxis of an Institutional Form* (New York: Columbia University Press, 1993), 8–14.
2. On China's involvement in the ARF, see Rosemary Foot, "China in the ASEAN Regional Forum: Organizational Processes and Domestic Modes of Thought," *Asian Survey* 38 (May 1998): 425–40; Ding Kuisong, "The ASEAN Regional Forum and the Asian Pacific Security Cooperation," *Xiandai Guoji Guanxi* [Contemporary international relations] 7 (1998): 7–12; and Alastair Iain Johnston, "The Myth of the ASEAN Way? Explaining the Evolution of the ASEAN Regional Forum," in Helga Haftendorn, Robert Keohane, and Celeste Wallander, eds., *Imperfect Unions: Security Institutions over Time and Space* (Oxford: Oxford University Press, 1999), 287–324.

3. Author interviews of Chinese policy analysts and Foreign Ministry officials, Beijing, September 2002–January 2003.
4. Foot, "China in the ASEAN Regional Forum," and Johnston, "The Myth of the ASEAN Way?"
5. Cheng-Chwee Kuik, "Multilateralism in China's ASEAN Policy: Its Evolution, Characteristics, and Aspiration," *Contemporary Southeast Asia* 27 (April 2005): 102–22.
6. Thomas J. Christensen, "Fostering Stability or Creating a Monster? The Rise of China and U.S. Policy toward East Asia," *International Security* 31 (Summer 2006): 81–126.
7. This section is drawn from Cheng-Chwee Kuik, "Multilateralism in China's ASEAN Policy" and "China's Participation in the ASEAN Regional Forum (ARF): The Exogenous and Endogenous Effects of International Institutions," in James K. Chin and Nicholas Thomas, eds., *China and ASEAN: Changing Political and Strategic Ties* (Hong Kong: Centre of Asian Studies, University of Hong Kong, 2005), 141–69.
8. Evan S. Medeiros and M. Taylor Fravel, "China's New Diplomacy," *Foreign Affairs* 8 (November/December 2003): 22–35; Francis Fukuyama, "China: Global Citizen or Growing Menace?" *The Daily Yomiuri*, May 16, 2004, available at www.unitar.org/hiroshima/programmes/ief04/Powerpoint/Yomiuri.PDF; Bates Gill, "China's New Security Multilateralism and Its Implications for the Asia Pacific Region," in *SIPRI Yearbook 2004* (Oxford: Oxford University Press, 2004), 205–30; David Shambaugh, "China Engages Asia: Reshaping the Regional Order," *International Security* 29 (Winter 2004–5): 64–99; Francis Fukuyama and G. John Ikenberry, *Report of the Working Group on Grand Strategic Choices* (Princeton, N.J.: Princeton Project on National Security, 2005), 14–25; and Christensen, "Fostering Stability or Creating a Monster?"
9. Exceptions are, inter alia, Wang Yizhou, ed., *Mohe zhong de Jiangou: Zhongguo yu Guoji Zuzhi Guanxi de Duoshijiao Toushi* [Construction in contradiction: A multiple-insight into relationship between China and key international organizations] (Beijing: China Development Press, 2003); Su Changhe, "Discovering China's New Diplomacy: Multilateral International Regimes and China's Foreign Policy New Thinking," *Shijie Jingji yu Zhengzhi* [World economics and politics] 4 (2005): 11–16; and Men Honghua, "Pressure, Perception, and International Image: A Historical Analysis of China's Strategy for International Institutions," *Shijie Jingji yu Zhengzhi* [World economics and politics] 4 (2005): 17–22.
10. Fukuyama, "China: Global Citizen or Growing Menace?"
11. This model is adapted from Alastair Iain Johnston, "Learning versus Adaptation: Explaining Change in Chinese Arms Control Policy in the 1990s and 1990s," *China Journal* 35 (January 1996): 27–61. However, instead of con-

trasting "adaptation" (a tactical adjustment) with "learning" (a more fundamental process whereby a state internalizes new definitions of security and alters its strategic actions) as Johnston did, I choose to contrast "adaptation" (determined largely by the *external* conditions of relative capabilities across the system) with "internally driven necessity" (demanded by a regime's *internal* need to strengthen its authority to rule). Unlike the learning-adaptation model, which reflects the "constructivism versus rationalism" debate, our model is aimed at exploring how domestic politics, specifically the imperative of regime preservation, affect foreign policy choices.

12. Kenneth N. Waltz, *Theory of International Politics* (Reading, Mass.: Addison Wesley, 1979), especially 88–99. See also John J. Mearsheimer, *The Tragedy of Great Power Politics* (New York: W. W. Norton, 2001).

13. On *Aussenpolitik* and *Innenpolitik,* see Fareed Zakaria, "Realism and Domestic Politics: A Review Essay," *International Security* 17 (Summer 1992): 177–98, and Gideon Rose, "Neoclassical Realism and Theories of Foreign Policy," *World Politics* 51 (1998): 144–72.

14. On neoclassical realism, see Rose, "Neoclassical Realism and Theories of Foreign Policy."

15. On legitimation or what Max Weber calls "inner justifications" of domination, see Weber, "Legitimacy, Politics, and the State," in William Connolly, ed., *Legitimacy and the State* (New York: New York University Press, 1984), 32–62, and Carol Lee Hamrin, "Elite Politics and Foreign Relations," in Thomas W. Robinson and David Shambaugh, eds., *Chinese Foreign Policy: Theory and Practice* (Oxford: Clarendon, 1994), 70–114, esp. 76–79.

16. Because of the focus on *Asian* institutions in this book, this study excludes China's accession to the World Trade Organization and its involvement in peacekeeping operations, despite the fact that they are important aspects of China's multilateral involvement. On these issues, see David M. Lampton, *Same Bed, Different Dreams: Managing U.S.-China Relations 1989–2000* (Berkeley: University of California Press, 2001), 159–203.

17. In this study, the terms *multilateral institutions, international organizations,* and *international institutions* are used interchangeably.

18. Men, "Pressure, Perception, and International Image," and Yongjin Zhang, *China in International Society since 1949: Alienation and Beyond* (London: Macmillan, 1998).

19. The U.S.-influenced General Assembly passed a resolution to brand the PRC as an "aggressor" and urged all countries to embargo exports of strategic and military materials to Beijing. See Wang Jianwei, "Chinese Perspectives on Multilateral Security Cooperation," *Asian Perspective* 22 (1998): 104–6.

20. Samuel S. Kim, "China's International Organizational Behaviour," in Thomas W. Robinson and David Shambaugh, eds., *Chinese Foreign Policy: Theory and Practice* (Oxford: Clarendon, 1994), 401–34.

21. Zhang Baijia, "Changing Thy Self, Influencing Thy World," *Zhongguo Shehui Kexue* [Chinese social sciences] 1 (2002): 4–19.
22. H. Lyman Miller, "China: An Uneasy Alliance," *Hoover Digest* 3 (2002), available at www.hooverdigest.org/023/lmiller.html.
23. William C. Kirby, "Traditions of Centrality, Authority, and Management in Modern China's Foreign Relations," in Robinson and Shambaugh, *Chinese Foreign Policy*, 13–29, and Hamrin, "Elite Politics."
24. Richard H. Solomon, *Mao's Revolution and the Chinese Political Culture* (Berkeley: University of California Press, 1971), and Chen Jian, *Mao's China and the Cold War* (Chapel Hill: University of North Carolina Press, 2001).
25. Li Shenzhi, "On the People's Republic of China's Foreign Policy," *Zhanlue yu Guanli* [Strategy and management] 4 (2002): 1–8; Wang Jisi, "International Relations Theory and the Study of Chinese Foreign Policy: A Chinese Perspective," in Robinson and Shambaugh, *Chinese Foreign Policy*, 484.
26. Chen, *Mao's China and the Cold War,* 50–51, and Steven M. Goldstein, "Nationalism and Internationalism: Sino-Soviet Relations," in Robinson and Shambaugh, *Chinese Foreign Policy*, 224–65, esp. 228.
27. Hamrin, "Elite Politics."
28. Chen, *Mao's China and the Cold War,* 49–84; Harold P. Ford, "Calling the Sino-Soviet Split," available at www.cia.gov/csi/kent_csi/pdf/v42i5a05%20p.pdf; and Goldstein, "Nationalism and Internationalism."
29. David M. Lampton, "A Growing China in a Shrinking World: Beijing and the Global Order," in Ezra F. Vogel, ed., *Living with China: U.S.-China Relations in the Twenty-first Century* (New York: W. W. Norton, 1997), 120–40; Kim, "China's International Organizational Behavior."
30. David Shambaugh, "Patterns of Interaction in Sino-American Relations," in Robinson and Shambaugh, *Chinese Foreign Policy*, 197–223, quote on 198.
31. Kim, "China's International Organizational Behavior," and Lampton, "A Growing China in a Shrinking World," 120–40.
32. Elizabeth Economy and Michel Oksenberg, eds., *China Joins the World: Progress and Prospect* (New York: Council on Foreign Relations, 1999), and Wang, *Construction in Contradiction.*
33. Shambaugh, "Patterns of Interaction in Sino-American Relations," 203.
34. Ibid., 204.
35. Harry Harding, "China's Changing Roles in the Contemporary World," in Harding, ed., *China's Foreign Relations in the 1980s* (New Haven: Yale University Press, 1984), 177–223, and Wang, "International Relations Theory and the Study of Chinese Foreign Policy," 485.
36. Deng Xiaoping, *Deng Xiaoping Wenxuan* [Selected writings of Deng Xiaoping], Vol. 3 (Beijing: Xinhua, 1994), 370. See also Susan Shirk, *The Political Logic of Economic Reform in China* (Berkeley: University of California Press,

1993), 23–37, and Kenneth Lieberthal, *Governing China: From Revolution through Reform* (New York: W. W. Norton, 1995), 122–27.

37. Lieberthal, *Governing China,* and Yongnian Zheng and Liang Fook Lye, "Political Legitimacy in Reform China: Between Economic Performance and Democratization," in Lynn White, ed., *Legitimacy: Ambiguities of Political Success or Failure in East and Southeast Asia* (Singapore: World Scientific Publishing, 2005), 183–214.

38. Economy and Oksenberg, *China Joins the World.*

39. Zhang, "Changing Thy Self," 4–19.

40. Harold K. Jacobson and Michel Oksenberg, *China's Participation in the IMF, the World Bank, and GATT: Toward a Global Economic Order* (Ann Arbor: University of Michigan Press, 1990).

41. Wang, "International Relations Theory and the Study of Chinese Foreign Policy," and Li, "On the People's Republic of China's Foreign Policy."

42. Johnston, "Learning versus Adaptation."

43. Meetings of four of these institutions are attended by the United States, namely those of APEC, ARF, and CSCAP, as well as the Six-Party Talks.

44. Cheng-Chwee Kuik, "Analyzing China's Interest in Joining the ASEAN-led Regional Institutions," *Shijie Jingji yu Zhengzhi* [World economy and politics] 9 (2004): 53–59, and Men Honghua, "Participation, Creation, and Domination: Promoting East Asian Integration via Institutional Building," *Guoji Wenti Luntan* [International issues forum] 1 (2005): 1–16.

45. Lee Lai To, "Domestic Changes in China since the 4 June Incident and Their Implications for Southeast Asia," *Contemporary Southeast Asia* 13 (June 1991): 17–43; Chen Jie, "Major Concerns in China's ASEAN Policy," in Chandran Jeshurun, ed., *China, India, Japan and the Security of Southeast Asia* (Singapore: Institute of Southeast Asian Studies, 1993), 144–80.

46. Susan Shirk, "Chinese Views on Asia-Pacific Regional Security Cooperation," *NBR Analysis* 5 (1994); Banning Garrett and Bonnie Glaser, "Multilateral Security in the Asia Pacific Region and Its Impact on Chinese Interests: Views from Beijing," *Contemporary Southeast Asia* 16 (June 1994): 14–34.

47. Yuen-Foong Khong, "Evolving Regional Security and Economic Institutions," *Southeast Asian Affairs 1995* (Singapore: Institute of Southeast Asian Studies, 1995), 59.

48. Foot, "China in the ASEAN Regional Forum," and Johnston, "The Myth of the ASEAN Way?"

49. Michael Leifer, *The ASEAN Regional Forum: Extending ASEAN's Model of Regional Security,* Adelphi Paper 320 (Oxford: Oxford University Press, 1996); Yuen-Foong Khong, "Making Bricks Without Straw in the Asia Pacific?" *Pacific Review* 10 (1997): 289–300; and Amitav Acharya, *Constructing a Security Community in Southeast Asia* (London: Routledge, 2001).

50. Foot, "China in the ASEAN Regional Forum," 428.
51. Pan Zhenqiang, "The Future of the ARF: A Chinese Perspective," in Khoo How San, ed., *The Future of the ARF* (Singapore, Institute of Defence and Strategic Studies, 1999).
52. Qimao Chen, "New Approaches in China's Foreign Policy: The Post–Cold War Era," *Asian Survey* 33 (March 1993): 237–51.
53. Lampton, *Same Bed, Different Dreams.*
54. Avery Goldstein, *Rising to the Challenge: China's Grand Strategy and International Security* (Stanford, Calif.: Stanford University Press, 2005), 8.
55. Yan Xuetong, *Meiguo Baquan yu Zhongguo Anquan* [American hegemony and Chinese security] (Tianjin: Tianjin People's Publication, 2000), and Zhang Ruizhuang, "Qingxing Renshi Zhongmei Guanxi de Fuzhaxing [Clearly recognizing the complexity of Sino-U.S. relations]," *Wenweipo* (Hong Kong), September 7, 2005, available at http://paper.wenweipo.com/2005/09/07/ww 05090700-03.htm.
56. See Robert S. Ross, "The 1995–1996 Taiwan Strait Confrontation: Coercion, Credibility, and the Use of Force," *International Security* 25 (Fall 2000): 87–123, and Christensen, "Fostering Stability or Creating a Monster?"
57. Yang Jiemian, "Big Power Relations and International Order: Interaction and Impact," *Guoji Wenti Luntan* [International review] 39 (Summer 2005): 1–113, and Robert G. Sutter, *China's Rise in Asia: Promises and Perils* (New York: Rowman and Littlefield, 2005), esp. 43–47.
58. Yong Deng, "Hegemon on the Offensive: Chinese Perspectives on U.S. Global Strategy," *Political Science Quarterly* 116 (2001): 343–65.
59. Ibid. and Goldstein, *Rising to the Challenge,* 133.
60. Jia Qingguo, "Learning to Live with the Hegemon: Evolution of China's Policy toward the US since the End of the Cold War," *Journal of Contemporary China* 14 (August 2005): 395–407.
61. Yan, *American Hegemony and Chinese Security.*
62. Deng, "Hegemon on the Offensive," 350.
63. Shi Yinghong, "Correctly Evaluating International Structure and Its Evolving Trend," *Zhanlue yu Guanli* [Strategy and management] 4 (1999): 103–5, and Zhang Ruizhuang, "Reevaluating Chinese Foreign Policy's International Environment," *Zhanlue yu Guanli* [Strategy and management] 1 (2001): 20–30.
64. David M. Finkelstein, *China Reconsiders Its National Security: The Great Peace and Development Debate of 1999* (Alexandria, Va.: CNA Corporation, December 2000).
65. Shen Jiru, "Multilateral Diplomacy and a Multipolar World," and Meng Xiangqing, "Participating in Multilateral Security Cooperation: A Challenge, but also an Opportunity," both in *Shijie Jingji yu Zhengzhi* [World economy and politics] 10 (2001): 20–24, and 25–29, respectively.

66. Chu Shulong, "China's National Interests, National Power, and National Strategy," *Zhanlue yu Guanli* [Strategy and management] 4 (1999): 13–18.

67. Pang Zhongying, "China's Asia Strategy: A Flexible Multilateralism," *Shijie Jingji yu Zhengzhi* [World economy and politics] 10 (2001): 30–35, and Men Honghua, "The International Strategic Framework of China's Peaceful Rise," in Men, ed., *Zhongguo: Daguo Jueqi* [The rise of modern China] (Hangzhou: Zhejiang People's Publication, 2004), 205–30.

68. Men, "Participation, Creation, and Domination."

69. Ahmed Rashid, *Jihad: The Rise of Militant Islam in Central Asia* (New Haven, Conn.: Yale University Press, 2002), 201–7.

70. Goldstein, *Rising to the Challenge,* 132.

71. Yan Xuetong, "China's Foreign Policy Must Stand on Periphery Ground," *Liaowang* 11 (2000): 49–50.

72. Christensen, "Fostering Stability or Creating a Monster?" 83; Michael A. Glosny, "Heading toward a Win-Win Future? Recent Developments in China's Policy toward Southeast Asia," *Asian Security* 2 (2006): 24–57; and Serene Hung, *China in ASEAN-led Multilateral Forums,* Maryland Series in Contemporary Asian Studies 185 (Baltimore: University of Maryland School of Law, 2006).

73. Thomas G. Moore and Dixia Yang, "Empowered and Restrained: Chinese Foreign Policy in the Age of Economic Interdependence," in David M. Lampton, ed., *The Making of Chinese Foreign and Security Policy in the Era of Reform* (Stanford, Calif.: Stanford University Press, 2001), 221–22.

74. Amitav Acharya, "Realism, Institutionalism, and the Asian Economic Crisis," *Contemporary Southeast Asia* 21 (April 1999): 1–29.

75. H. E. Tang Jiaxuan, Minister of Foreign Affairs, People's Republic of China, opening statement, Seventh ARF, Bangkok, July 27, 2000.

76. Robert Sutter, "China's Regional Strategy and Why It May Not Be Good for America," in David Shambaugh, ed., *Power Shift: China and Asia's New Dynamics* (Berkeley: University of California Press, 2005), 295.

77. Although the PRC had long advocated strengthening its "solidarity with Third World countries" as early as during the Maoist era, its relations with many neighboring countries were obstructed by various political and ideological problems throughout the Cold War period. It was not until the early 1990s that China made real progress in promoting close and comprehensive relations with its neighbors, as highlighted by its normalization and establishment of diplomatic ties with Indonesia (August 1990), Singapore (October 1990), Brunei (September 1991), Vietnam (November 1991), and South Korea (August 1992).

78. Andrew J. Nathan, *China's Crisis: Dilemmas of Reform and Prospects for Democracy* (New York: Columbia University Press, 1990).

79. Wu Xinbo, "China: Security Practice of a Modernizing and Ascending Power," in Muthiah Alagappa, ed., *Asian Security Practice: Material and Ideational Influences* (Stanford, Calif.: Stanford University Press, 1998), 132.

80. Jia, "Learning to Live with the Hegemon," 397. Three more principles were added later: "keeping low key and biding our time [*taoguang yahui*]," "accomplishing something [*yousuo zuowei*]," and "never aspiring to lead [*juebu dangtou*]," thereby forming the "twenty-four-character strategy [*ershisi-zi fangzhen*]."

81. Zhang Baijia, "China's Domestic Politics and Foreign Relations in the 1990s," *Zhonggong Dangshi Yanjiu* [CCP history studies] 6 (2001): 29–34.

82. Chen, "New Approaches in China's Foreign Policy."

83. Zhang Yunling, "How to View Our Periphery Relations and Security Problems," available at www.iapscass.cn/XueShuWZ/showcontent.asp?id=356; China Institute of Contemporary International Relations, "A Research Report on China's ASEAN Policy," *Xiandai Guoji Guanxi* [Contemporary international relations] 10 (2002): 1–10.

84. Chen, "Major Concerns in China's ASEAN Policy," 162.

85. Zhang Yunling and Tang Shiping, "China's Regional Strategy," in Shambaugh, *Power Shift,* 50.

86. Cheng-Chwee Kuik, "Regime Legitimation and Foreign Policy Choices: A Comparative Study of Southeast Asian States' Hedging Strategies toward a Rising China, 1990–2005," dissertation prospectus submitted to the Paul H. Nitze School of Advanced International Studies (SAIS) (Washington, D.C.: The Johns Hopkins University, September 2006).

87. Kuik, "Multilateralism in China's ASEAN Policy."

88. Termsak Chalermpalanupap, "ASEAN-China Dialogue: Towards Enhancing Friendship and Good Neighbourliness," *China-ASEAN Review 1999* (Hong Kong: University of Hong Kong, 1999).

89. Wang Yi, "Yulin Weishan, Yulin Weiban [Friendliness and companionship to neighbors]," *Qiushi* [Seeking truth] 4 (2003): 19–22.

90. Yongnian Zheng and Sow Keat Tok, *China's 'Peaceful Rise': Concept and Practice,* China Policy Institute Discussion Paper 1 (Nottingham, England: University of Nottingham, 2005), 14.

91. Lucian Pye, "China: Erratic State, Frustrated Society," *Foreign Policy* 69 (Autumn 1990): 56–74, and Minxin Pei, "China's Governance Crisis," *Foreign Affairs* 81 (2002): 96–109.

92. Wang Gungwu and Zheng Yongnian, *Reform, Legitimacy, and Dilemmas: China's Politics and Society* (Singapore: Singapore University Press and World Scientific, 2000), esp. 1–20; Harry Harding, "The Halting Advance of Pluralism," *Journal of Democracy* 9 (1998): 11–17; and Thomas J. Christensen, China," in Richard J. Ellings and Aaron L. Friedberg, eds., *Strategic Asia 2001–2002: Power and Purpose* (Seattle, Wash.: National Bureau of Asian Research, 2001), 27–69.

93. Deng, *Deng Xiaoping Wenxuan,* Vol. 3, 370.

94. Jiang Zemin, "Accelerating Reform and Opening-Up," *Beijing Review* 35 (1992): 9–32.

95. Chinese Ministry of Commerce Web site, available at http://yzs.mofcom .gov.cn/aarticle/date/c/200601/20060101431338.html.

96. Feng Xiaoming, "China and ASEAN Can Enjoy Prosperity Together," *Guoji Jingji Pinglun* [International economy review] 1–2 (2002): 60–62.

97. Takahara Akio, "Beijing Embraces Regionalism," *Japan Echo* 29 (2002): 38–49.

98. Deng, *Deng Xiaoping Wenxuan,* Vol. 2, 417.

99. Tang Shiping, *Shuzhao Zhongguo de Lixiang Anquan Huanjing* [Construct China's ideal security environment] (Beijing: CASS Publishing, 2003), 86–96.

100. Yan Xuetong, "Whatever-It-Takes Would Ensure China's National Unification," *Lianhe Zaobao* (Singapore), November 28, 2003, 19, and Shi Yinghong, "China's External Difficulties and the New Leadership's Challenges: International Politics, Foreign Policy, and the Taiwan Problem," *Zhanlue yu Guanli* [Strategy and management] 3 (2003): 34–39.

101. Chien-Peng Chung, "The Defense of Xinjiang," *Harvard International Review* (Summer 2003): 58–62; Bates Gill and Matthew Oresman, *China's New Journey to the West: A Report of the CSIS Freeman Chair in China Studies* (Washington, D.C.: Center for Strategic and International Studies, 2003).

102. See Yan Xuetong, "The Rise of China in Chinese Eyes," *Journal of Contemporary China* 10 (2001): 33–39, and Ye Zicheng, *Zhongguo Da Zhanlue: Zhongguo Chengwei Shijie Daguo de Zhuyao Wenti ji Zanlue Xuanzhe* [China's grand strategy: The major problems and strategic choices for China's quest to become a world major power] (Beijing: China Social Sciences Publishing, 2003). For a historical view of "the rise of China," see Wang Gungwu, "The Fourth Rise of China: Cultural Implications," *China: An International Journal* 2 (September 2004): 311–22.

103. On China's "peaceful rise," see Zheng Bijian, *Peaceful Rise—China's New Road to Development* (Beijing: Central Party School Publishing House, 2005).

104. On China's nationalism, see Peter Hays Gries, *China's New Nationalism: Pride, Politics, and Diplomacy* (Berkeley: University of California Press, 2004), and Shuisheng Zhao, "China's Pragmatic Nationalism: Is It Manageable?" *Washington Quarterly* 29 (Winter 2005–6): 131–44.

105. Tang, *Construct China's Ideal Security Environment,* and Men, "Participation, Creation, and Domination."

106. Steven I. Levine, "Sino-American Relations: Practicing Damage Control," in Samuel Kim, ed., *China and the World: Chinese Foreign Policy Faces the New Millennium,* 4th ed. (Boulder, Colo.: Westview, 1998), 91.

107. Christensen, *Useful Adversaries,* and Chen Jian, *Mao's China and the Cold War.*

108. Both incidents are widely regarded as "political-military crises" that could have led to acute consequences for China-U.S. relations. For an excellent analysis of how Chinese and American leaders managed these crises, see Michael D. Swaine and Zhang Tuosheng, eds., *Managing Sino-American Crises: Case Studies and Analysis* (Washington, D.C.: Carnegie Endowment for International Peace, 2006), esp. 327–452.

109. Li Shaojun, *Guoji Zhengzhixue Gailun* [Study of international politics] (Shanghai: Shanghai People's Publication, 2002), 520–26.

110. Zhang and Tang, "China's Regional Strategy," 50, and Zhang Yunling, "Comprehensive Security and Some Thoughts on Our National Security," *Dangdai Yatai* [Contemporary Asia Pacific] 1 (2000): 4–16. Emphasis added.

111. Alastair Iain Johnston, "Is China a Status Quo Power?" *International Security* 27 (Spring 2003): 5–56.

112. M. Taylor Fravel, "Regime Insecurity and International Cooperation: Explaining China's Compromises in Territorial Disputes," *International Security* 30 (Fall 2005): 46–83.

CHAPTER 6

China and the Impracticality of Closed Regionalism

Daniel H. Rosen

WILL THE NATIONS OF NORTHEAST ASIA continue to embrace global financial and economic institutions as their economic weight in the world increases, or will they turn to local, regionally based structures? To what extent will Asia, particularly China, evolve its own internally oriented economic system? China's perspectives on these questions are of special importance for several reasons. China's growth trajectory is expected soon to give it the political and economic heft to realistically lead a "governance block" independent of the West and of existing Western-led governance institutions. Because its marginal growth is so important to its immediate neighbors' economic welfare, China could induce their participation through the influence of soft power (including allure rather than compulsion). The rise of a Northeast Asian governance structure could also lead to the relative decline of multilateral structures that the United States typically dominates, and thus the diminution of U.S. influence.

In exploring this topic from the perspective of economics, my approach centers on *markets*. In the succeeding pages I identify the economic systems and markets on which China's interests depend, explore what governance systems are necessary to sustain these systems, and draw conclusions as to whether China's interests could thus be met through an Asian-led governance system, Beijing-dominated or otherwise, rather than through the multilateral alternatives that exist today. Generally, China cannot hope to manage its economic interests within Asia-centric alternatives to multilateral institutions in the near or the medium term. While in the long term Asianism cannot be ruled out, there is no reason to presuppose its evolution until much greater progress is made on preconditions.

Introduction: What We Know about China's View

Over the past 25 years, China's actions have manifested a commitment to market economics that goes far beyond mere rhetoric. China has radically dismantled obstacles to market economic activity both internally and at its periphery. Intraprovincial trade barriers and external tariffs have been trimmed to a fraction of their previous autarkic levels, nontariff barriers of all sorts have been greatly reduced, investment barriers and price controls largely abolished, and so on. The extent of such reforms is impressive and widely acknowledged.[1] Ironically, China is a good example of the properly understood Washington Consensus school of thought on the political economy of policy reform and marketization.[2]

While still poor in absolute terms, China has grown many times wealthier in recent years and is on track to achieve moderate wealth in absolute terms within a few decades. Yet its past, present, and future achievements rest on the foundation of China's engagement with a set of economic systems that lie beyond Beijing's sovereign authority and require collective governance. These include

- external capital markets,
- external markets for China's exports and imports,
- international regimes to manage regional and global economic volatility,
- security and governance regimes to manage international energy and resource flows, and
- global regimes that support regional development and stability.

China could reasonably expect to manage each of these external needs through regional rather than global multilateral mechanisms, as discussed in detail later. However, the conclusions drawn from this study are necessarily uncertain and speculative for the following reasons:

- The track records of those attempting to guess the views of senior Chinese leadership on matters of national strategy are notoriously bad, both among foreign intelligence communities and among insiders who claim to have exceptional access to Beijing. We simply do not have a certain channel of insight into how Beijing thinks about such issues.

- There is *no single China*. Views in China change often these days; a seminal shift is under way in the educational backgrounds of Chinese leaders and hence in their modes of thinking.[3] Within Chinese leadership there is no consistent ideology regarding many issues, with nationalists and internationalists competing for influence over policy.[4] Even within camps, views change depending on the technical sophistication of the individuals involved and on policy details.
- Vested interests are evolving in China as new wealth is created. As the costs and benefits of better engagement with external markets change, so too do China's national interests, especially as wealth management becomes a major preoccupation of China's 100 million–strong managerial/technical/intellectual middle class.[5]
- A minority of Chinese leaders are still engrossed—some would say neurotically so—with eliminating their nation's vulnerability to the outside world. This camp was stronger previously than it is today, but still cannot be ignored when considering senior discourse. This remains the "wild card" in China's ruling psychology.[6]

For these reasons and more, we must speculate when we consider China's perspective on Northeast Asian economic integration (just as we would be speculating if we were to explore America's perspective on continued military engagement in Iraq). This does not imply that our speculation cannot be reasonable and predictive.

Another preliminary point: the question I address is not whether China has a *desire* to exercise leadership or power over the external economic systems on which it depends, but rather whether it is feasible for it to do so any time soon. Many people consider it debatable whether China even wants to hold management responsibility in many economic areas, given that this entails entanglement in Byzantine cross-cultural conflicts and political dramas for which Beijing seems to have a limited taste. However, let us assume that China does aspire to embrace these headaches at some point, and ask whether its efforts to do so could reduce U.S. primacy.

External Capital Markets

Could China seek a Northeast Asian supplier to meet its external capital needs, perhaps even a regime that it could dominate? To answer this question we need to clarify the nature of China's external capital needs, and what multinational regimes dealing with capital have to offer.

Since World War II, economic development theory has long held that increasing the formation of capital is the key to fostering economic development in poor countries. Starting poor, China indeed needed investment. Today, Chinese companies still need to raise money. Obtaining funds from government sources is not the way preferred by the more dynamic firms because that would entail a loss of managerial independence and hence competitiveness. Because China still has a system dominated by state banks, domestic equities and bond markets are inadequate to raise funds. Some in Beijing believe domestic capital-raising can be "outsourced" to foreign markets because China has grown at such a fast rate without the benefit of good domestic markets thus far. That is a mistake, but for our purposes the point is that Chinese firms—both quality private firms and rickety state-owned firms—look abroad for money.

There are three types of external capital flows into China today: foreign direct investment (FDI), multilateral development bank (MDB) investment, and portfolio investment in equity markets.

Foreign Direct Investment (FDI)

China's FDI is the envy of the developing world. Annual FDI inflows grew over 100 percent between 2000 and 2005, from U.S.$38.4 billion in 2000 to $79.1 billion in 2005, making China the largest or second largest FDI recipient in the world. Yet FDI is only around 5 percent of total investment in China (now over $1 trillion following recent GDP revisions).[7] And a significant though uncertain share of this FDI is "round-tripped"— originating in China, then flowing out and back in to enjoy preferential terms for foreign investors. Therefore, it is not the capital formation of $60 billion or so of FDI that matters, but its catalyzing role. FDI is often the prime mover that sets off a cascade of other investments, either directly or indirectly. FDI often brings technological progress to Chinese industries, it spawns spin-off investments as Chinese copycats pile on to imitate foreign production processes, it creates back-linkages to the home market that opens up both inbound and outbound trade flows, and it generates new construction for facility and supply chain partners.

China has two main strategic interests regarding FDI. The first is the integration of manufacturing value chains throughout East Asia, which is driven and achieved through FDI. Japanese, Korean, and Taiwanese firms have flocked to China over the past decade, setting up foreign-owned enterprises or joint ventures to provide final assembly of manufactured goods built from intermediate components imported from East Asian neighbors. This integration brings economic efficiencies that accrue partly to China. However, it also brings interdependence, which is healthy for China and the East Asian political-economic system because it creates an expectation that international problems must be resolved cooperatively and that unilateral solutions are prohibitively costly.

China's second main strategic interest in FDI is related to the explicit or implicit technology transfers that usually accompany it. Chinese leaders are eager to move up the manufacturing value chain in order to realize their goals of quadrupling per capita incomes between 2000 and 2020. The Chinese leadership sees high-technology-related FDI as key to this process.

Although there is no international regime governing FDI, both multinational and regional regimes have tried to provide rules that encourage cross-border investment. A Multilateral Investment Agency was proposed, but this effort has foundered in recent years. The World Trade Organization (WTO) accord on Trade-Related Investment Measures (TRIMs) goes part way toward disciplining unfair investment policies, and regional accords increasingly include investment-related provisions. In late 2005, China, Japan, and South Korea conducted preliminary talks on the inclusion of investment provisions in a Northeast Asian economic arrangement that might facilitate future inclusion of such provisions in an Association of Southeast Asian Nations (ASEAN) Plus Three undertaking.[8]

Deeper Asian economic integration and regional governance can facilitate achievement of the strategic goal of regional value chain integration, but only partly. Critical sources of new technology and know-how lie outside Asia. Europe and the United States still have high-end manufacturing and R&D assets that China needs a robust FDI environment to take advantage of. Figure 6.1 shows that, although East Asia is an important source of FDI, over half of all non–Hong Kong inflows come from non-Asian countries. If China were to direct its cross-border investment regime-building energies toward a regional structure and away from structures involving Europe and the United States, it would suffer a decline in technology transfer and trade back-linkages with these key markets.

Multilateral Development Banks (MDBs)

Loans and grants from MDBs such as the World Bank once played an important part in Chinese capital accumulation, financing major infrastructure and environmental projects. In recent years, however, as World Bank funding to China has declined, Asian Development Bank (ADB) loans have increased. In 2004, the World Bank provided China with U.S.\$1 billion in new loans (down from \$2.9 billion in 1996), while the ADB approved \$1.3 billion in loans (up from roughly \$600 million in 1997).[9] Yet both banks play a marginal and declining role in satisfying China's total

Figure 6.1 FDI Flows into China, 1995–2005

Billions of U.S.$

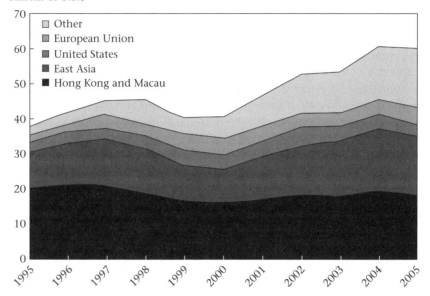

Sources: Estimates from CEIC Data Co. and China's National Bureau of Statistics.
Note: East Asia consists of Indonesia, Japan, Korea (ROK), Malaysia, the Philippines, Taiwan, and Thailand.

capital needs, as demonstrated by Figure 6.2, which compares World Bank funding to FDI and overall investment.

Foreign Portfolio Investment

Although MDBs and FDI are becoming marginal in terms of China's overall capital needs, foreign financial markets play a large and growing role. While Asian markets such as Hong Kong and Singapore have attracted a large number of Chinese firms seeking to raise money, the evolving norms of these capital markets and of the domestic Shanghai and Shenzhen exchanges are still dominated by the high standards of European and U.S. regulatory thinking. As a result, Chinese giants such as Petro-China, China Mobile, and China Life Insurance have all decided to list on the New York Stock Exchange (NYSE). The 17 Chinese firms listed on the Big Board in 2005 had a combined market capitalization of U.S.$329 billion at the end of 2005.[10] Chinese technology firms such as Baidu have

Figure 6.2 World Bank Funding and FDI, 1995–2005

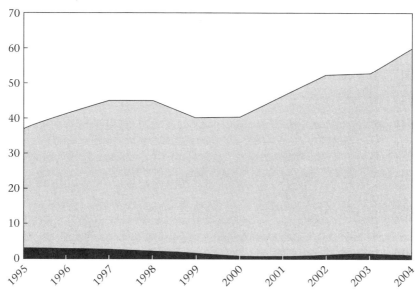

Billions of U.S.$

Sources: World Bank annual reports, 1996–2005 (World Bank FY2005 is listed under 2004, etc.). FDI data for 1994–2004 from the United Nations Conference on Trade and Development. Total investment figures are from the Economist Intelligence Unit, derived from national sources and IMF, *International Financial Statistics.*
Note: The black fill indicates new World Bank loans; the gray fill indicates foreign direct investment.

also sought U.S. listings on NASDAQ.[11] As shown in Figure 6.3, the stock value of Chinese firms traded in New York outstrips the market capitalization of the firms' tradable shares on the Hong Kong, Singapore, and domestic exchanges combined.

How long will it take for Asia to rival the United States as a highly competitive location for raising capital? The diversity and depth of U.S. markets, coupled with the well-established regulatory institutions that govern them, have traditionally attracted huge amounts of global capital to the United States. Through U.S. markets, Chinese companies will be able to access a wide range of investors from all over the world.

To surpass the United States as a preferred venue for raising capital, Asia has to attract more international investors to tap its markets for prof-

Figure 6.3 Market Capitalization of Chinese Firms as of
December 31, 2005

Billions of U.S.$

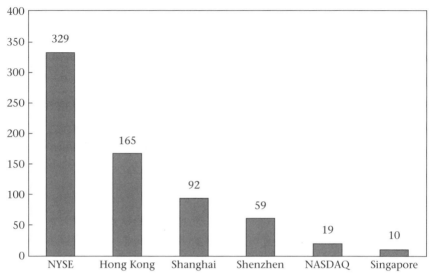

Sources: CEIC Data Co. and the Web sites for Thomson Financial and the stock exchanges
listed.

itable investments. To draw large, sophisticated investors, Asia has to establish a reliable regulatory infrastructure, develop international standards
of financial expertise, and introduce a wide range of products to satisfy the
investment and hedging needs of international investors. Asian markets
are developing quickly in these areas, particularly Hong Kong due to its
proximity to China and its traditional role as the entry point for international capital looking to invest in Chinese companies.

It is worth noting that the Hang Seng Index ended 2004 with HKD300
billion (U.S.$40.1 billion) in initial public offering (IPO) funding, making
it the second most lucrative market after New York.[12] In fact, China Construction Bank is planning to launch its expected $7.7 billion IPO in Hong
Kong rather than the United States.[13] Postulated reasons include the high
costs of listing in New York and the strenuous compliance standards for
IPOs on the NYSE and NASDAQ. Complying with the 2002 Sarbanes-
Oxley Act is mentioned as an onerous financial and accounting disclosure
requirement that increases the liability of company directors for wrong-
doing.[14] According to Dealogic Holdings, there has been a sharp drop in

the amount of cash raised by Chinese companies on the NYSE, with only $1.37 billion raised in January–August 2005 compared with $7.26 billion in all of 2004.[15] If this trend continues into the future, Asian markets may eventually surpass the United States as favorite grounds for Chinese capital-raising.

However, the standards set in U.S. capital markets will be a factor influencing the standards Chinese capital-seekers from abroad will prepare to meet for some time. U.S. asset management firms can move money to Asian investments outside of U.S. capital markets as well, but when they do so they continue to apply fiduciary standards developed and enforced in the United States.

External Markets for China's Exports and Imports

Chinese leaders depend on a strong domestic economy to validate and perpetuate the political and economic system they sit atop. Manufacturing for export (with a high proportion of re-export) has been a key engine of Chinese economic growth and reform, and net export surplus currently accounts for the bulk of annual Chinese GDP growth. China relies equally on external markets for access to the raw materials, goods, and services it consumes and processes.

As mentioned in the discussion of FDI, investment in Chinese manufacturing by Japanese, Korean, and Taiwanese firms is progressively integrating East Asia, with China serving as the final assembly point for raw materials and intermediate goods imported from its neighbors. China has become a more important trading partner for all East Asian nations over the past 10 years (Figure 6.4). In 2004, China accounted for 22 percent of Japan's total trade, up from 8 percent in 1994. China's share of Korea's total trade rose from 6 percent to 19 percent over the same period.

Yet China's accession to the WTO, which stabilized Western markets for Chinese exports, has resulted in a diminished role for East Asia in terms of China's total trade. While South Korea and the ASEAN nations constitute a slightly larger share of China's trade flows now than in 1993 (Figure 6.5), these increases do not offset reductions in the standing of Hong Kong and Japan in the trade portfolio.

The result of increasing East Asian dependence on trade with China, in conjunction with acceptance of China's exports by Western markets, is an integrated Asian value chain. As shown in Figure 6.6, Japan's declining share of East Asia's trade with the world mirrors China's growing share over the past 10 years. Japanese capital goods, intermediates, and raw materials now stop off in China for final assembly before being exported to the

Figure 6.4 Asian Countries' Trade with China as a Share of Their Total Trade, 1993–2004

Share of total trade (%)

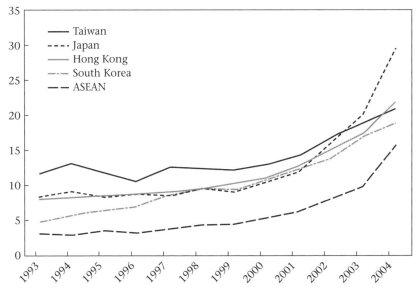

Source: UN Comtrade, July 14, 2005.
Note: Classification: HS 1992.

West. So while U.S. imports from China have boomed over the past decade, U.S. imports from all of East Asia have declined as a share of total imports, from 37.3 percent in 1996 to 34.5 percent in 2004.[16]

Economic integration in East Asia has led to a great deal of speculation about the prospect of a pan-Asian free trade agreement (FTA). The idea was first proposed by former Malaysian prime minister Mohamad Mahathir in 1990 but was shelved in favor of the Asia-Pacific Economic Cooperation (APEC), which includes Australia, Canada, New Zealand, Russia, and the United States. Because APEC has done little on the trade liberalization front since its inauguration, is it possible that a regional trade bloc on the scale of the European Union or the North American Free Trade Agreement is in the works?

While a regionwide initiative exists in the form of ASEAN Plus Three (which includes China, Japan, and Korea), China, Japan, and Korea are all putting more energy into bilateral FTAs, many of which are with non-Asian countries. In the Institute for International Economics working paper "Prospects for Regional Free Trade in Asia," Gary Clyde Hufbauer

Figure 6.5 China's Trade with Asian Countries as a Share of Its Total Trade, 1993–2004

Share of total trade (%)

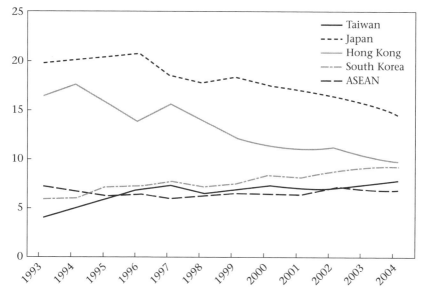

Source: UN Comtrade, July 14, 2005.
Note: Classification: HS 1992.

and Yee Wong document the long list of FTAs implemented, under negotiation, or proposed by East Asian nations. From 1992 to 2005, some
15 FTAs were implemented, 9 of which were with partners outside of
East Asia. Of the 27 FTAs under negotiation, only 9 were with East Asian
partners.

China, reliant on non-Asian markets for raw materials, capital goods,
and intermediates, has been particularly active in seeking bilateral FTAs
outside Asia. As shown in Figure 6.7, the United States remains critical to
Beijing, receiving 25.6 percent of China's non–Hong Kong global exports
in 2005. The European Union accounts for an additional 22.6 percent of
China's non–Hong Kong exports. And of course a significant portion of
what China exports to Hong Kong is destined for the West as well.[17]

The importance of the U.S. market to China is amplified by the competition between China and the rest of Asia. High-income Asian economies,
including those of Singapore, South Korea, and Taiwan, compete with
China in high-technology exports. China is also a significant competitor
of labor-abundant nations such as Indonesia, Thailand, and Vietnam, mak-

Figure 6.6 Asian Countries' Trade with the World Excluding Intra-Asian Trade, 1993–2004

Share of total trade (%)

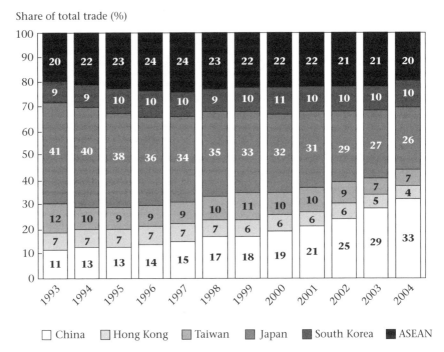

☐ China   ☐ Hong Kong   ▨ Taiwan   ▨ Japan   ■ South Korea   ■ ASEAN

Source: UN Comtrade, July 14, 2005.
Notes: Classification: HS 1992. East Asia (EA): ASEAN + China + Hong Kong + Japan + South Korea + Taiwan. Quantity unit differences ignored in UN Comtrade search. UN Comtrade does not accept Taiwan as reporter; therefore, search inverted to make global exEA the reporter and EA (which includes Taiwan) the partner. Rest of the world = global exEA = world minus East Asia.

ing such labor-intensive products as clothing, footwear, toys, and consumer electrical goods.

The size of the U.S. market leaves little doubt that it will remain highly influential in Chinese and Asian trade strategy well into the future. The importance of the U.S. market will plateau as China and Asia gradually restructure their production patterns to reflect changes in their comparative advantages and move toward an increasingly complementary trade relationship, but it is not likely to decline.

China is also reliant on non-Asian markets for many of its raw material and capital goods imports. As shown in Figure 6.8, imports from East

Figure 6.7 China's Exports to the World, 1995–2005

Billions of U.S.$

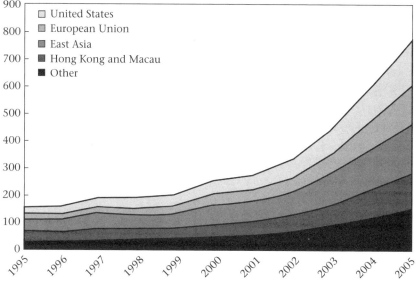

Sources: Estimates from CEIC Data Co. and China's National Bureau of Statistics.
Note: East Asia consists of Indonesia, Japan, Korea (ROK), Malaysia, the Philippines, Singapore, Taiwan, and Thailand.

Asia account for only 17 percent of the animal products and foodstuffs, 13 percent of the mineral products, and 28 percent of the pulp and paper imported by China. Because of commodity trade patterns such as these, Beijing has proposed bilateral FTAs with Australia, Brazil, Chile, and Peru.[18] In fact, of the 18 currently proposed by China, only 6 involve East Asian partners.

While East Asia plays a larger role in supplying the intermediate and capital goods that fuel China's manufacturing might, the European Union and the United States are still important partners and cannot easily be excluded from the value chain, although in other product areas, such as optical equipment, much of the industry has already moved to Asia (see Figure 6.9). Because of the long-standing U.S. history of extensive R&D investment, access to American technology will likely remain critical for China in the foreseeable future.

Finally, the role of the U.S. Navy in ensuring the security of the world's sea lanes is unlikely to be supplanted over the next 50 years. A large por-

Figure 6.8 China's Commodity Imports, 2005

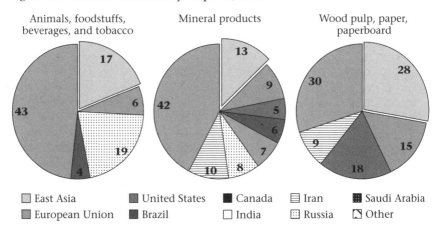

Sources: Estimates from CEIC Data Co. and China's National Bureau of Statistics.
Note: East Asia consists of Indonesia, Japan, Korea (ROK), Malaysia, the Philippines, Singapore, Taiwan, Thailand.

Figure 6.9 China's High-Value Imports, 2005

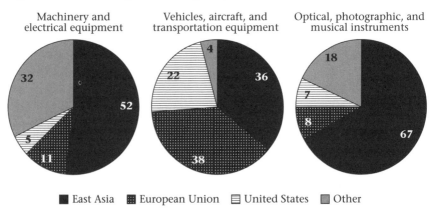

Sources: Estimates from CEIC Data Co. and China's National Bureau of Statistics.
Note: East Asia consists of Indonesia, Japan, Korea (ROK), Malaysia, the Philippines, Singapore, Taiwan, and Thailand.

tion of China's trade with the world travels through choke points such as the Straits of Malacca. The vulnerability of commodity import flows to a terrorist attack at one of these points is a growing preoccupation of the Chinese leadership.[19] While hesitation to rely on America for trade security has prompted Beijing to strengthen its naval capacity, the ability to replace the United States as provider of the police force protecting Asia's sea lanes will elude China for some time.

Regimes to Manage Regional and Global Economic Volatility

Because China's economic and political footprint is broadening, regional and global economic vitality are becoming more than "someone else's problem." External economic strength is integral to China's continued economic growth and its ascent to the status of a first-rate global power, a point emphasized by U.S. Treasury Secretary John Snow and Federal Reserve Chairman Alan Greenspan on their October 2005 visit to Beijing for a meeting of G20 officials. In China this message did not fall on deaf ears.

Presently, the United States maintains the leading role in fostering global economic growth and managing volatility through international financial institutions such as the International Monetary Fund (IMF), the WTO, the World Bank, and others. Although Asia plays a lesser role by comparison, this role is set to expand as China becomes an increasingly significant participant in the world economy. In fact, the formation of ASEAN Plus Three is often seen as a move to form an Asian economic *and* political bloc less beholden to the United States. It is widely postulated that in coming years China could take over the role of the United States as the principal guardian of regional stability in Asia.

To date, however, regional institutions including the ADB, APEC, and ASEAN Plus Three have not established effective coordinating mechanisms that can push forward economic reforms or resolve crises. These institutions tend to adopt an approach that emphasizes informality, consensus-building, and nonconfrontational bargaining styles, and members have been less willing to bind themselves to agreements, making it difficult to establish coordinating mechanisms. For instance, APEC is committed to the notion that members will undertake agreements unilaterally rather than negotiate formally and sign treaties. Therefore, there is little discipline when it comes to reducing trade barriers. Although financial integration has also received attention at the regional level, there are limits to the ability of an Asian Monetary Fund (AMF) to replace the IMF as the principal economic stabilizer of East Asia.

The notion of an AMF was proposed, principally by Japan, after the 1997 Asian financial crisis, in part as a response to Asian misgivings about the policy emphasis of the IMF. In 2000, ASEAN Plus Three took a step toward realizing this notion through the creation of a currency swap arrangement known as the Chiang Mai Initiative.[20] Some hope an AMF will grow out of this agreement in the future. However, the resources of an AMF would not likely be sufficient to truly address systemic Asian economic volatility. The United States has been wary of an Asia-only monetary fund. Moreover, other Asian countries have been reluctant to empower a strong AMF for the same reasons that an Asia-only trade reform organization has been slow to take off: they harbor mutual mistrust on such a sensitive matter as monetary policy and are reluctant to submit to one another's discipline. Mutual trust and willingness to submit to mutual discipline are both necessary for effective response to crises.

An alternative for East Asian nations is to seek greater representation at the IMF. While China, Japan, and Korea together controlled 43 percent of the world's foreign exchange reserves in 2004, they represented only 9.8 percent of the total votes at the IMF (Figure 6.10). Meanwhile, Europe and the United States, which controlled only 5.2 percent of global foreign exchange reserves, represented 46.82 percent of the voting power. Presiding IMF Managing Director Rodrigo de Rato and former director Michael Camdessus both made speeches in the fall of 2005 calling for reallocation of IMF representation.[21] Although almost everyone agrees that the IMF must reform its governance in order to maintain its effectiveness, views differ over who should cede influence to the East Asian giants. At the World Economic Forum in January 2006, European finance ministers rejected the notion of a diminished E.U. voting share without a corresponding reduction in U.S. representation.[22]

The outcome of reform discussions at the IMF's spring 2006 meeting had considerable bearing on whether China, Japan, Korea, and ASEAN look to the fund to manage regional economic stability or direct their energy toward strengthening ASEAN Plus Three and a potential AMF. Yet for the latter to be successful, there will have to be a stronger sense of Asian solidarity to improve the cooperative framework of the existing regional organizations. With continuing tensions in the region—not the least between China and Japan, the two largest and most important economies—prospects are still distant. Absent a record of mutual action to coordinate economic management in Asia, it is hard to see how China or a China-led Asian caucus could act collectively in a meaningful way to support the vitality of the global economy in which they are embedded. For the foreseeable future, existing regimes led by the United States will play the predominant roles in addressing economic volatility in Asia and worldwide.

Figure 6.10 IMF Voting Shares and Foreign Exchange Reserves, 2004

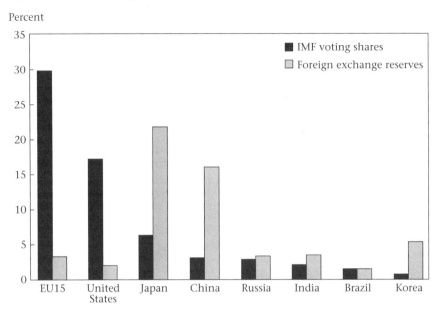

Sources: "IMF Members' Quotas and Voting Power, and IMF Board of Governors," February 14, 2006, available at www.imf.org, and the Economist Intelligence Unit. Foreign exchange reserve figures derived from IMF, *International Financial Statistics,* 2004.

Regimes to Manage International Energy Resource Flows

Increasing reliance on imported oil, coal, and liquefied natural gas (expected to be a major factor in the years ahead) has made international energy security one of Beijing's primary interests. Although China has made dramatic improvements in its energy efficiency over the past 20 years, GDP growth consistently above 8 percent will cause overall Chinese energy demand to skyrocket in the years ahead (see Figure 6.11). With domestic coal mines running at capacity and oil fields like Daqing in the Northeast maturing, China will become increasingly reliant on energy sources imported from abroad. Ensuring and securing the uninterrupted supply and delivery of energy is a major policy objective of the Chinese government. The most pressing concern is the country's dependence on foreign oil.

China has been a net oil importer since the mid-1990s and in 2003 surpassed Japan to become the world's second largest importer of crude oil after the United States. The International Energy Agency (IEA) reports that

Figure 6.11 Chinese Energy Consumption and Intensity, 1980–2025

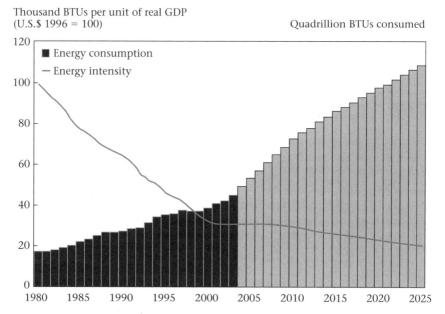

Thousand BTUs per unit of real GDP
(U.S.$ 1996 = 100)   Quadrillion BTUs consumed

Sources: GDP data from national statistics derived by the Economist Intelligence Unit and IMF, *International Financial Statistics.* Energy consumption data and forecasts from the Energy Information Agency's *International Energy Annual, 2003,* and projections from *International Energy Outlook, 2005.*

China's oil demand grew by 15.4 percent in 2004. Although in 2005 the growth rate in oil demand pulled back to 3.2 percent as a result of heavy-handed state controls, in 2006 it is expected to snap back, with more than 7 percent growth in oil consumption.

More than 80 percent of all oil imported to most Asian countries, China included, is transported through the South China Sea / Straits of Malacca.[23] In spite of this, there is little concerted effort to safeguard energy supplies by combating maritime piracy in those waters or to provide an alternative to the U.S. Navy in protecting transit routes from the Middle East and North Africa. Japan's proposal of multinational patrols in both territorial and international waters was met with resistance from Indonesia and Malaysia. Mutual suspicion and concerns over sovereignty violations are primary factors hampering solidarity among Asian nations in energy cooperation. In fact, energy competition has become a flashpoint for tensions between China and Japan. Drilling rights in the East China Sea and the destination of Russian oil and gas pipelines have become issues of significant contention in Northeast Asia.

At the multilateral level, Asia remains, to date, a minor player in the coordination of international energy policies, even though its share of global energy consumption is rising (see Figure 6.12). Only two of Asia's 26 economies, those of Japan and South Korea, are members of the IEA, the main international organization that coordinates among energy importers. China has a relationship with the IEA, and there is much talk about formalizing its membership. But to do so, it will need to construct a strategic petroleum reserve (SPR) that can hold 90 days' worth of oil supply. China has begun construction of a 30-day SPR, but has shrouded its stockpiling efforts in secrecy for fear of raising international oil prices.

Meanwhile, the United States continues to have significant influence over international energy resource flows and policies through its partici-

Figure 6.12 Oil Consumption, 1983–2003

Share of global oil consumption (%)

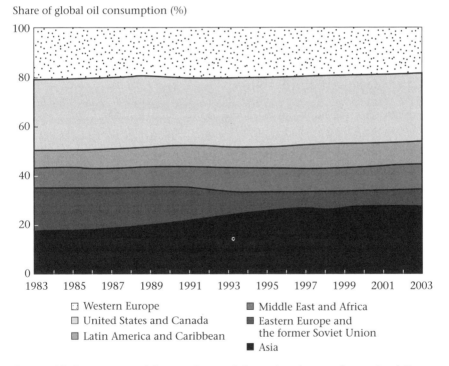

Legend:
☐ Western Europe
☐ United States and Canada
☐ Latin America and Caribbean
■ Middle East and Africa
■ Eastern Europe and the former Soviet Union
■ Asia

Source: U.S. Department of Energy, Energy Information Agency, *International Energy Annual,* 2003.

pation in the IEA. Its traditional global military presence results in de facto U.S. policing of major sea lanes, including the Persian Gulf and the Strait of Hormuz. In fact, the United States has recently reinforced its ability to protect major sea lanes in the South China Sea and the Strait of Malacca in the absence of an East Asian alternative.[24]

For Asia to expand its role on the energy front, Asian nations must increase their cooperation and the coordination of their respective views on energy issues. This could open the door to greater cooperation in safeguarding sea lanes. But all the issues of regional trust and history that make coordination difficult in trade and monetary affairs are even more problematic in energy because energy is such a sensitive strategic commodity. It is doubtful that China, or any other Asian country, can find a local alternative to the U.S.-led IEA to address international energy issues on the demand side any time soon. Although Beijing is responding to its increased energy dependence by seeking equity oil deals with producers in Africa, Central Asia, and the Middle East, China is too large to ensure its energy security unilaterally. The kind of supply disruptions and price spikes that present the most potent risks to China's economic growth can be handled only through multilateral approaches like that of the IEA.

Global Regimes to Support Regional Development and Stability

Regional economic development is crucial to China's continued domestic economic growth and political stability. Volatility in Asia has the potential to disrupt and damage the economies of China and its neighbors. Indeed, the main external drivers of Asian economies—external trade and inflows of foreign investment—are contingent on regional political stability. Clearly, it is in China's interest to promote regional economic development through investment and foreign policy for both commercial and political reasons. More cynically, one could say it is also in China's interest to provide an alternative to Western development support tied to the promotion of liberal democratic governments over authoritarian regimes.

Examples of potential triggers for Asian regional instability include Muslim fundamentalism in Indonesia, the fragility of the North Korean state, and the dependence of Central Asia on the opium trade, to name just a few. Asia, particularly China, plays a significant role in countering these risks. Acknowledging that poverty may exacerbate these threats and ignite political tumult, Japan and South Korea have been disbursing development aid to poorer Asian countries both bilaterally and through regional and international institutions such as the ADB and the United Nations

Figure 6.13 Official Development Assistance to East Asia, 1984–2004

Billions of U.S.$

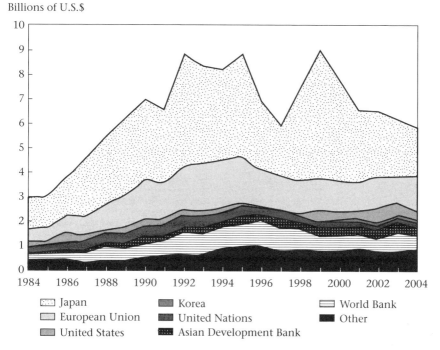

Japan
European Union
United States

Korea
United Nations
Asian Development Bank

World Bank
Other

Source: Organisation for Economic Co-operation and Development, *International Development Statistics.*

(Figure 6.13). Although China has played a central role in the multilateral Six-Party Talks over the fate of North Korea's nuclear program and in the Shanghai Cooperation Organization in Central Asia, it has only recently become a significant source of development assistance for countries in the region. According to official statistics, Chinese foreign aid grew from U.S.$19 million in 1993 to $186 million in 2004.[25] While this is a small amount compared to the $9 billion Japan disbursed that year, it approaches the $423 million in aid given by South Korea.[26]

Under many of the bilateral agreements China has inked with developing nations in Asia, such as Cambodia, Myanmar, and Vietnam, the money disbursed goes mainly to build infrastructure that facilitates economic growth (not the least, trade with China). In response to accusations that China's development assistance comes with strings attached, Chinese officials are not shy about admitting privately that resources are used to promote Chinese interests, and generally are not provided as part of a tradition of charity.

In the years ahead, will China have the capacity to promote regional stability and development unilaterally or through Asia-only vehicles? That is unlikely. The regional development institution that has the strongest developmental profile, the ADB, includes U.S. participation, and, of the total bilateral development assistance provided to Asia, only Japan makes a significant contribution in comparison to America and Europe. Figure 6.13 shows both bilateral and multilateral official development assistance (ODA) provided to East Asia from 1984 to 2004. While Japan offered the largest portion of ODA, that proportion declined steadily from its peak in 1999. European funding, on the contrary, increased in recent years. And although official U.S. aid appears marginal in comparison, it does not include Asia's portion of the $6.8 billion disbursed in 2004 by American nongovernmental organizations and foundations worldwide.[27]

On certain issues, such as North Korea, many in Asia perceive the United States as having divergent goals from China, Japan, and South Korea, and even as posing a threat to regional stability through confrontational posturing. Yet mutual distrust between the major powers in Northeast Asia means that a rival source of power is unlikely to emerge that can replace the United States as the preeminent military force in the region. At the same time, the significance of the U.S. role will probably decline over time as Asia gains strength through both economic growth and political development. Over the long term, peace in Asia may well have more to do with the "peaceful descendance" of the United States than with the "peaceful ascendance" of China. But for the next several decades, Asia will rely on the United States, and on U.S.-dominated institutions, to ensure economic prosperity and regional stability.

Conclusion: The Centrality of the U.S. Role

Asia plays a significant and growing role in providing external markets to buy Chinese goods and services and to supply resources and intermediates. In the future, China could play a significant role in regional development efforts. In terms of managing regional and global economic vitality, Asia (along with China) still plays a limited role. With the exception of Hong Kong, Asia's role in providing Chinese firms with external capital markets to raise money is also limited. The United States, on the other hand, plays a significant role in all these areas of Chinese economic interest, and will continue to do so for some time.

It would be a severe mistake for the United States to conclude that its influence over regimes and institutions that are critical to China's interests is unassailable. If confronted with a complacent regime leader, even if that complacence is benign or justified as a matter of short-term priorities, other international stakeholders will move to devise alternative structures to secure their interests. But it is a mistake for America to operate as though its leadership role is under assault on all fronts, when in fact it is not. The United States will maximize the influence it has crafted and in which it has invested over many decades not through a defensive attitude, but through realizing, with a sense of confidence, that existing institutions are supportive of U.S. interests even as new powers come to enjoy an increasing role in their administration.

Acknowledgments

Trevor Houser of China Strategic Advisory contributed extensive research assistance for this chapter.

Notes

1. For a good review, see Barry Naughton, *Growing Out of the Plan* (Cambridge: Cambridge University Press, 1996).
2. I say "ironically" because many assume that China's economic growth is a counterpoint to the Washington Consensus family of policy prescriptions, and some have even suggested there is something like a "Beijing Consensus" as an alternative for other would-be developing nations to emulate.
3. See, for example, Li Cheng, "Educational and Professional Backgrounds of Current Provincial Leaders," *China Leadership Monitor* 8 (Fall 2003).
4. See, for example, one of my favorite analyses of internal Chinese debate, Erika Downs, "The Chinese Energy Security Debate," *China Quarterly* 177 (2004).
5. On the changing outcomes of policy making as vested interests shift, I recommend as an example Scott Kennedy, "China's Porous Protectionism: The Changing Political Economy of Trade Policy," *Political Science Quarterly* 120 (2005). Kennedy demonstrates how vested Chinese interests are competing against one another to determine the level of protection affecting imports. On the translation of economic interest to the demand for political participation at the civic level, see Benjamin Read, "Democratizing the Neighborhood? New Private Housing and Homeowner Self-Organization in Urban China," *China Journal* 49 (January 2003): 31–59.
6. Dan Rosen, Scott Rozelle, and Jikun Huang, *Roots of Competition* (Washington, D.C.: Institute for International Economics, 2004), examines this impulse as it appears in the form of grain self-sufficiency even though such policies per-

petuate agrarian poverty in China (China generally has little comparative advantage in land-intensive grains; therefore, such farmers will be unproductive on average and hence relatively poor).

7. See details of the GDP revision at www.stats.gov.cn/english/newsandcoming events/t20051220_402297118.htm (accessed December 28, 2005).

8. See "Japan, China, S. Korea to Conclude Investment Talks in Nov.," *Kyoto News,* October 14, 2005.

9. Asian Development Bank and World Bank Annual Reports, from www.adb .org and www.worldbank.org, respectively (accessed February 19, 2005).

10. New York Stock Exchange, "NYSE 2005 Year-End Review: New Records in Average Daily Volume, NYSE Composite Index and Seat Prices New Listings Outpace 2004 Level," December 30, 2005, available at www.nyse.com/ Frameset.html?displayPage=/press/1135252289621.html.

11. "Update: Nasdaq Sees Pace of China IPOs Continuing in 2006," Dow Jones Newswires, December 8, 2005, available at www.djnewswires.com.

12. E-line Financials, "Dynamic Market Opportunities," available at financials .com, January 20, 2005.

13. "China Construction Bank to Launch IPO on Oct 27 or 28," Agence France-Presse, September 27, 2005.

14. Keri Geiger, "Chinese Cos Favour Hong Kong over US for IPOs," Economic Times Online, Associated Press, August 20, 2005.

15. Ibid.

16. U.S. International Trade Commission, DataWeb, available at www.usitc.gov.

17. Chinese and U.S. bilateral trade figures vary considerably due to Hong Kong transshipment, which the Chinese statistics do not incorporate. While the U.S. Census estimates that the total imports from China in 2005 were U.S.$243 billion, Chinese figures put the number at $163 billion. In examining the composition of China's trade with the world, which is done using Chinese data, we look only at non–Hong Kong trade in an attempt to address this disparity.

18. See Hufbauer and Wong, "Prospects for Regional Free Trade in Asia," Working Paper WP 05-12 (Washington, D.C.: Institute for International Economics, October 2005).

19. Erica Downs, "The Chinese Energy Security Debate," *China Quarterly* 117 (2004): 21–41

20. See Hufbauer and Wong, "Prospects for Regional Free Trade in Asia."

21. Edwin M. Truman, "A Strategy for IMF Reform," Policy Analysis in International Economics 77 (Washington, D.C.: Institute for International Economics, February 2006).

22. Stella Dawson, "US Upbeat on IMF Quota Deal, Europe Holds Out," *Reuters News,* January 28, 2006.

23. Energy Information Administration, U.S. Department of Energy, "South China Sea Region," Country Analysis Briefs, September 2003, available at www .eia.doe.gov/emeu/cabs/schina.html.

24. Michael T. Klare, "Global Economy—The Oil That Drives the U.S. Military," Global Policy Forum, October 9, 2004, available at www.globalpolicy.org/ security/oil/2004/1009protection.htm.

25. CEIC Data Co.

26. Organisation for Economic Co-operation and Development, International Development Statistics, available at www.stats.oecd.org/wbus/default/aspx.

27. Ibid.

CHAPTER 7

Japan and the New Security Structures of Asian Multilateralism

Kazuhiko Togo

WHAT IS JAPAN'S PERSPECTIVE on security multilateralism in Asia and its role in that process? I describe the three security-related multilateral organizations that have developed in Asia beginning in the 1990s: (1) the Association of Southeast Asian Nations (ASEAN) Regional Forum (ARF), established in 1994 in the Asia-Pacific region, which has pursued moderate activities to date; (2) ASEAN Plus Three, which began in 1997, along with the East Asia Summit (created as its extension) and the emerging concept of the East Asian Community; and finally (3) the Six-Party Talks, which were first convened in 2003 in Northeast Asia. Then I discuss the future of Asian security multilateralism from Japanese and U.S. perspectives.

The ASEAN Regional Forum

The idea that led to the ARF was first discussed in June 1991 at the ASEAN Institutes of Strategic and International Studies (ASEAN-ISIS) conference in Jakarta, where a proposal was made to hold a conference initiated by the ASEAN Post Ministerial Conference (PMC) to discuss stability and peace in the Asia-Pacific region.

Japan's Initiative in the ARF

Yukio Sato, director general of the Information and Analysis Department of Japan's Ministry of Foreign Affairs (MOFA), participated in the

ASEAN-ISIS meeting and agreed that the time was ripe for establishing an Asia-Pacific regional security dialogue. In July of that year, at the ASEAN PMC meeting in Manila, Taro Nakayama, Japanese minister for foreign affairs, offered a proposal based on Sato's idea—that a mutual reassurance dialogue be initiated among friendly countries in the region. Nakayama's proposal was not received with enthusiasm by ASEAN or the United States. Lack of sufficient prior consultation was one of the reasons, but Nakayama's idea also differed from the ASEAN-ISIS agenda in that it did not include socialist countries and envisaged the ASEAN PMC itself as the appropriate forum within which to conduct security dialogues.[1] Despite the cool reaction by ASEAN and the United States, Japan continued to advance its proposal to establish an ASEAN PMC–based security forum, as Prime Minister Kiichi Miyazawa did in a speech he gave in Washington in July 1992.[2]

Two factors characterized Japan's positive approach to East Asian regionalism in this period. First, Japan made a considerable effort to conceptualize East Asian regionalism as just one part of its "multitiered [*jyuusouteki*]" security strategy. Kuniko Ashizawa argues that four distinct tiers of this strategy could be discerned in this period and cites Nakayama's July 1991 speech in Kuala Lumpur as well as Sato's own writing. The first tier refers to existing bilateral security relationships, such as the Japan-U.S. alliance; the second tier refers to case-by-case, ad hoc arrangements to deal with specific issues, such as North Korea or Cambodia; the third tier refers to a regional multilateral framework for security dialogue; and the fourth tier refers to nonsecurity arrangements, particularly in the economic realm.[3] By 1991–92, three tiers already existed, but the fourth tier had yet to be developed. The main purpose of this conceptualization was to clearly indicate the unwavering importance to Japan of its bilateral ties with the United States while it sought an acceptable forum for developing cooperative regional security agreements. The concept of a multitiered strategy in four phases was explained in detail in the *Gaiko Seisho* (Diplomatic bluebook) of 1992 and 1993,[4] and since then it has continued to appear as a mainstay of MOFA thinking.[5]

Second, as both Paul Midford and Ashizawa have pointed out, the Japanese leadership emphasized that Japan was promoting the idea of a regional forum because it wanted to create an appropriate environment in which to explain Japan's policy of becoming a more proactive and responsible power on matters related to peace and security and at the same time reassure its neighbors that it had no intention of becoming a "military power." Prime Minister Toshiki Kaifu, in addition to Sato and Nakayama, made clear statements to that effect.[6]

By the middle of 1991, the post–Cold War geopolitical reality was already seriously affecting Japan. On the one hand, it was clear that the U.S.

contraction from Asia could lead to an important reorientation of its alliance with Japan, and that Japan was bound to play a more responsible role. The first real alarm came in April 1990, when the United States issued a report on reducing its forces in East Asia by 14,000 to 15,000 personnel, including 5,000 to 6,000 from Japanese bases.[7] But the most decisive incident was the 1990–91 Gulf War. The U.S.$14 billion of economic assistance Japan provided to the United States and countries in the Gulf region was not appreciated by the international community, partly because it was perceived as "too little too late," but, more important, because "checkbook diplomacy" without any engagement of personnel, to shed sweat if not blood, was considered selfish and irresponsible. Japan had to act in order to show the world that it was not an irresponsible and selfish power. It had reached the point at which its economic standing required responsible behavior. That was the reality facing Japan in the wake of the Cold War.

But there was another reality. This was a product of the memory deeply entrenched in the minds of Japan's Asian neighbors, particularly in China and Korea, which "reacted with the most suspicion" toward Japan.[8] Developing a multilateral forum in which to explain that Japan intended to become a responsible but nonaggressive power was thus of real importance. For Japan it was a matter of regaining the trust and confidence of its Asian neighbors. Actions were naturally important, but how those actions were perceived and recognized was even more important.

Thus, in the wake of the Cold War, the establishment of a regional security forum based on the principle of cooperative security met Japan's need for both power and identity, that is, the realists' requirement that it become a responsible and proactive power and the constructivists' requirement that it establish an intersubjective identity by being accepted as a harmonious power in Asia.[9] Actions followed in 1991. Japan adopted the International Peace Cooperation Law in June 1992, and this paved the way for the dispatch of its Self-Defense Forces to Cambodia in September. China, which had cautioned Japan until the last moment before the dispatch, also sent construction troops, and the two forces were engaged in similar reconstruction work. When two Japanese peacekeepers were killed in April and May 1993, the leaders of Malaysia and Singapore asked Japan not to withdraw its troops.[10] Any possible U.S. reservations about a multilateral forum were removed in July 1993, when President Bill Clinton, during his trip to Korea, called for "the promotion of new multilateral regional dialogues on the full range of common security challenges."[11] Later that month, the ASEAN PMC decided to start the ARF the following year. The ARF was launched with Japan's full support in July 1994.

The Development of the ARF and China's Role

During the latter part of the 1990s, the ARF mechanism of confidence-building developed, albeit slowly. The subjects discussed ranged from traditional to nontraditional security matters, and the forum took a cooperative security approach based on a consensus-led "ASEAN way."[12] Through this process, China became much more active in enhancing cooperative security in the region. In 1996, just after the establishment of the ARF, Japan and the United States reconfirmed their alliance, igniting harsh criticism from China. But since then, China has become a much more active participant in the ARF dialogue. Akiko Fukushima argues that China wanted to strengthen its security position through enhancing common regional security,[13] a view supported by Thomas Christensen.[14] China hosted and co-chaired a confidence-building group in 1997, and in November 2004 it hosted and co-chaired the first ARF Security Policy Conference, at which "defence policy officials contributed further to building confidence and fostering mutual understanding."[15]

But in reality, did this engagement bring about a real change in China's defense and security behavior? Using an ongoing problem as an example, Donald Weatherbee states, "The South China Sea problem is a prime example of the ARF's relative irrelevance to real conflict management." The ARF had to be content with welcoming negotiations on the Code of Conduct of Parties in the South China Sea, which was formulated as a declaration in 2002.[16]

But one may also argue that having a declaration is better than having nothing to guide actions for the future. Moreover, if China is prepared for or even enthusiastic about the formulation of regional norms, is it not worthwhile for it to influence these norms rather than remain outside the process? Masashi Iida argues that, if enhanced mutual confidence between China and ASEAN could be achieved, expansionist activities by China might be restrained.[17] The ARF might be one of the catalysts for such movement. Christensen cautions against dismissing the regional cooperative developments as "mere rhetoric or showmanship."[18] Cheng-Chwee Kuik sees an underlying Chinese "aspiration to shape the 'rules of the game' for regional institutions for the ultimate ends of fulfilling the needs of a range of foreign policy concerns."[19]

As has been openly recognized, the effectiveness of the ARF in solving concrete security issues is limited. Nevertheless, Japan has found merits in the ARF. At present, faced with the phenomenon of a rising China, Japan realizes that it is in its interest to become engaged with China in multilateral security regionalism and enhance cooperative security. Principles of realism suggest that countries with different values can coexist, but mutual understanding, cooperation, and, if possible, trust would facilitate that coexistence. An effort to agree on a vision of cooperation based on values that Japan cherishes would also be worthwhile. At the same time, there are important issues regarding its future security and defense policy that Japan will have to explain. In Japan, many envisage the amendment of Article 9 of the constitution in order to make Japan a responsible and proactive power, not a militaristic power that will threaten its neighbors.[20] This is an important issue, and one about which a multilateral forum like the ARF can enhance understanding. Japan's long-term objective of reentering Asia would be better served by its active engagement in the ARF. The 2004 *Gaikou Seisho* declared that "Japan will be contributing further so that the ARF will develop into an organization that contributes effectively for the security of the region."[21]

ASEAN Plus Three, the East Asia Summit, and the East Asian Community

In the first half of the 1990s, the ARF was the leading multilateral organization dealing with security in the Asia-Pacific region, whereas the Asia-Pacific Economic Cooperation (APEC), initiated in 1989, was the leading organization in economic cooperation. APEC gained political clout after the leaders' meeting in 1993. But when APEC faced considerable difficulty in 1998 because of the rift between Japan and the United States over the liberalization of fish and forestry markets,[22] another mechanism of regional cooperation emerged in East Asia. The ASEAN Plus Three (APT) was convened at the time of the Asian financial crisis in 1997–98. Its mission was first conceived of as promoting dialogue in the area of economic cooperation, but was gradually expanded to cover a wider area, including political-security issues. The idea of holding an East Asian summit was presented at the APT summit in 2001. And the notion of an East Asian Community (EAC) began to be discussed widely after that.

The Chronological Development of the EAC

The Period of Formation (1997–99). It was the Asian financial crisis of 1997–98 that triggered Japan's active interest in regional cooperation. The Asian Monetary Fund (AMF) initiative in August–November 1997 failed,[23] but the assistance Japan provided amounted to U.S.$10 billion for South Korea, $5 billion for Indonesia, and $4 billion for Thailand.[24] Thus ASEAN invited Japan, together with China and Korea, to its summit in December

1997 in Kuala Lumpur, held to commemorate its thirtieth anniversary. The main topics of discussion were currency and financial matters.[25]

In August 1998, Vietnam, the host country for the ASEAN summit, again extended invitations to Japan, China, and South Korea to attend the second APT summit in December. There Prime Minister Keizo Obuchi expressed his determination to work for early implementation of the $30 billion Miyazawa Initiative declared in October.[26]

But it was at the third APT summit, held in November 1999, that the APT began to seriously attract the attention of the Japanese leadership. They adopted a "Joint Statement on East Asia Cooperation," in which they declared that political-security and transnational issues were objects of cooperation in addition to issues in the economic and social fields.[27] Obuchi launched an initiative for human resource development in the APT,[28] but his most striking initiative was to convene a Japan–China–South Korea tripartite breakfast meeting on the fringe of the APT meeting. This gathering concentrated on trade and economic matters, avoiding any political matters such as North Korea. But whatever the central theme of the talks, given the complexity of Japan's relations with China and South Korea, a tripartite gathering under the auspices of ASEAN was like a fresh breeze. It provided Japan with a golden path by which to reenter Asia through regionalism.[29]

In December 1999, Obuchi also undertook an important initiative with Singapore's Prime Minister Goh Chok Tong, under which a group of experts began studying the feasibility of a Japan-Singapore Free Trade Agreement (FTA).[30] It was the first initiative to explore "spider-web bilateralism" as a way to structure a regional trade organization.[31]

Mori's Initiative and China's Rise (2000–2001). In the area of financial cooperation, the May 2000 finance ministers' meeting in Chiang Mai established a network of swap arrangements that came to be known as the Chiang Mai Agreement.[32] Spider-web bilateralism produced a tangible result, and the Japanese Ministry of Finance (MOF) was instrumental in this success. Ministerial meetings on many issues began to be held regularly during these years.

At the 2000 APT summit, Prime Minister Yoshiro Mori proposed cooperation based on three principles: establishment of partnerships, open regionalism, and comprehensive dialogue and cooperation on political and security matters. He also proposed an Asian conference on piracy and engaged Indonesia and Korea in the context of a security dialogue with other leaders. Meanwhile, China moved rapidly on concrete cooperation in trade. In its 2000 bilateral talks with ASEAN, it proposed to conclude a China-ASEAN FTA, and in 2001 a framework agreement was reached to conclude the FTA in principle by 2010.

Koizumi's Initiative (2002–3). To the surprise of many, in a speech Prime Minister Junichiro Koizumi gave in Singapore in January 2002, he named Australia and New Zealand as "core members" of the EAC. This move succeeded in creating an impression of inclusiveness, in contrast with China's paying such close attention to the 13 countries of the APT.[33]

In another speech, given in Australia in May of that year, Koizumi emphasized "functional cooperation" as the mainstay of East Asian cooperation. It was wise to use this concept to guide cooperation with Australia, which was not a member of the APT but which, he urged, "should become a core member." This notion of functionality has become for Japan the core concept guiding EAC cooperation.[34]

Since the latter part of 2002, however, the swing toward inclusiveness with regard to Australia and New Zealand has reversed itself, and the pendulum has shifted back to the original notion of cooperation within the APT. The moderate step taken in November 2002 at the sixth APT summit in Cambodia, at which Koizumi and the ASEAN leaders adopted a Joint Declaration on a Comprehensive Economic Partnership Agreement (EPA),[35] was overtaken in 2003 by three major steps to enhance cooperation in East Asia. First, in October the seventh APT summit was held in Bali, and India was also present. Japan and ASEAN at last signed a Framework for Comprehensive Economic Partnership,[36] and they finally agreed to establish an EPA/FTA in principle by 2012.[37]

Second, Japan, China, and South Korea signed a Joint Declaration on the Promotion of Tripartite Cooperation, the first agreement among just those three countries.[38] It was a stunning document because it included "across-the-board and future-oriented cooperation in a variety of areas" and defined tripartite cooperation as "an essential part of East Asian cooperation." Given the difficulties in bilateral Japan-China and Japan-Korea relations, to focus only on future-oriented relations without reference to history was amazing.

Third, in December Japan hosted an ASEAN-Japan summit in Tokyo, the first meeting in ASEAN's history held outside Southeast Asia. In a section of the resulting document headed "Deepening East Asian Cooperation for an East Asian Community," the participants agreed to "uphold Asian traditions and values, while respecting universal rules and principles."[39] What was meant by "Asian values" was still vague, but for Japan—which had long been rejected as an acceptable partner for Asia because of its war in the Pacific—this manifestation of its greater acceptance in Asia was an important step toward the reestablishment of its Asian identity.

The Polarized Search for an EAC (2004–5). As the time drew near for the eighth APT summit in Laos, which was to be held in November 2004, interest in holding an East Asian summit (EAS) heightened among member countries.[40] But the government of Japan prepared "issue papers" in June 2004 signaling caution in differentiating between the APT summit and an EAS.[41] There was some confusion at the Laos ASEAN summit and the eighth APT summit in November, but ultimately ASEAN decided to hold an EAS the following year in Malaysia. At the APT summit, Koizumi was somewhat surprised by this turn of events, stating, "There is a need to discuss the concept of the conference"; but he accepted ASEAN's conclusion.[42]

Thus, in Japan the year 2005 began with an affirmative feeling toward an EAC. On January 21, in his General Policy Speech to the Diet, Koizumi declared for the first time, "The Government will play an active role in the creation of an East Asian community, an open community that shares economic prosperity while embracing diversity."[43] Haruki Wada has stated that "the declaration at the Diet of a new regionalism after its oblivion for sixty years was an extremely important event."[44]

But a demonstration by Chinese students in April 2005 revealed an increasing geopolitical rivalry and a deepening rift on issues of history, fueled by Koizumi's yearly visit to the Yasukuni Shrine, where war dead are enshrined. All this brought Sino-Japanese political relations to their lowest point since World War II, dooming Japan-China cooperation on an EAC.

At this point, striking U.S. opposition to an exclusive EAC emerged. U.S. opposition to the East Asia Economic Caucus proposed in 1990 by Malaysian Prime Minister Mohamad Mahathir was well known.[45] But after the 1997–98 Asian financial crisis, the United States offered no resistance to the embryonic APT. After President George W. Bush came to power in 2001, the United States even perceived Asian regionalism positively, as a means of launching a common fight against global terrorism.[46]

However, this tolerant view was replaced by open criticism of an exclusive EAC at the end of 2004. Sudden politicization of the EAS and underlying U.S. concern over the rise of China may have been primary reasons for this change of attitude. The Bush administration did not make its position public,[47] but the views of public opinion leaders were expressed unambiguously.[48] A clear message came from Richard Armitage, perceived as the guardian of the Japan-U.S. alliance. In a May 2005 article in the Japanese magazine *Wedge*, Armitage emphasized the soundness and effectiveness of the alliance and raised objections to an exclusive EAS without a clearly defined content, purpose, and agenda, stating that "India, Australia and the United States should be given the right of participation."[49]

By then, there had been numerous reports that China was resolute about enhancing cooperation based on the framework of the APT. In Japan, the pendulum quickly swung back toward "inclusivity" as it had been manifested in early 2002. Given the deteriorating political relations with China and with such clear objections from the United States, geo-political thinking shifted toward expanding the number of participants in the East Asian regional cooperation. In a press conference held at the end of February, Shotaro Yachi, vice minister for foreign affairs, stated that "Japan-U.S. relations are the cornerstone of our policy; anything which may not be compatible with [them] must really be scrutinized thoroughly."[50] On March 22, Foreign Minister Nobutaka Machimura stated in a public lecture that the EAC "has to be an open community; India and Australia are welcomed; the United States is welcomed as an observer; it is important that Russia participate in some form as well."[51]

On April 11, the foreign ministers of the ASEAN countries agreed that all countries participating in the EAS should be ASEAN dialogue partners and would have to sign a Treaty of Amity and Cooperation with ASEAN. That decision set a course for resolving the question of membership. On July 27, the foreign ministers of the APT members agreed in Vientiane that, in addition to the thirteen APT countries, Australia, India, and New Zealand would participate in the first EAS in Malaysia in December. After this lively disagreement over membership in the EAS, the leadership struggle between Japan and China reportedly quieted down.[52]

In fact, this quiet proved to be merely a lull before the storm. At the December meeting of the APT and in the EAS in Malaysia, all media reports indicated that China pressed the APT as a major vehicle for developing the EAC,[53] whereas Japan tried to exert leadership to let the newly emerging EAS play a decisive role. The resulting declarations stated that the APT was to "continue to be the main vehicle in achieving that goal [of realizing an East Asian community]" and that the EAS "could play a significant role in community building in this region." From the point of view of the Japanese delegation, it was a compromise to agree on the Chinese "main vehicle" formula for the APT while ensuring the Japanese a "significant role" in the EAS.[54] Be that as it may, from the point of view of Japan's reentry into and reconciliation with Asia, it was a grave setback to Japan for both China and Korea to be part of a regularized tripartite meeting (among Japan, China, and Korea) under the auspices of an APT summit.

Proponents, Modifiers, and Opponents of the EAC

Thus, by the end of 2005 the position of the Japanese government on the EAC had taken an acute shift toward "inclusiveness," and Northeast Asian regional cooperation was becoming a distant goal. Against this background, it may be worthwhile to reexamine the range of Japanese thinking on the EAC among ministries, business and opinion leaders, and others in order to understand the breadth and complexity of this issue.

Proponents of the EAC. The primary uncontested reason that some favor regional integration is economics. East Asia's exports, domestic direct investment, and GDP rose sharply in the past 15 years.[55] So did regional trade.[56] The three leading Japanese ministries are all in favor of regional economic integration. The Ministry of Economy, Trade, and Industry's *Tsusho Hakusho* [White paper on trade and industry] for 2005 for the first time devoted a large section to the nature of the developing East Asian economy. Its main conclusion was that Japan needed deeper integration with East Asia in order to overcome its own demographic and structural problems. MOF is continuing to enhance the Chiang Mai agreement and is also supporting the establishment of a bond market for each country of the region while simultaneously promoting the establishment of its own Yen bond market.[57] MOFA's efforts to conclude EPAs and FTAs continue, with an emphasis on the five founding ASEAN countries.[58] The 2004 *Gaiko Seisho* categorized the reasons Japan needs EPAs and FTAs as follows: economic reasons, which include enhancing free trade and supplementing the World Trade Organization; security reasons, which include improving the conditions of developing countries together with overseas development assistance; and political and strategic reasons, which include consolidating relations with the countries that Japan considers important.[59] Opinion leaders discuss why Japan and Asia need the East Asian economic community. For example, Toshio Watanabe and other scholars strongly support the gradual expansion of EPAs and FTAs, but add that further integration will be accomplished through common recognition, governance support, and political dialogue.[60] Makoto Taniguchi writes, based on his long-time service in the Organisation for Economic Co-operation and Development, that Japan should become a real partner of the East Asian economic community and take a leadership role so that Asia, Europe, and the United States can lead the development of the world economy.[61] Haruki Yoshida, based on his research on the EAC in 2003, proposes to establish an economic community of Ten Plus Five, including Hong Kong and Taiwan, with possible eventual inclusion of Mongolia and North Korea.[62]

Some Japanese view Japan's quest for East Asian regionalism as emanating from its desire to regain its Asian identity, which was shattered in 1945. They feel that supporting East Asian regionalism has become a means of reconciling Japan with East Asia. And they see Prime Minister Obuchi's move toward Asia, the 2003 Japan-ASEAN Tokyo Declaration that singled out "Asian values," and MOFA's clear recognition that the EAC's final stage will involve the creation of a "sense of community" as moves toward repairing Japan's historically soured relations with the region. Toshiaki Arai describes Japan's identity as the issue underlying its search for an East

Asian economic sphere.[63] Haruki Wada states on his home page that Japan needs reconciliation with its two major neighbors, China and Korea, for the sound development of regionalism.[64]

These views beg the question: What is the Asian identity? From Japan's point of view, apart from merely being accepted by other Asian countries as a true member and their friend, what are the specific values that distinguish Asia and create an Asian identity? In May 2004, the Council of the East Asian Community (CEAC) was established to study the East Asian Community, and prominent Japanese intellectuals from all areas gathered. They prepared a *Seisaku-houkokusho* (policy report) that was published in August 2005.[65] The CEAC report makes two points that may shed light on the question of an Asian identity: It points out that a common identity in East Asia may already be developing based on a "similar life style of urban middle class workers" that was developed in Japan in the process of its postwar economic development and is now shared by many newly industrialized Asian economies, Southeast Asian countries, and China. The report also raises a second issue that lies at the border between the constructivist search for identity and the liberal search for democratic values. It proposes that, as guiding values to unite East Asia, Japan promote the values it has cherished in its own development since World War II: freedom, democracy, and human rights. Kenichi Ito, the chairman of CEAC, argues that Japan must develop an EAC motivated by these "strategic principles," not just by its anti-China sentiments.[66]

The essential issue is China. Relations between Japan and China are becoming strained, particularly under Prime Minister Koizumi. But if Japan realizes that it is in its own national interest to reduce this tension, it should also see that one way to do this is to follow a multilateral process and to engage China in common projects to enhance understanding. China's activism within multilateral frameworks has been increasing. Its proactive position since 2000 has been remarkable when compared to its passive involvement (1990–95) and later active participation (1996–99) in ASEAN-led multilateral institutions in the past decade.[67] Its reassuring "trade and smile" diplomacy allows China to play a deepening security role.[68] Its regional policy rests on four main pillars: participation in regional organizations, deepening of bilateral relations, expansion of economic ties, and reduction of distrust in the security sphere.[69] Is the EAC not an appropriate forum within which Japan can positively engage with this kind of China?

On June 24, 2004, Hitoshi Tanaka, deputy minister for foreign affairs in charge of political matters, explained why MOFA believes an EAC is necessary: (1) It would be in Japan's long-term national interest. (2) It might create a system within which Japan could cooperate with China. (3) It would help to absorb unhealthy nationalism. The second point mentioned by Tanaka is that regional multilateralism may help Japan establish better relations with China. Makoto Iokibe argues that both Japan and China should make an effort to redress their grievances, and that, even if Japan's relations with the United States are sound, Japan must not criticize China, because Japan's doing so might someday be awkward if there is U.S.-China rapprochement.[70]

Modifiers of the EAC. Rising tensions with China and clear objections from the United States to the formation of an exclusive EAC have shaken Japan's thinking, and at least two modifying lines of thought have begun to take shape. The first favored opening up the scope of cooperation to outside countries across the Pacific Ocean and the Indian Ocean. The participation of Australia, India, and New Zealand in the EAS was seen as the first step. Japan favored the inclusion of Russia and the United States. From all indications, in the first half of 2005 the Japanese government set a course in this direction. Japan's fundamental geopolitical interest in engaging and cooperating with China was replaced with a short-term geopolitical interest in competing with China. The question of participation in the EAS by Russia (after it was present at the 2005 EAS as a guest of the hosting Malaysian government) and by the United States (after its emphasis shifted more clearly to APEC) lost political impetus, but the Japanese emphasis on inclusiveness remained influential.

The second line of thought favored limiting cooperation to the economic arena, where the reasons for cooperation are the strongest. The totalitarian character of the Chinese government and the anti-Japanese attitude of the Chinese people cautioned Japan against going too far in the establishment of a "community." Noboru Hatakeyama, former president of Japan External Trade Organization, advocates this approach.[71]

Opponents of the EAC. Although those who advocated modifying the EAC could be understood as trying to adjust the vision of East Asian cooperation to the reality, skepticism about China led some opinion leaders to negate entirely the idea of East Asian regional cooperation. Taro Yayama argued that the EAC was a Chinese stratagem to drag Japan into the sphere of Sino-centrism and that the solution for Japan lay in the creation of an "Asia-Pacific Community" with Australia, ASEAN, India, New Zealand, and the United States as participants, or else the creation of an "Alliance of Maritime States."[72] Mineo Nakajima drew a distinction between China's continentality, Japan's insularity, and Korea's peninsularity, emphasizing a wide range of discrepancies in the recognition of modern history, and stated that during the "new cold war" between China and the United States, the EAC might be an illusion.[73] A speech given on November 30, 2006, by Foreign Minister Taro Aso, titled "Arc of Freedom and Prosperity:

Japan's Expanding Diplomatic Horizons," might be considered an extension of this line of thinking.[74]

Security Implications of the EAC

If cooperation were "functional" and all relevant countries were included, cooperation based on the EAC might produce tangible results, which would benefit all participating countries. Avoiding duplication, however, is a legitimate concern. Demarcation between the cooperation under the ARF and the EAC may be a worthwhile consideration, just as, on economic matters, demarcation between APEC and the EAC might be helpful.

But the real security issue is China, that is, how we should understand present-day China and consider the issue of multilateral cooperation in that context. Does it make sense to enhance cooperative security with China? If China is rising to manifest its Sino-centrist historical tradition, based on its rapidly developing power on the military, political, and economic fronts and using hatred of Japan to promote national unity, it may not be wise for Japan to flirt with regionalism in East Asia, at least without U.S. participation. Although dialogue is essential for constructive engagement, such dialogue is very different from joint efforts to create an EAC.

But if China is a rapidly growing power that has not adjusted to the speed of its rise, misunderstands the outside world, and has ideas that Japan must listen to and understand—as Sakutaro Tanino, former Japanese ambassador to Beijing, argues[75]—efforts aimed at cooperative security and enhancing an appropriate form of regionalism are crucial to Japan's national interest. Naturally, even in the latter case the importance of guarding security in the traditional sense by means of strategic defense forces and the alliance firmly stands. In addition, Japan should not yield to undue pressure in the foreign policy sphere. But Japan's overall behavior would change depending on how one views China.

If the second scenario presents the most accurate picture of China, there were good reasons for Japan to have been active in the work related to the APT and EAC. But in that situation, from the point of view of Japan's security and alliances, there remains a serious question. The question has four parts: Is Japan's policy consistent if it tells the United States (1) that there is no need to worry about Japan's participation in an EAC in which the United States might not take part; (2) that Japan's purpose in participating in an EAC is to ensure that China will be harmonized with the region; (3) that there is a dire need for Japan to create a viable regional multilateral structure, not only for economic reasons but also to satisfy its long-time desire to be accepted as a partner in Asia; (4) and that its alliance with the United States since World War II should be a good basis for the United States to trust Japan not to harm U.S. interests? Looking back at Japan's Asian policy since the turn of the new century, another question undermines Japan's position regarding part (3) of the previous question: if "reentering Asia" is so important to Japan, how could it have behaved in such a way as to antagonize China, bringing the political relationship between the countries to its lowest point since World War II?

The EAC cannot be understood properly without an appreciation of the fact that Japan is trying to regain the Asian identity it lost after its defeat in August 1945. But in Japan that defeat also resulted in a contradiction between complete negativism toward the country's prewar activities and a legitimate desire to protect its honor.[76] Japan's inability to resolve this contradiction is creating a crisis of national identity. The two approaches on which it has staked it search for identity—"reentering Asia" and "reestablishing national values"—are on a collision course.

Although this identity crisis has a strong domestic character, its international repercussions are strongly affecting Japan's foreign policy. At a time when national identity seems to be gaining the upper hand over Asian identity, no one in Japan can responsibly and persuasively explain how the EAC is important for Japan's economic prosperity and geopolitical stability and also for the reestablishment of its honor in Asia. Among the eleven "lessons for successful regionalism" in Northeast Asia given by Gilbert Rozman, the most sensible is that Japan is back-pedaling by not pursuing "an accord between China and Japan over security" with maximum intensity and giving up its opportunity to "foster a regional identity."[77]

Owing to this confusion, Japan is moving to a position of seeking an EAC with an enlarged membership to counter China and to include the United States. But is this position really serving Japan's best security interests? From an immediate geopolitical perspective, when relations with China are so strained and when the United States is so openly against the EAC, taking the "expansionist modifier" position is the only option. The classical theory of balance of power applies. But in the long run, if Japan were able to participate in a robust EAC, in which it could harmonize China with the outside world and gain greater understanding and trust in the region, would not such an EAC best serve Japan's security interests? Power is still a key consideration. But conciliating as well as balancing may become the key. Besides, the search for an Asian identity may be at least as important as that for a national identity. After one year of unexpectedly harmonious Asian policy under Prime Minister Shinzo Abe, Yasuo Fukuda, known to be more Asia-friendly, was elected prime minister in September 2007. From the U.S. point of view, would not an EAC that improved relations between Japan and China also contribute to U.S. security interests?

From the point of view of its national interest, the United States may legitimately require an inclusive East Asian cooperation in which it plays an integral part. But even in such a case, a key question still remains: would the United States prefer to have a Japan capable of managing its relations with China or bear with a weakened and dependent Japan? Today, Japan-China political relations are so strained that the relevance of such a question seems remote.[78]

The Six-Party Talks

At the end of the 1990s, while Japan's interest in regionalism was manifested mostly within a cooperative framework comprising both Northeast and Southeast Asia, an important scheme was also taking shape to address cooperation around the Korean peninsula. In response to the first North Korean nuclear crisis of 1993–94, the Korean Peninsula Energy Development Organization (KEDO) had been established in 1995,[79] and Four-Party Talks had begun in 1996. But KEDO was in principle a technical body whose purpose was to construct a light water reactor, and the Four-Party Talks did not have a concrete task to accomplish within a set time frame.

The Six-Party Talks (6PT) were entirely different. From a geopolitical perspective, the task of the 6PT was to stop North Korean nuclearization; their mission was to eliminate a threat to regional security in the most traditional sense. Or, as Francis Fukuyama indicated, the 6PT (or possibly 5PT) could develop into an entity that could profoundly influence the future peace and stability of Northeast Asia.[80] From the point of view of Japanese identity, because what was at stake was so fundamentally related to the core issue of traditional security, the presence of the United States was a prerequisite. Whether Japan would seek its identity through reentering Asia or through reestablishing its national pride, it was important that the players in the game include its key trans-Pacific partner, the United States, and its two continental neighbors, China and Korea; there was no room for membership agony.

Japan–North Korea Relations before the 6PT

During the 1990s, after the end of the Cold War, relations between Japan and North Korea swung between two poles: relatively warm relations and cold relations with an absence of communication (see Table 7.1). These pendulum swings exactly reflect North Korea's relations with the entire outside world.

The significance of Prime Minister Koizumi's visit to Pyongyang in September 2002 must be analyzed in the context of these relations. By the

Table 7.1 Japan–North Korea Relations, 1991–2005

Years	Japan–North Korea relations	North Korean external relations
1991–92 P	Kanemaru's visit; eight rounds of talks	North-South joint UN declaration
1993–94 N	Nuclear crisis	Nuclear crisis
1995–97 P	Housewives' return, food aid	KEDO established; Four-Party Talks
1998–99 N	Missile crisis, vessels' encroachment	Provocations at South Korea's eastern coast
1999–2000 P	Three rounds of talks, rice aid	North-South summit; Russia; China
2001 N	Vessel shot down and sunk (–)	Europe establishes relations (+)
2002 P	Koizumi's visit (September) (+)	Axis of Evil speech (January) (–)
2003–5 N	Abduction, nuclear crisis	Nuclear crisis

Note: P, (+), positive; N, (–), negative.

time of his visit, numerous problems separated Japan from North Korea, and public opinion was sensitive in demanding justice for Japanese victims of North Korean abductions.[81] But Koizumi's visit resolved all of these issues, most of them as prescribed in the Pyongyang Declaration of September 17, 2002, which included an acknowledgment of and apology for the abductions.[82] On Northeast Asian security, the declaration included a statement of the countries' shared recognition "that it is important to have a framework in place in order for these regional countries to promote confidence-building, as the relationships among these countries are normalized."[83]

For a very short period of time, it seemed as if this diplomatic success gave Koizumi a small but unprecedented opportunity to take a leadership position in the negotiations regarding North Korea. Makoto Iokibe stated that "abduction is abominable, but in order not to repeat such tragedy, normalization of relations must be accomplished without making mistakes."[84] Shinichi Kitaoka praised Koizumi's visit as "a success to be remembered in post-WWII foreign policy."[85] But it goes without saying that, when the nuclear issue exploded in October, the perspective on normalization changed substantially. North Korea's holding nuclear weapons was a clear violation of the Pyongyang Declaration and a grave threat to Japan's security. Japan's taking a rigorous position against North Korean nuclearization was natural and unavoidable. But had Koizumi maintained his diplomatic stance and channel to the North, Japan's ability to communicate with North Korea might have had a different kind of impact on the 6PT process.

However, events developed in a different direction. The Japanese public was shocked and angered that 8 out of 13 abductees had been pronounced dead under mysterious circumstances. Media coverage of the return of the remaining 5 abductees to Japan on October 15 was rife with national emotion, and on October 24 the Koizumi government, despite the basic understanding of several weeks that the 5 abductees would return to North Korea, decided not to let them go back to the North.[86]

This decision had a profound impact. It was supported by public opinion, as influenced by the families and relatives of the abductees, now organized as the Association of the Families of Victims Kidnapped by North Korea (AFVKN) and supported by the National Association for the Rescue of Japanese Kidnapped by North Korea (NARKN).[87] The families, after years of suffering in isolation, had begun to cooperate in the 1990s, forming the AFVKN in 1997 and gaining the "strength to fight against Kim Jong Il."[88] Their anger was also directed against the Japanese government for its longtime negligence in protecting Japan's citizens from abduction. Whereas the majority of the abductions had taken place in 1977–78, no precautionary measures had been taken then,[89] and it was only in 1988 that the government officially acknowledged that "there were enough doubts to suspect that North Korea [had] abducted six Japanese citizens."[90]

Deciding whether to let the five abductees return to North Korea was difficult: their families genuinely feared that they might not be allowed to come back again, but North Korean negotiators reportedly maintained that not returning them would constitute a breach of trust that, given the nascent relationship between the two countries, would jeopardize the whole process. It was reported that Yasuo Fukuda, chief cabinet secretary, and Hitoshi Tanaka, director general of the Asian Bureau and the chief negotiator with the North, were of the latter view, whereas Shinzo Abe, deputy chief cabinet secretary, and Shotaro Yachi, the highest MOFA official in the prime minister's office, took the former position.[91]

When the view of Abe and Yachi prevailed, North Korea virtually withdrew from the entire process initiated on September 17. In Japan, the abductions became the national priority in dealing with North Korea. The idea of introducing economic sanctions, with the ultimate aim of forcing a regime change, gathered increasing support.[92] Tanaka began to be portrayed in the media as a "national traitor" for having acted out of perceived self-interest, not paying enough attention to the alliance with the United States, and being too willing to compromise with North Korea.[93] Koizumi maintained his trust in Tanaka, who had kept a communication channel open with North Korea, but in reality Japan's ability to negotiate seemed to have been shattered.

Koizumi's decision to keep the abductees at home should be seen partly as reflecting the dynamics of Japanese internal politics. Public opinion was overwhelmingly sympathetic to the families of the abductees, who maintained that the returned abductees must not be sent back to North Korea. At the same time, the widely shared support for that decision was a reflection of a new feeling of national identity: it seemed appropriate for the state to take measures to protect its citizens and thus protect Japan's national honor and identity.

Japan's Security Position in the 6PT

With the interested parties facing a deadlock over the North Korean nuclear issue, Japan did not stay idle. As was recently disclosed by former U.S. Assistant Secretary of State Jim Kelly, Japan proposed holding either five-party talks among North Korea, the United States, China, South Korea, and itself, or six-party talks, adding Russia, to Secretary of State Colin Powell during his Asian trip in February 2003. Powell agreed, but reformulated this as a U.S. idea and proposed it to China, which did not immediately agree.[94] Eventually China agreed, and North Korea finally expressed its support for six-party talks through Russia on July 31, 2003.[95]

Japan's position in the six rounds of the 6PT can be summarized as follows:

- As stated clearly in the keynote speech of each round, the resolution of the abduction issue together with the nuclear issue was a prerequisite to the normalization of bilateral relations.[96]
- North Korea should dismantle "all nuclear programs." The dismantling should be comprehensive, verifiable, and irreversible.[97]
- Japan was willing to assist North Korea, provided that adequate conditions were met. In the fourth round, Japan stated that "under adequate conditions, Japan was ready to join the energy support program" that had been proposed by South Korea in the second round.[98]
- Cooperation with Washington and consolidation of the U.S. and Japanese positions were vital.[99]

Japan's emphasis on the abductions put it in the most difficult position of the five countries negotiating with North Korea. This at least saved the United States from isolation from the other four countries. Assisting North Korea as appropriate was consistent with Japanese policy. But Japan's position of remaining tough on North Korea was put in jeopardy when the United States turned toward a policy of seeking agreement with the North at the fifth round of the talks in February 2007. Japan decided not to join in providing financial support as agreed in that round. Its insistence on the abductions isolated Japan from the other four countries, and its role did not compare with that of China in hosting the meeting and becoming the major interlocutor in setting the direction of the negotiations, or that of South Korea in making concrete proposals to tempt North Korea to abandon its nuclear program, or that of the United States in acting decisively to achieve some kind of agreement with North Korea.

How should this situation be considered in the context of Japanese-U.S. relations? Is Japan's position harming the U.S. position in resolving the North Korean nuclear issue? It is difficult to tell. Japan's reactive approach is based on conditions that have faced Japan since Koizumi's decision about the abductees on October 24, 2002, when Japan's potential to play a more proactive role was greatly reduced. Yoshihide Soeya provides one of the rare straightforward analyses: "[Japanese–North Korean] negotiations broke down as the result of the Japanese government's decision not to return the abductees, and foreign policy strategy to lead the transformation of East Asia through the normalization of Japan–North Korean relations collapsed."[100] If Japan had continued its basic policy, expressed in September 2002, and succeeded in influencing Kim Jong-il on the nuclear issue, Japan's relations with the United States would have been even further strengthened.

From the realists' point of view, preserving Koizumi's channel with Kim Jong-il could have been a priority, because there are enormous stakes involved in North Korea's developing nuclear weapons. But from the point of view of regaining Japan's national identity, protecting the five abductees at all costs became a prerequisite. The Japanese people thought it only fair that, after so many years of neglect, the government had at long last taken the actions necessary to protect its citizens. Assuming a geopolitical leadership role on the Korean peninsula was an extremely difficult and remote objective anyway; in contrast, the task of protecting the five abductees was a tangible objective, in which Koizumi could not fail. Internal politics were also at stake. The choice was clear: identity overwhelmed realism.

Conclusion: What Kind of Japan Is the Most Credible Security Partner for the United States?

Japan's security in East Asia is best ensured through multilateral forums when geopolitical power, economic efficiency, and its search for a national and Asian identity are harmonized and policy is well coordinated based on these three factors. At present, the conflict between power and identity is creating real difficulties that are weakening Japan's security position.

Japan's policy with regard to the ARF is being conducted reasonably successfully. The ARF was conceived as an Asia-Pacific forum that would include both the United States and China, and Japan's major aim was to use it as an environment in which to harmonize its defense security policy with the policies of its Asian neighbors. The fundamental structure and purpose of the forum eliminated conflicts between power and identity.

With regard to the EAC, cooperation among East Asian countries has a potential for conflict with the United States: Japan's search for an Asian identity could clash with its geopolitical interests in maintaining a solid alliance with the United States. When cooperation was attempted under the APT, motivated by economics with an emphasis on "functionality," contradictions did not appear on the surface. But when that cooperation began to develop a political momentum, it invited U.S. objections. This coincided with the deterioration of Japan's bilateral relations with China, and the delicate balance between power and identity under the APT began to disintegrate. With tension with China as a backdrop, Japan's search for a national identity began to enjoy stronger support than its search for an Asian identity. Balancing power with Australia, India, and New Zealand vis-à-vis China was preferred to seeking a harmonization of power with China within an EAC. National identity and geopolitics took priority over Asian identity.

The 6PT started without membership contradictions. Both the United States and China were there as founding members. The 6PT had the potential to serve as a cradle for effective security multilateralism in Northeast Asia. As Francis Fukuyama states in his chapter of this book, a new five-power organization (counting Korea) might be a viable option to enhance security cooperation in the region, particularly to overcome differences among member countries on democracy and human rights. Japan's security interests could have been maximized by taking a leadership position in the 6PT, and Koizumi's visit to Pyongyang in September 2002 might have provided a rare opportunity to accomplish that. But Japan's decision to take a tough stance on the abduction issue froze the channel with North Korea that had opened the way for Koizumi's visit. In the 6PT, Japan began to take an even harder position toward North Korea than the United States. National identity overwhelmed geopolitical realism.

From the U.S. perspective, what is Japan's multilateral security outlook in East Asia? In both the EAC and the 6PT, Japan is strongly supporting the U.S. position. Japan's proposal to include the United States among the 13 APT countries, albeit as an observer, was the closest to the U.S. position.

Japan's tough position vis-à-vis North Korea in the 6PT was effective in not isolating the United States until the fifth round of the talks, when the U.S. delegation began to adopt a more flexible policy to reach agreement with the North.

At the same time, in relation to both China and North Korea, Japan failed to maximize its foreign policy potential under Prime Minister Koizumi. Japan's security position vis-à-vis China is weakened by its failure to conduct solid dialogue at the level of the top leaders and to manage difficulties between the two countries, ranging from history to geopolitics. Japan failed to use a small window of opportunity to maximize its influence over North Korea with regard to the nuclear issue. As a partner in the Japan-U.S. alliance, one might argue that present-day Japan is a weakened partner unable to maximize its foreign policy–security potential.

Thus, an important question that the United States might consider from the point of view of its long-term national interests is: What kind of Japan does it prefer as an alliance partner? A strong partner that is maximizing its security potential; capable of harmonizing its power, efficiency, and identity; and developing sound political relations with China through its bilateral and multilateral ties? Or a weakened partner whose security position is troubled because of its conflict between identity and power, a partner experiencing difficulties with China both bilaterally and multilaterally and becoming increasingly dependent on the United States in East Asia? The United States has the right to choose the type of partner it prefers.

From Japan's perspective, the harmonization of its power, efficiency, and identity can ultimately be achieved through its two fundamental postwar policy objectives: strengthening its alliance with the United States and reentering Asia. If the international situation compels Japan to choose one of the two, the consensus is clear: alliance will be given precedence. But this kind of zero-sum picture is not desirable for Japan. It must achieve both objectives in order to maximize its diplomatic posture and satisfy its national interest.[101]

The situation in which Japan found itself in 2005—successive deterioration of its political relations with other Asian countries, notably China—simply contradicted Japan's fundamental desire to reenter Asia and its efforts in that regard. Regardless of the expectation that a "principled" approach toward China will maximize Japan's long-term international posture, Japan's inability to govern and manage present-day difficulties is weakening its international reputation. From a Japanese point of view, this is regrettable, and such a Japan may not really be the best alliance partner for the United States.

Japan's relations with China improved substantially under Prime Minister Abe. Under Prime Minister Fukuda Japan's relations with Asia may be further improved. If Japan begins to behave as a stronger partner capable of conducting a more responsible and effective policy in governing and managing its relations with China and other Asian countries, it would be in the best interest of the United States to consider how best to deal with that kind of Japan, whether to encourage and acknowledge or to disapprove of and object to Japan's fundamental desire to reenter Asia. The answer may not be simple, depending on the preference of the United States regarding its involvement in East Asia. Whatever that preference, I strongly believe that 60 years of consolidation of its alliance with Japan provides sufficient grounds for the United States to trust Japan in its efforts to reenter Asia.

Acknowledgments

I thank Professors Thomas Berger, Kent Calder, Rosemary Foot, Francis Fukuyama, and Gilbert Rozman, along with an anonymous reader, for their valuable comments, and Ms. Serene Hung for her helpful research and comments.

Notes

1. Paul Midford, "Japan's Leadership Role in East Asian Security Multilateralism: The Nakayama Proposal and the Logic of Reassurance," *Pacific Review* 13 (2000): 380.
2. Kuniko Ashizawa, "Japan's Approach toward Asian Regional Security: From 'Hub-and-Spoke' Bilateralism to 'Multi-Tiered,'" *Pacific Review* 16 (2003): 367.
3. Ibid., 363–64.
4. Ibid., 367–68.
5. Expressions have differed somewhat from year to year, but that difference has not affected the fundamental principles. It is interesting to note, though, that in the editions of *Gaiko Seisho* for the years 2001–4, explicit statements to the effect that U.S. engagement and presence should be considered "prerequisite" to multitiered cooperation were included, but those for the years 1999–2000 did not have such statements. The wording used in these years was as follows: 2001–4—"with the prerequisite of US presence and engagement in the region, Japan advances bilateral and multilateral dialogue in a multi-tiered manner (the 2003 and 2004 editions used the wording "with the form of laying dialogues in a multiple manner"); 2000—"advance bilateral and multilateral dialogue and cooperation in a multi-tiered manner"; 1999—"advance bilateral and multilateral dialogue in a multi-tiered manner"; 1998—"with the prerequisite of US presence, accumulate various efforts to enhance (a) bilateral and multilateral dialogue and cooperation to resolve conflicts; (b) political and security dialogue to raise transparency and reassurance in the Asia-Pacific region; (c) political stability through economic

assistance." From the MOFA Web site: www.mofa.go.jp/mofaj/gaiko/bluebook/ index.html (accessed August 11, 2005).

6. In May 1991, Kaifu said: "Japan has very recently decided to send minesweepers to the region. This action does not mean that Japan is assuming a military role in the international community and does not represent any change in Japan's basic defense policy." The following month, Sato wrote: "In the coming years, Japan will engage herself more positively than before in the process to enhance political stability and security in the Asia and Pacific region. . . . Yet, anxiety on the part of many Asian countries about the possibility of Japan becoming a 'military power' will persist unless . . . [Japan involves] herself in the process of regional dialogue on this question." In July of the same year, Nakayama said: "This expansion of the Japanese political role in the Asia-Pacific region has caused anxiety and concern among other countries. . . . [These] concerns and apprehensions about the future direction of Japanese foreign policy are a worthy topic for such types of political dialogue[, where] friendly countries in this region could engage in frank exchanges of opinion on matters of mutual interest." Midford, "Japan's Leadership Role," 376, 381, 382–83.

7. Ashizawa, "Japan's Approach toward Asian Regional Security," 370.

8. Midford, "Japan's Leadership Role," 375.

9. The terminology of "realists" versus "constructivists" is used in accordance with the latest theory of international relations, in such works as those by Muthiah Alagappa, John Ikenberry, Peter Katzenstein, Alexander Wendt, and others.

If Japan was truly disposed to be a harmonious power, there is a question: why did Nakayama's 1991 proposal for a regional forum not include China as a founding member of such a forum? Korea joined ASEAN-PMC in 1991, but China joined only in 1996. Paul Midford presents a convincing argument that this omission was due to Japan's reluctance to include the Soviet Union (Midford, "Japan's Leadership Role," 376–78).

10. Tadashi Ikeda, *Kanbojiawaheiheno Michi* [The road to Cambodian peace] (Tokyo: Chuou Seihan, 1996), 179–80.

11. From President Clinton's speech before the Korean National Assembly, in Akiko Fukushima, *Japanese Foreign Policy: The Emerging Logic of Multilateralism* (London: Macmillan, 1999), 144.

12. Cooperative security directs its attention to the way each state deals with the threat. David Dewitt and Amitav Acharya present three key ways: inclusively, habits of dialogue, and cooperation among actors and within states. Akiko Fukushima, David Capie, and Paul Evans, *Rekishikon, Ajiataiheiyo Anzenhoshotaiwa* [The Asia Pacific security lexicon] (Tokyo: Nihonkeizai Hyoronsha, 2002), 96. The ASEAN way could be characterized as "patience, progressiveness, informality, realism and consensus" (ibid.). Kusuma Snitwongse

defined it as "a practice of consultation and compromise through frequent contacts" (ibid., 25).

13. Fukushima, *Japanese Foreign Policy*, 146–47. Common security is defined by the Palme Commission as "ensuring security through cooperation rather than competitive power politics." Fukushima, Capie, and Evans, *Rekishikon, Ajiataiheiyo Anzenhoshotaiwa*, 109.

14. Thomas Christensen, "China, the U.S.-Japan Alliance, and the Security Dilemma in East Asia," in Michael Brown et al., eds., *The Rise of China* (Cambridge, Mass.: MIT Press, 2000), 158.

15. From the ARF's chairman's statement on the 12th meeting of the ARF on July 29, 2005, available at www.aseanregionalforum.org/Default.aspx?tabid=67 (accessed August 12, 2005).

16. Donald Weatherbee, *Southeast Asia: The Struggle for Autonomy* (New York: Rowman and Littlefield, 2005), 151.

17. Masafumi Iida, "Chuugoku-ASEAN Kankeito Higashiajia Kyouruoku [China-ASEAN relations and East Asia cooperation]," in Kokubun Ryousei, ed., *Chuugokuseijito Higashiajia* [Chinese politics and East Asia] (Tokyo: Keio University Press, 2004), 334.

18. Christensen, "China and the U.S.-Japan Alliance," 158.

19. Cheng-Chwee Kuik, "Multilateralism in China's ASEAN Policy: Its Evolution, Characteristics, and Aspiration," *Contemporary Southeast Asia*, April 1, 2005, 11.

20. Article 9 prohibits Japan's exercise of "the right of belligerency" and its maintenance of "land, sea and air forces." It has been interpreted as not allowing the country to engage in collective self-defense. Some Japanese politicians and opinion leaders have criticized the article as the cause of excessive passive pacifism.

21. Available at www.mofa.go.jp/mofaj/gaiko/bluebook/2004/hakusho/h16/index.html (accessed August 19, 2005).

22. J. Ravenhill, *APEC and the Construction of Pacific Rim Regionalism* (Cambridge: Cambridge University Press, 2001), 183–84.

23. Michael Green provides an excellent analysis of the nature of the Asian financial crisis and how Japan's AMF proposal emerged, was negotiated, and disappeared. Michael Green, *Japan's Reluctant Realism* (New York: Palgrave, 2001), 239–50.

24. Available at www.mofa.go.jp/policy/economy/asia/crisis0010.html (accessed October 4, 2007).

25. Available at www.mofa.go.jp/mofaj/kaidan/kiroku/s_hashi/arc_97/asean97/kaigi.html (August 13, 2005).

26. See www.mofa.go.jp/policy/economy/asia/crisis0010.html (accessed October 4, 2007).

27. Available at www.mofa.go.jp/region/asia-paci/asean/pmv9911/joint.html (accessed August 12, 2005).

28. See www.mofa.go.jp/mofaj/kaidan/kiroku/s_obuchi/arc_99/asean99/3shuno .html (accessed August 12, 2005).

29. On the eve of the breakfast, Obuchi said to the accompanying Japanese press corps: "I feel much obliged to the ASEAN which gave us this occasion, but I simply cannot miss this opportunity." *Asahi Shinbun,* November 29, 1999.

30. An Economic Agreement for a New Age Partnership was signed between Japan and Singapore on January 13, 2002.

31. Julie Gilson, "Complex Regional Multilateralism: 'Strategising' Japan's Responses to Southeast Asia," *Pacific Review* 17 (March 2004): 78. *Spider-web bilateralism* refers to a network of bilateral agreements among multiple actors. The arrangement consists of pro forma bilateral agreements, but in substance it is tantamount to a multilateral agreement.

32. This agreement consisted of arrangement to supply short-term financial resources through bilateral currency swap agreements.

33. Koizumi's speech left another striking impression: he argued that the EAC should be opened to *outside* regional entities such as APEC and the Asia-Europe Meeting (ASEM). The EAC is geographically inside the Asia-Pacific sphere, and therefore is technically a part of APEC; it faces Europe and is therefore outside the ASEM. Japan was clearly putting a greater emphasis on cooperation in East Asia than in the Asia-Pacific sphere. The invitation to Australia and New Zealand might have been made to balance this retreat from the wider range of Asia-Pacific cooperation.

34. The 2004 MOFA paper summarizes the reason this approach became important as follows: "(a) the idea of community building in East Asia was originally inspired by the progress of various functional cooperation [such as coping with the Asian financial crisis or engaging in transnational issues]; (b) such an approach accommodates the diversity of the region in which application of unified rules and establishment of region-wide mechanisms are less feasible in comparison to other regions; and (c) promotion of the functional cooperation does not lead to constraints on the sovereignty which no country in the region is ready to accept." The paper is available at www.mofa.go .jp/region/asia-paci/issue.pdf (accessed August 13, 2005).

35. Koizumi put forward a "two-track approach" of targeting both a comprehensive EPA with ASEAN and bilateral EPAs and FTAs with its constituent countries. See www.mofa.go.jp/region/asia-paci/asean/conference/asean3/ overview0211.html (accessed August 13, 2005).

36. Available at www.mofa.go.jp/region/asia-paci/asean/pmv0310/framework .html (accessed August 13, 2005).

37. With this agreement, ASEAN agreed to conclude EPAs or FTAs with China by 2010, with India by 2011, and with Japan by 2012.

38. Available at www.mofa.go.jp/region/asia-paci/asean/conference/asean3/joint 0310.html (accessed August 13, 2005).

39. Available at www.mofa.go.jp/region/asia-paci/asean/year2003/summit/tokyo _dec.pdf (accessed August 13, 2005).

40. The idea of holding an East Asian summit was proposed by the East Asian Vision Group in 2001, and the East Asian Study Group concluded that it was a "desirable long-term objective" in 2003.

41. Available at www.mofa.go.jp/region/asia-paci/issue.pdf (accessed August 13, 2005).

42. Kyodo Tsushin news agency, November 29, 2004; *Asahi, Sankei,* and *Mainichi Shinbun,* November 30, 2004.

43. Available at www.kantei.go.jp/foreign/koizumispeech/2005/01/21sisei_e.html (accessed August 13, 2005).

44. Available at www.wadaharuki.com/newpaper.html (accessed August 13, 2005).

45. Fukushima, *Japanese Foreign Policy,* 138.

46. Yoshihide Soeya, "Higashiajia Anzenhosho Shisutemuno Nakano Nihon [Japan inside the East Asian security system]," in Yoshihide Soeya and Masaaki Tadokoro, eds., *Nihon-no Higashi-Ajia Kousou* [Japan's East Asian initiatives] (Tokyo: Keio University Press, 2004), 207. The height of U.S. tolerance of Japan's leadership in East Asian regionalism was marked by Gerald Curtis's article in the spring of 2004, which argued that "East Asian regionalism was a key path for Japan to overcome its deep rooted identity crisis between the West and Asia" and that "the United States has potentially much to gain from the strengthening of a security dialogue and cooperation among the nations of East Asia." Gerald Curtis, "For the United States and Japan Multilateralism Is the Key," *Foreign Affairs* (March–April 2004).

47. *Jiji Press,* June 24, 2005.

48. Yoshihisa Komori summarized the U.S. reaction on the EAC as questioning "whether it was not a Chinese stratagem aiming to exclude the United States from East Asia" and quoted Marcus Noland, Kent Calder, Francis Fukuyama, Max Beaucus, Fred Bergstein, Harry Harding, and Edward Lincoln as having expressed concerns about an EAC without U.S. participation in several seminars at the end of 2004. Yoshihisa Komori, *Chugoku Hannichino Kyomou* [Lies and hollows of China's 'anti-Japanism'] (Tokyo: PHP, 2005), 102–12.

49. Richard Armitage, "Higashiajaikyoudoutaiheno Sankaha Kokuekininarunoka [Does joining the East Asian community suit national interests?]," in *Wedge* (Tokyo), May 2005, 6.

50. *Asahi Shinbun,* March 31, 2005.

51. Ibid.

52. *Asahi Shinbun,* July 28, 2005.

53. In my interviews with Chinese opinion leaders in June 2005, there was a unanimous view that practical, step-by-step cooperation among the nations of the APT was most important and that politicizing the issue was of no in-

terest to any East Asian country. Interviews by author, Shanghai, June 22–23, 2005, and Beijing, June 27–28, 2005.

54. *Sankei Shinbun,* December 13, 2006.

55. The 2002 figures, compared with those for 1980, show that exports grew by a factor of 7.8, domestic direct investment by a factor of 25.6, and GDP by a factor of 25.6. World Bank, *World Development Indicators 2004,* CD-ROM, and Council of the East Asian Community (CEAC), *Seisaku-houkokusho* [Policy report], August 2005, available at www.ceac.jp/j/pdf/policy_report.pdf (accessed August 17, 2005), 22.

56. Comparing the figures for 1980 to those for 2003, East Asian regional exports increased from 33.9 percent to 50.5 percent of total exports and regional imports from 34.8 percent to 59.7 percent of total imports. Figures from Japan External Trade Organization. CEAC, *Seisaku-houkokusho,* 23.

57. CEAC, *Seisaku-houkokusho,* 27–28.

58. Japan concluded FTAs with Chile, Malaysia, Mexico, the Philippines, Singapore, and Thailand. Basic agreement was also reached with Brunei and Indonesia. Negotiations have begun or are under consideration with ASEAN, Australia, the Gulf Cooperation Council, India, Korea, Switzerland, and Vietnam. See www.mofa.go.jp/mofaj/gaiko/fta/pdfs/kyotei_0703.pdf (accessed October 4, 2007).

59. Available at www.mofa.go.jp/mofaj/gaiko/bluebook/2004/hakusho/h16/index.html (accessed August 14, 2005).

60. Yuji Miura, "Nihonwa Higashiajiakeizairenkeijidaini Ikanitaiousubekika [How should Japan respond in this age of East Asia economic partnership?]," in Toshio Watanabe, ed., *Higashiajia Keizairenkeino Jidai* [Partnerships for economic development in East Asia] (Tokyo: Toyokeizaisha, 2004), 228–35.

61. Makoto Taniguchi, *Higashiaajia Kyoudoutai* [East Asian Community] (Tokyo: Iwanami Shinsho, 2004), ii.

62. Haruki Yoshida, "Higashiajaisamittoha Nichibeidoumeiwo Sokonauka [Does the EAS harm the Japan-U.S. alliance?]," *Sekai Shuuho,* April 26, 2005.

63. Toshiaki Arai, *ASEAN to Nihon, Higashiajia Keizaiken-no Yukue* [ASEAN and Japan: How far does the East Asian economic sphere extend?] (Tokyo: Nichyuu Shuppan, 2003), 152–73.

64. Muthiah Alagappa, *Asian Security Order* (Oxford: Oxford University Press, 2001), 244–54.

65. The report is available at www.ceac.jp/j/pdf/policy_report.pdf (accessed August 17, 2005).

66. *Sankei Shinbun,* July 14, 2005.

67. Kuik, "Multilateralism in China's ASEAN Policy," 4–7.

68. David Lampton, "What Growing Chinese Power Means for America," statement prepared for testimony presented before the U.S. Senate, June 7, 2005, 9.

69. David Shambaugh, "China Engages Asia, Reshaping the Regional Order," *International Security* 29 (Winter 2004–5): 72–78.

70. Makoto Iokibe, "Nichyuuno Mizoha Umarunoka? [Would the gap between Japan and China be bridged?]," discussion, *Gaikou Forum* (Tokyo), July 2005, 11, 19.

71. Noboru Hatakeyama, "Higashiajiakyoudoutraino Gensowo Suteyo [The illusion of the EAC should be forsaken]," *Chuuou Kouron* (Tokyo), September 2005, 154–61.

72. *Sankei Shinbun,* May 23, 2005.

73. *Sankei Shinbun,* August 1, 2005.

74. The speech is available at www. mofa.go.jp/mofaj/press/enzetsu/18/easo_ 1130.html (accessed October 4, 2007).

75. Tanino, "Nichyuuno Mizoha Umarunoka?" 14, 17.

76. Muthiah Alagappa, *Asian Security Order: Instrumental and Normative Features* (Stanford, Calif.: Stanford University Press, 2003), 4.

77. Gilbert Rozman, *Northeast Asia's Stunted Regionalism: Bilateral Distrust in the Shadow of Globalization* (Cambridge: Cambridge University Press, 2004), 366.

78. In September 2005, the Working Group on Grand Strategic Choices of the Princeton Project on National Security issued a report that included the option of creating an FTA between Japan and the United States that would capitalize on the countries' shared value of democracy. This is certainly a creative and interesting idea along the lines of encouraging deeper U.S. involvement in East Asia. But a key haunting question remains: can Japan overcome its inability to govern its relations with China? The report is available at www.wws.princeton.edu/ppns/conferences/reports/fall/GSC.pdf (accessed February 13, 2006).

79. Japan, South Korea, and the United States were expected to become major contributors.

80. Francis Fukuyama, "Re-envisioning Asia," *Foreign Affairs* (January–February 2005): 75.

81. At the end of the 1970s, North Korea abducted Japanese citizens, primarily from the coastal area along the Sea of Japan, mostly for the purpose of educating North Korean spies and agents. The Japanese government now recognizes 17 abductees.

82. The declaration included a road map for the establishment of diplomatic relations; Kim's acknowledgment (that 8 out of 13 had already died), an apology, and a promise not to repeat the abduction; and a statement of North Korea's intention to comply with international agreements on nuclear issues. The declaration is available at www.mofa.go.jp/region/asia-paci/n_korea/ pmv0209/pyongyang.html (accessed August 17, 2005).

83. Pyongyang Declaration, clause 4.

84. *Asahi Shinbun,* October 1, 2002.
85. Shinichi Kitaoka, "Sengo Nihongaikoushini Nokoru Seikoudearu [It was a success to be remembered in the post-WWII foreign policy]," *Chuuoukouron,* November 2002, 46–57.
86. *Asahi Shinbun,* October 25, 2002.
87. See www.sukuukai.jp/narkn/index.html (accessed October 4, 2005).
88. Teruaki Masumoto, deputy director general of AFVKN, in *Asahi Shinbun,* November 10, 2002.
89. Out of 16 abductees so recognized by the government of Japan, 12 were abducted in 1977–78, 4 in 1980, and 2 in 1983. See the NARKN Web site, www .sukuukai.jp/narkn/. By 1978, the police had arrested 39 North Korean agents on charges including one abduction. Politicians and opinion leaders now argue that the government should have been in a position to know the danger and take appropriate measures to protect Japanese citizens. See Tooru Maeno, *Boukokunihonheno Ikarino Shougen* [Testimony of anger at Japan's disintegration] (Tokyo: PHP, 2004), 31.
90. Tsutomu Nishioka, vice president of NARKN, in *Asahi Shinbun,* December 8, 2002.
91. *Yomiuri Shinbun* has unusually detailed accounts of the intergovernmental strife over whether to keep the five in Japan or let them go back to North Korea, then call them back with their children. See *Yomiuri Shinbun,* October 25, October 27, and December 1, 2002.
92. Tsutomu Nishioka, *Kinshojitsugashikaketa "Tainichi Daibouryaku" Rachino Shinjitsu* [The truth of abduction: "Great stratagem" by Kim Jong-il] (Tokyo: Tokuma, 2002), 183.
93. To give just a few examples: in December 2002, *Chuuoukouron* carried an article by the editorial board, "Nichibeidoumeino Sahouwomushishita 'Taibeihimitsugaikou' ["Confidential diplomacy" excluding the U.S. ignored rules among the Allies]" (38–57), strongly criticizing the way Tanaka had secretively pushed forward the preparation of Koizumi's visit to Pyongyang; in November 2002, *Bungeishunju* carried an article by Tatsuya Shiroyama, "Dokudangaikoukan Tanaka Hitoshitoha Nanimonoka [Who is that despotic diplomat, Hitoshi Tanaka?]" (186–90), and followed it up in the August 2003 edition with an article by Hiroshi Kodama, " 'Boukokuno Gaikoukan' Tanaka Hitoshino Shoutai [The hidden reality of Hitoshi Tanaka, a diplomat who will ruin Japan]" (198–206). The titles indicate the content. *Chuuoukouron* and *Bungeishunju* are usually considered the most highly respected monthly magazines.
94. Jim Kelly, interview in *Asahi Shinbun,* June 18, 2005.
95. *Asahi Shinbun,* August 1, 2003.
96. Accounts of the four rounds are available as follows (Internet sources all accessed on August 18, 2005): first round: www.mofa.go.jp/mofaj/area/n_ korea/abd/6kaigo_gh.html; second round: www.mofa.go.jp/mofaj/area/n_korea/

abd/6kaigo2_gh.html; third round: www.mofa.go.jp/mofaj/area/n_korea/ abd/6kaigo3_gh.html; fourth round: *Asahi Shinbun,* July 27, 2005.

97. For the first three rounds, see the MOFA Web site, www.mofa.go.jp/; for the fourth round, see *Asahi Shinbun,* August 3–4, 2005.

98. For Japan's official position in the third round, www.mofa.go.jp/mofaj/ area/n_korea/abd/6kaigo3_gh.html (accessed August 18, 2005). See also *Sankei Shinbun,* February 29 and June 27, 2004, and *Asahi Shinbun,* July 28, 2005.

99. *Sankei Shinbun,* August 30, 2003, and February 27 and 29, 2004.

100. Soeya, "Higashiajia Anzenhosho Shisutemuno Nakano Nihon," 214.

101. As for Japan's efforts to achieve this dual objective of consolidating alliance with the United States and reentering Asia in the period prior to Koizumi, see Kazuhiko Togo, "The Second Half of the 1990's," in Gilbert Rozman, Kazuhiko Togo, and Jody Ferguson, eds., *Japan's Strategic Thought toward Asia* (New York: Palgrave, 2007), 79–108.

CHAPTER 8

Korean Perspectives on East Asian Regionalism

Sook-Jong Lee

AS A SMALLER POWER surrounded by stronger nations, South Korea has been susceptible to the idea of multilateralism from the perspective of a regional balance of power. Late-nineteenth-century Korean strategists like Queen Minbi had to be conscious of the regional balance of power for the survival of their weak Chosun Dynasty. Since Korea lost national sovereignty to Japan because it failed to strike a balance between Japan, China, and Russia in the early twentieth century, Korea's ruling elite have had an understandable aversion to letting any single power dominate the East Asian region. As a result, architects of Korea's national security have attempted to safeguard the country's independence by simultaneously linking Korea to numerous regional actors.

The Korean War made South Korea's quest for a balance of power unnecessary because the country was integrated into the West's Cold War defense strategy for the Asia-Pacific region. Anchored in a strong bilateral alliance with the United States, South Korea successfully modernized its economy while deterring North Korea's military threat. Strong military, political, and economic bilateral ties with the United States naturally allowed South Korea to develop a trans-Pacific interdependence: the United States supplied aid, investment, technology, and, most important, the country's largest export market. Japan became another major trans-Pacific partner after South Korea normalized diplomatic relations with its former colonial master in 1965. South Korea maintained a virtual alliance with Japan through a common ally, the United States, despite historical animosity and occasional rancor.[1] South Korea also developed its economic ties with other Pacific countries, especially Australia, Canada, and New Zealand.

The end of the Cold War renewed South Korea's interest in multilateralism. Under the changing atmosphere of easing Cold War tension, South Korea's President Roh Tae-woo proposed the idea of a "Consultative Conference for Peace in Northeast Asia" in his address to the UN General Assembly in October 1988. The proposal called for laying a solid foundation for durable peace and prosperity in the region through a conference to be attended by China, Japan, the Soviet Union, and the United States in addition to the two Koreas—the exact members of the current Six-Party Talks. Although the idea was not seriously promoted at that time, South Korea became one of the earliest proponents of a multilateral security architecture. It gained confidence after rejuvenating previously antagonistic relations with Russia and China through normalization in 1991 and 1992, respectively. South Korea officially introduced a proposal for a Northeast Asia Security Dialogue (NEASED) at the 1994 Asia Regional Forum Senior Officials' Meeting in Bangkok.

South Korea has been actively participating in Track II or "1.5" security-related multilateral talks in the Asia-Pacific framework in such forums as the Council for Security Cooperation in the Asia Pacific (CSCAP) and the Northeast Asia Cooperation Dialogue (NEACD). CSCAP was created in 1994 as a body for cooperation among private research organizations, and South Korea has been actively participating in it since it created CSCAP-Korea in 1994, with about 50 members including scholars, businessmen, and journalists.[2] NEACD was formed in 1993 by the Institute on Global Conflict and Cooperation (IGCC) at the University of California–San Diego to encourage cooperation among Northeast Asian countries. Nongovernmental participants have gathered together with officials from the foreign and defense ministries of South and North Korea, China, Japan, and Russia. However, overall, regionwide intergovernmental dialogue, Track II processes, and bi- or trilateral coordination mechanisms in the Asia-Pacific region remain embryonic, and a qualitatively new multilateralism has yet to take hold in the Asia-Pacific.[3] These less government-driven multilateral networks served Korean interests well until recently, because the region is still plastic and Korea has yet to develop a regional policy that is independent of its conventional bilateral ties.

Earlier Korean ideas on multilateralism were limited in the following senses. First, multilateralism was bounded by bilateralism. It was conceived of as a supplement to, not a substitute for, existing bilateral arrangements. This position has been supported rather vigorously in the security area.

Leaders of the Republic of Korea (ROK) have maintained the position that the linchpin of Korean security should continue to be the ROK-U.S. alliance. Multilateral security arrangements are viewed as having added value for South Korea only as a means of preparing for strategic uncertainties in the Asia-Pacific following the Cold War.[4] The 1993 conference between the Institute for Foreign Affairs and National Security and the Brookings Institution produced a report that concluded by calling for the inauguration of a multiparty security dialogue to address specific problems in Northeast Asia. Such a dialogue would complement, not compete with, the system of American bilateral alliances in the region.[5] Although leftist nationalists have recently challenged this concept, thus far the political leadership in South Korea has successfully defended it.

Second, earlier ideas on multilateral arrangements did not clearly map out a specific geographic strategic boundary. South Korea has long vowed to maintain the principle of undiscriminating openness in regional affairs. South Korea rationalized its active participation in the Asia-Pacific Economic Cooperation (APEC) by portraying the group as the embodiment of "open regionalism." Even NEASED was portrayed more as a channel for dialogue among the countries of the region in which the United States had a stake than as an active mechanism for the resolution of conflicts within the region. South Korea itself was reluctant to change its long-held position that the issue of the peace and reunification of the Korean peninsula should be addressed by the two Koreas. Only after the North Korean first nuclear crisis of 1993–94 were the Four-Party Talks and later the Six-Party Talks legitimized as a mechanism for dealing with the North Korea question.

The thinking about how to situate South Korea in a dynamic regional order started to evolve slowly in the late 1990s. The overall regional milieu of the late 1990s, especially after the financial crisis of 1997–98, was an important factor in shaping South Korea's interests in East Asia, as well as its definition of an "imagined community" that would mainly emphasize economic relations. This chapter analyzes the emerging interests and ideas of South Korea regarding regionalism by examining the country's changing responses to new and existing regional institutions and how its domestic politics and political coalitions have influenced its national leadership to choose specific policies at "critical junctures."[6]

The Evolution of East Asian Regionalism in South Korea

Riding on Southeast Asian Regional Institutions

Since the 1990s, Southeast Asia has played a catalyzing role in the emergence of East Asian regional institutions. When Malaysian Prime Minister Mohamad Mahathir suggested the idea of an East Asian Economic Grouping (EAEG) whose ultimate goal would be to create an exclusive East Asian free trade area, many Koreans were impressed by this bold idea while dismissing it as unrealistic. Among the suggested members (China, Japan, Hong Kong, South Korea, and Taiwan) outside of the Association of Southeast Asian Nations (ASEAN), South Korea and Japan were particularly cool to the idea. They had strong political as well as economic ties with the United States, and, because China's economy was not yet perceived as a dominant economic force in Southeast Asia, they could not use ASEAN to balance China. As a result of clear opposition from the United States, Mahathir's EAEG was incorporated into APEC in 1993 in the modified form of an East Asian Economic Caucus. Weighing the importance of its U.S. export market and security alliance, at the time South Korea viewed its national interests as solidly grounded in trans-Pacific cooperation.

Such cooperation was seen as a loose but successful consolidation of Southeast and Northeast Asian regionalism. As a result, Korea began to take ASEAN more seriously. The ASEAN Regional Forum (ARF) was launched in 1994 as the first regional forum to discuss the possibility of security cooperation in the Asia-Pacific region. Barry Buzan argues that this creation of institutional security connections linking Northeast and Southeast Asian states was accompanied by the parallel development of a shared concern regarding growing Chinese power as well as the development of an East Asian regional economy thought to be strongly linked to political and regional stability.[7] Although the ARF was not a sophisticated multilateral security arrangement, its formation was a stimulus for Northeast Asian countries to view ASEAN as a part of their own strategic calculus. The creation of the ASEAN Plus Three (South Korea, China, and Japan) framework in 1995 was originally a by-product of preparations for the first Asia-Europe Meeting in Bangkok a year later. However, this meeting became institutionalized as an annual event after the Kuala Lumpur ASEAN summit in 1997. As a result, three Northeast Asian countries that could not form their own subregional body started to use ASEAN Plus Three for their own Asian diplomacy. Starting in November 1999, South Korea, China, and Japan used this political space to create their own summit meeting, and they used trilateral or bilateral summit meetings for subregional cooperation. For example, China proposed to examine the feasibility of a Korea-China-Japan free trade agreement at the trilateral summit meeting of 2002, held in Cambodia.

ASEAN Plus Three became a strong regional institution because three Northeast Asian countries that account for about 90 percent of East Asia's GDP joined. The unexpected Asian financial crisis of 1997 allowed the "Plus Three" countries to see themselves as an integral part of East Asia and contributed to the consolidation of the ASEAN Plus Three formula. At the height of the crisis, Japan proposed the establishment of a U.S.$100 billion Asian Monetary Fund (AMF) that was expected to weaken the strictures of the Anglo-American-style capitalism imposed on countries receiving financial aid by international financial institutions. The U.S. opposition that derailed this initiative was viewed negatively within the region. As a result, alternative arrangements for self-help among East Asian countries were devised. Japan modified its proposed AMF into the U.S.$30 billion Miyazawa Plan. The ASEAN Plus Three finance ministers gathered in Chiang Mai, Thailand, in 2000 to announce the creation of a network of bilateral currency-swap agreements to prevent future currency crises. The three Northeast Asian countries held the largest foreign exchange reserves among participants, and thus played a central role in this swap network. China initially opposed the AMF idea for fear of Japanese leadership in the region, but provided financial resources to the region through the International Monetary Fund (IMF) and pledged not to devalue the renminbi in the early years after the crisis.[8]

East Asia's regionalism immediately after the financial crisis was linked to a desire to limit the influence of the United States and international financial institutions controlled by the United States.[9] This also reflected a realization that the region had been underrepresented in global institutions. Harris rightly points out that regional cooperation in East Asia is crisis driven.[10] In the years since the financial crisis, regionalism has weakened as Asia's economies have recovered. In order for East Asia to build regional institutions, policy makers will need to realize that cooperation is the only feasible way of addressing certain issues. In this sense, common problems such as how to deal with the North Korean nuclear threat or how to socialize China as a peaceful power can promote East Asian regionalism.

Incipient Regionalism during President Kim Dae-jung's Administration

The Asian financial crisis was crucial in planting the seeds of East Asian regionalism for South Korea. The country was hit by a liquidity crisis and subjected to a restructuring that was perhaps the IMF's harshest. This economic crisis was so psychologically traumatic for Koreans that they labeled it the second greatest national disaster after the Korean War of 1950. The crisis helped long-time opposition leader Kim Dae-jung win the 1997 presidential election, and he vigorously pursued reforms during the first two years of his administration.

Kim was the first Korean president to envision East Asia as a community. The Asian financial crisis made South Korean leaders review their long-held position of "open regionalism," and they discredited APEC for impotence both before and after the crisis. This changing identity was evident both in Korea's diplomacy toward Japan and in its pursuit of free trade agreements. Kim's concept of adopting toward Japan a forward-looking policy that laid to rest historical issues was based on the idea that a common East Asian identity and Japan's cooperation would be needed to foster prosperity and peace in the region. President Kim's visit to Tokyo in October 1998 and his summit meeting with Japanese Prime Minister Keizo Obuchi opened a new stage in bilateral relations. The official apology of the Japanese government to South Korea for its colonial past and the action plan for bilateral cooperation included in the summit's joint communiqué were accepted as unprecedented signs of progress in the Korea-Japan relationship.[11]

In the past, South Korea's interest in regional economic cooperation had revolved around the territories surrounding the Tuman River or the Yellow Sea. Local governments and the private sector had been mainly responsible for cooperation, and state-level cooperation had not been considered. However, after the financial crisis discussions of regional economic cooperation referred to cooperation between individual Asian states. Interestingly, the Korean government's pursuit of a regional policy was accompanied by its quest for bilateral free trade agreements (FTAs). The Korean government had previously shown no interest in forging such agreements, but this changed at the November 1998 meeting of the Coordinating Committee of the External Economy. The meeting participants concluded that South Korea would pursue an active FTA policy in order to prevent its economic isolation amid the international trend of spreading regional FTAs and to expand export markets and foreign direct investment into Korea. The country aimed to conclude FTAs with major trading partners such as China, the European Union, Japan, and the United States. An FTA with Chile was intended to test the waters, both politically and economically, for larger agreements to come. Chile was a relatively small trading partner, and its FTA with Korea was expected to do less damage to domestic industries.[12]

Under President Kim's forward-looking diplomacy, Japan became Korea's major object of FTA interest. There was heated debate regarding the concept of a Korea-Japan FTA among top trade bureaucrats as a result of the economic redundancies between the two countries and the restructuring such an FTA would inevitably entail.[13] The feasibility of the idea was examined starting in November 1998, when the two countries' trade ministers agreed to investigate the idea through their respective think tanks. The idea was also analyzed by the business community of each country and later by a tripartite study group consisting of representatives of think tanks, business, and government. Despite an intervening dispute about the Japanese government's approval of a right-wing middle school history textbook that whitewashed Japan's oppressive colonial rule of Korea, the pursuit of Korea-Japan FTA was succeeded by the opening of official negotiations with Japan on the agreement in October 2003 by the government of President Roh Moo-hyun. Korea's policy shift toward bilateral FTAs with Asian trading partners was clearly linked to an emerging regionalism.

South Korea was most active in developing region-oriented proposals and policies during Kim's presidency. At the 1998 Hanoi ASEAN Plus Three summit meeting, Kim proposed forming an East Asia Vision Group (EAVG) and East Asia Study Group (EASG) to allow the private sector to research future cooperation within ASEAN Plus Three.[14] Seoul hosted the inaugural meeting of the East Asia Forum in December 2003. This meeting was held to promote cooperative programs of the EASG. By late 2003, ASEAN Plus Three comprised about a third of the world's population, a fifth of global GDP, and a fifth of world trade volume. South Korea's trade with this region accounted for about 40 percent of its total trade, and ASEAN alone was South Korea's fifth largest trading partner (following the United States, China, Japan, and the European Union), accounting for 11 percent of Korea's total trade. South Korea spent 21 percent of its total grant aid and 42 percent of its development assistance funds in the ASEAN Plus Three region.[15]

South Korea's new focus on ASEAN Plus Three has been accompanied by China's increased interest in Southeast Asia. China's move to push for the formation of an FTA between China and ASEAN was a sign of its burgeoning confidence. Chinese Premier Zhu Rongji proposed the idea at the ASEAN Plus Three summit in November 2000. At a meeting of senior ASEAN and Chinese economic officials in Brunei the following summer, China proposed tariff reductions and other measures to be phased in over the next seven years, 2003–9. ASEAN responded cautiously, proposing a 10-year phase-in period without a specified start date. Premier Zhu formally proposed that a China-ASEAN FTA be realized within 10 years at the ASEAN-China summit in November 2001. ASEAN accepted this proposal and announced its plan jointly with China at the November 2002 summit held in Cambodia.[16] The China-ASEAN FTA reflects China's new security concept, which advocates a multipolar world and multilateralism to dilute U.S. unilateralism. China emphasized multilateralism and cooperation as the best route to a more peaceful Asia in order to rise above one-sided security and seek common security. In addition to protecting China against the economic shocks of globalization, the Chinese approach to economic integration with ASEAN was strategically conceived.[17] China also ratified the ASEAN Treaty of Amity and Cooperation in 2003. Although Beijing's multilateralism in Southeast Asia is motivated by a nationalistic desire to strengthen China's presence in the region in the face of competition from Japan and the United States,[18] Korea was drawn to Southeast Asia to counteract the increased dominance in East Asia China acquired through its ASEAN linkage.

The Venture into Northeast Asian Regionalism by Roh Moo-hyun

In his regional policy, President Roh Moo-hyun essentially maintained the previous government's regional emphasis on East Asia. Nevertheless, the strategic boundary was reduced so as to focus on Northeast Asia. In his February 2003 inaugural speech, Roh put forward the concept of a "Northeast Asian era of peace and prosperity" as the new government's major policy goal. The Presidential Committee on the "Northeast Asian Business Hub" was created in April 2003 to form a comprehensive policy, and in June 2004 changed its name to the Presidential Committee on the Northeast Asian Cooperation Initiative. To create a new order, the initiative called for a three-level strategy. The first level was regional cooperation to create a virtuous circle of peace and prosperity by establishing a new order of integration and cooperation. The second level was the establishment of peace and prosperity on the Korean peninsula. The third level was the strengthening of national competitiveness through innovation and reform. This strategy defined South Korea's role as that of a "bridge nation" to link continental and maritime powers, a "hub nation" to emerge as the center of ideas to ensure peace and prosperity in the region and for interregional networks, and a "cooperator nation" to serve as a catalyst for regional cooperation to build a community of peace and prosperity in the region. It emphasized the link between security and economics in Northeast Asian cooperation.[19]

President Roh's focus on Northeast Asia rather than merely "East Asia" reflects the increased strategic importance of the Northeast Asian region to Korea. North Korea's nuclear threat and the beginning of the Six-Party Talks in August 2003 limited the Korean government's previously pro-North policy, which had been pursued through bilateral exchange and cooperation. South Korea dealt with the imperative of resolving the nuclear threat from North Korea through cooperation between the United States and regional powers including China, Japan, and Russia. At the same time, Roh remained committed to the inter-Korean reconciliation principle and to creating a soft landing for North Korea's security threat in the region through economic and political development. In this context, the political leadership in Korea inserted its regional policy as a buffer against potentially hawkish U.S. policy toward North Korea. The enhanced regional leadership of China had become visible in the Six-Party Talks, while the North Korea policy of U.S. President George W. Bush was perceived as adversarial and potentially destabilizing to the region.

In addition, Chinese economic clout had increased rapidly, so expanding South Korea's positive relations with China and simultaneously managing its long-standing economic and security relations with Japan became critically important. In this context, South Korea came to see its strategic position in Northeast Asia as a balancer between two regional leaders and developed its interest in subregional institutions.

China surpassed the United States as the number one trading partner for South Korea in 2004; the Chinese portion of Korea's total trade rose from 15.3 percent to 16.6 percent between 2003 and 2004, while that of the United States declined from 15.8 percent to 15 percent. In 2003, China accounted for 18.1 percent of Korea's total exports and 12.2 percent of its total imports, while the United States accounted for 17.6 percent and 13.8 percent, respectively. In 2004, China increased its share of Korea's total exports to 19.6 percent and its share of total imports to 13.2 percent, while the United States decreased its shares to 16.9 percent and 12.8 percent, respectively. In regional terms, Asia accounted for half of Korea's total trade in both 2003 and 2004, while the trans-Pacific areas of North America, South America, and Oceania together accounted for 23.8 percent of Korea's total trade in 2003 and 22.8 percent in 2004. In a nutshell, Korea's Asian trade linkages have thickened, and increased trade with China is primarily responsible for this.[20] South Korea is a trade-dependent country whose 2004 trade accounted for 70 percent of its annual GDP. In addition, Korea had a trade surplus with China of U.S.$13.2 billion in 2003 and $20.2 billion in 2004. On the other hand, Korea has consistently had a trade deficit with Japan. This deficit amounted to U.S.$19 billion in 2003 and $24.4 billion in 2004.

Recently, China has also been South Korea's number one destination for overseas investment. Asia as a region takes about 60 percent of South Korea's investment—47.1 percent in 2002, 59.3 percent in 2003, 56.5 percent in 2004, and 59.9 percent in 2005—and about 70 percent of the total investment in Asia goes to China. This means that China accounted for about 40 percent of South Korea's total overseas investment in 2005. On the other hand, anywhere from a fifth to a quarter of Korea's overseas investment goes to the United States. In 2005, investment in North America (19.8 percent), Europe (9.8 percent), South America (5.7 percent), and Oceania (2.4 percent) accounted for 37.7 percent of Korea's total overseas investment of U.S.$6.4 billion, a sum smaller than Korea's investment in China.[21]

Nevertheless, Europe and North America are major regions from which South Korea receives foreign direct investment. In 2005, reported investment from the European Union and the United States accounted for 42.2 percent and 23.3 percent, respectively, of total foreign direct investment (U.S.$11.56 billion) in South Korea. Investment from the Asian region was 30.3 percent, greater than North America's share of 26.9 percent. However, the Chinese share was a meager 0.6 percent.[22] This robust pattern of capital investment in Korea by the European Union and the United States is not likely to change in the near future because China and the rest of Asia, except for Japan, are still "catching up" to the West. Both of these economies are thirsty for capital investment in their own domestic industries. This phenomenon lends support to Pempel's argument regarding East Asian integration that East Asian integration has occurred primarily in the economic and private spheres rather than in the governmental and institutional spheres, and Asia's is likely to retain strong trans-Pacific ties as long as American and European capital continues to flow into the region.[23]

The earlier FTA policy of Kim Dae-jung's government, and to some extent the first two years of Roh's government, was linked to regional policy. Whether economically motivated or driven by security concerns, bilateral or trilateral FTA policies were more focused in East or Northeast Asia. But South Korea's more recent bilateral FTAs target many countries outside of Asia. Although there had been domestic opposition to the Korea-Chile FTA, FTAs between Korea and Singapore and between Korea and the European Free Trade Association (EFTA) were concluded without major incident. The Korea-Singapore FTA was concluded in November 2004 after just 11 months of official negotiations. The countries' trade ministers signed the FTA in August 2005, and it was to take effect in 2006. The Korea-EFTA FTA negotiations commenced in January 2005 and were successfully concluded in July and signed in December of that year. In addition to these three bilateral FTAs, the Korean government is engaged in other bilateral FTA negotiations or studies. A Korea-ASEAN FTA commenced negotiations in February 2005. The basic agreement and another agreement to resolve conflicts were signed in December of the same year. South Korea agreed with ASEAN to create a free trade area by 2010, meaning that South Korea's agreement with ASEAN is on course to be realized *before* the China-ASEAN FTA takes full effect, despite the fact that Korea's negotiations with ASEAN started three years after China's. The Korean government also agreed to negotiate an FTA with Canada in July 2005. Most recently, in April 2007, Korea concluded FTA negotiations with the United States. Korea has also explored FTAs with India and MERCOSUR (the Southern Common Market) as well as Korea-Japan-China and Korea-China FTAs.

South Korea's FTA bureau, newly created in 2004, has aggressively pushed through each of these trade agreements and studies. The bureau says that Korea's policy to create FTA networks through "simultaneous FTA strategy" aims at preventing the country's isolation in a regionalized global economy and at expanding its export markets. Korea's current FTA policy was formulated through the FTA Roadmap determined at a meeting of foreign affairs ministers on August 30, 2003. It states that the Korean government will pursue comprehensive FTAs with a multitrack approach to achieve a per capita GDP of U.S.$20,000 and emerge as the "hub state" of East Asia. The criteria for selecting FTA partners are economic validity, political implications, the potential partner's strong willingness to conclude an FTA with Korea, and linkage to a larger, more advanced economic bloc.[24]

It is interesting to note that the Korean government tries to create a strategic linkage between its goal of becoming a Northeast Asian hub state and a multitrack FTA policy that includes countries outside of East Asia.[25] Roh's earlier vision of Korea as a Northeast Asian hub state and his later idea of Korea as a balancer were supposed to bolster Korean autonomy with regard to the United States. Even when Korea was seeking bilateral FTA partners, it did not consider the United States. Therefore, it was a stunning surprise when the two governments announced in February 2006 that they would start FTA negotiations by May. In preparation for the negotiations, the Korean government halved the number of days the United States was required to show Korean films at movie theaters despite strong opposition to this move from the domestic film industry. The government believes that the Korea-U.S. FTA will consolidate the alliance of the two countries by expanding the security alliance into an economic alliance. It regards the United States as the best partner for an FTA that can increase Korea's trade volume, advance its economic institutions and customs, and increase foreign investment in Korea due to rising global confidence in the Korean economy.

Conclusion: Prospects for South Korea's Regional Policy

South Korea has long pursued modernization of the ROK-U.S. security alliance and now is pursuing the development of trans-Pacific economic and political ties. Because of its focus on bilateral ties with the United States, South Korea did not devise a regional policy until the late 1990s. Although the end of the Cold War renewed Korea's interest in multilateralism from the perspective of a balance of power, its multilateral ideas were not confined to a specific region and were subject to bilateralism. It was the consolidation of Southeast Asian regionalism through ASEAN and the creation of the ARF that made South Korea more seriously consider its own subregion. When an annual meeting of the ASEAN Plus Three was institutionalized in 1997, the linkage between Southeast and Northeast Asia emerged. South Korea came to actively participate in this framework to carry out its region-oriented policies. The financial crisis in East Asia facilitated crisis-driven regionalism, giving rise to the epistemic community emphasizing cooperation and consultation among the countries in the region. The government of Kim Dae-jung embraced this trend in its foreign policy. President Kim proposed the creation of the EAVG and warmed relations with Japan through working to address common regional concerns sympathetically. Bilateral or trilateral FTAs were sought as a way to provide links to the East Asian region. The government of President Roh Moo-hyun narrowed its regional scope to Northeast Asia and added a security dimension to its regional policy. Northeast Asia was factored into the new security calculus for South Korea to give it relative autonomy with regard to U.S. pressure on issues regarding North Korea and to allow South Korea to balance China against Japan. FTAs across regions, however, weakened South Korea's Northeast Asia policy. Thus, South Korea turned to a pragmatic policy of trying to deepen its ties with the United States through economic cooperation in the form of an FTA. President Roh, who had once vowed to pursue greater independence from the United States, gravitated back toward the conventional wisdom that South Korea should deepen its alliance with the United States to fortify its role in the region.

The question of how to interpret South Korea's recent efforts to seek bilateral FTAs across various regions is controversial. Some may argue that the country's FTA partners are best limited to Asian countries because intraregional trade patterns have created a de facto trade bloc in East Asia. Others may argue that bilateral FTAs with major individual countries or regions do not negatively affect regional policy. The latter would point out that the inflow of capital and technology into South Korea is still coming mainly from the European Union and the United States. Therefore, East Asian regionalism, even in an economic sense, is premature. Other countries in East Asia have also turned to bilateral FTAs. Bisley argues that optimism regarding East Asian regionalism has been replaced by skepticism due to the decline of concerted regional leadership by Australia, Japan, and the United States. After the financial crisis in East Asia, interstate collaboration gave way to bilateral trade agreements that distracted the countries in the region from the task of regional community-building.[26] Rising nationalism in China and Japan is expected to complicate the task of establishing regional leadership in East Asia, and crisis-driven East Asian regionalism seems to be dissipating with the return to normalcy.

If one defines the existence of collective norms and social purpose as the criterion for multilateralism, multilateral collaboration in East Asia is likely to remain functional rather than normative. If regionalization means the occurrence of increased economic and social interaction within a region, and if regionalism is the body of ideas, values, and concrete goals that direct such processes,[27] East Asia may remain a case in which the regionalization of economic activities does not lead to other forms of regionalism. Nevertheless, the conventional wisdom that regionalism in East Asia is bound to be economically driven, sans political cooperation and institutionalization, does not have to hold true.[28] East Asia must pay attention to new functional imperatives in order to build an East Asian or Northeast Asian multilateral security framework. The recent formation of a framework for the Six-Party Talks demonstrates that regional institutions in Northeast Asia can be realized in a security realm. It is too early to predict whether the current Six-Party Talks can develop into a meaningful multilateral security institution; however, it is clear that Northeast Asian countries have to deal with potential conflicts through multilateral security regimes, as Southeast Asia has. In addition to the specter of North Korea's nuclear threat, numerous territorial disputes and the potential for cross-strait conflict haunt Northeast Asia. Buzan predicts that bipolarity will be durable in the East Asian security context because no other state comes close to matching China or Japan, and a successful regional security regime can develop only in the context of a supportive global international environment. Because of this, the United States must stay engaged in East Asia.[29]

Currently East Asian or Northeast Asian multilateral cooperation is moving toward the realm of security. This trend is likely to strengthen in the future. Additionally, South Korea's stake in the Asian security regime will remain salient. Inter-Korean relations are still turbulent, and potentially dangerous. In addition, from the perspective of a balance of power, South Korea or a unified Korea, caught between China and Japan, will be a crucial balancer in East Asia. Using Korea's long-time ally, the United States, to increase Korea's strategic value to its powerful neighbors remains a good option. The nationalistic leadership in Korea must face the reality that it needs to make efforts to deepen U.S. engagement in regional security regimes as the ROK-U.S. alliance softens.

Notes

1. Victor Cha, *Alignment Despite Antagonism: The US-Korea-Japan Security Triangle* (Stanford, Calif.: Stanford University Press, 1999).

2. CSCAP aims to build confidence among countries in the region and support multilateral security cooperation among them. Ten countries joined at the time of its formation, and 20 countries were members as of the end of 2005. CSCAP has been reporting the results of its research to the ASEAN Regional Forum.

3. Nobuo Okawara and Peter Katzenstein, "Japan and Asian-Pacific Security: Regionalization, Entrenched Bilateralism and Incipient Multilateralism," *Pacific Review* 14 (2001): 165–94.

4. Jin-hyun Paik, "Multilateralism and the Korean Peninsula," *Korea and World Affairs* 21 (1997): 12–14.

5. Institute of Foreign Affairs and National Security (IFANS), *Evolving Multilateral Security Regime in Northeast Asia* (Seoul: IFANS, 1994).

6. Calder and Ye suggest employment of the critical juncture approach, which combines the analytical strengths of realism and historical institutionalism in explaining the creation of regional bodies. They emphasize the incentive structure of key decision makers at fluid moments of decision making. In doing so, this approach gives more weight to the variable of domestic politics, such as the motives and interests of individual countries' political leadership. See Kent Calder and Min Ye, "Regionalism and Critical Junctures: Explaining the 'Organization Gap' in Northeast Asia," *Journal of East Asian Studies* 4 (2004): 191–226.

7. Barry Buzan, "Security Architecture in Asia: The Interplay of Regional and Global Levels," *Pacific Review* 16 (2003): 155–61. Buzan points out that the ARF was formed because the United States ended its long-standing opposition to multilateral security dialogue in the region when less was at stake strategically and more was at stake economically in East Asia. The ASEAN countries were also disappointed with that body's inability to construct itself as a counterweight to China, and therefore saw the need to try to socialize China and make it a good citizen through the ARF.

8. Hiwatari argues that the compatibility of the East Asian countries' policy preferences and their domestic financial systems and external balance positions have caused these countries to devise bilateral and international arrangements rather than regional alternatives. See Nobuhiro Hiwatari, "Embedded Policy Preferences and the Formation of International Arrangements after the Asian Financial Crisis," *Pacific Review* 16 (2003): 331–50.

9. Paul Bowles, "Asia's Post-Crisis Regionalism: Bringing the State Back in, Keeping the United States Out," *Review of International Political Economy* 9 (Summer 2002): 244–70.

10. Stuart Harris, "Asian Multinational Institutions and Their Response to the Asian Economic Crisis: The Regional and Global Implications," *Pacific Review* 13 (2000): 495–516, passage cited on 513.

11. Victor Cha, "Positive and Preventive Rationales for Korea-Japan Security Co-

operation: The American Perspective," in Ralph A. Cossa, ed., *US-Korea-Japan Relations: Building toward a 'Virtual Alliance'"* (Washington, D.C.: Center for Strategic and International Studies Press, 1999), 84–85.

12. Ministry of Foreign Affairs and Trade (MFAT), *1999 White Paper on Diplomacy* (Seoul: MFAT, July 2000), 230. In contrast to bureaucrats' expectations, Korea's first FTA experiment was not smooth due to opposition from domestic grape producers. Governments of Korea and Chile entered official negotiations in September 1999, but it took three years to conclude negotiations and another two years for the results to become effective, as they finally did on April 1, 2004.

13. Lee Sook-Jong, "Political Economy of Korea-Japan Free Trade Agreement: Change in Trade Policy and Industrial Restructuring," in Lee Sook-Jong, ed., *Korea-Japan Relations in Transition* (Seoul: Sejong Institute, 2002), 37–78.

14. The EAVG is composed of 26 scholars, businessmen, and former or incumbent public officials, 2 from each of the 13 members of ASEAN Plus Three.

15. Chung Jae-wan et al., *ASEAN PLUS THREE Economic Trend and South Korea's Economic Cooperation* (in Korean) (Seoul: Korea Institute of External Economy, Policy Data, 2004).

16. The Framework Agreement on Comprehensive Economic Cooperation, a legal instrument to govern future ASEAN-China economic cooperation, covers cooperation in goods, services, and investment and other relevant areas. The inception year 2010 was set for China and the six original ASEAN states of Brunei, Indonesia, Malaysia, the Philippines, Singapore, and Thailand, and 2015 was set for the remaining less developed members, Cambodia, Laos, Myanmar, and Vietnam.

17. Sheng Lijun, "China-ASEAN Free Trade Area: Origins, Developments and Strategic Motivations," working paper (Singapore: Institute of Southeast Asian Studies, 2003).

18. Christopher R. Hughes, "Nationalism and Multilateralism in Chinese Foreign Policy: Implications for Southeast Asia," *Pacific Review* 18 (March 2005): 119–35.

19. See the brochure *Presidential Committee on Northeast Asian Cooperation Initiative,* available at www.nabh.go.kr.

20. See Ministry of Foreign Affairs and Trade (MOFAT), "Trends of Exports and Imports by Region" (in Korean), available at www.mofat.go.kr. Japan accounted for 8.9 percent of Korea's total exports and 20.3 percent of its total imports in 2003. In 2004, Japan's shares were 8.5 percent and 20.5 percent, respectively.

21. Korea Export-Import Bank, *Oversea Investment Trends for 2005* (in Korean), 2006, available at www.koreaexim.go.kr.

22. Ministry of Commerce, Industry and Energy, *Foreign Direct Investment Statistics, 2005,* available at www.mocie.go.kr.

23. T. J. Pempel, "International Finance and Asian Regionalism," *Pacific Review* 13 (2000): 57–72, passages cited on 59 and 70.

24. Ministry of Foreign Affairs and Trade (MOFAT), *Roadmap to Pursue FTA* (in Korean) (Seoul: MOFAT, September 2003).

25. Chung Jin-Young, "Northeast Asian Economic Cooperation and South Korea's FTA Strategy: Policy Appraisal of Roh Government" (in Korean), National Strategy Panel Report 12 (Seoul: East Asian Institute, January 2006).

26. Nick Bisley, "The End of East Asian Regionalism?" *Journal of East Asian Affairs* 17 (Spring/Summer 2003): 148–69, passage cited on 157–58.

27. Helge Haveem, "Political Regionalism: Master or Servant of Economic Internationalization?" in Bjorn Hettne, Andras Inotai, and Osvaldo Sunkel, eds., *Globalism and the New Regionalism* (London: Palgrave Macmillan, 1999), 86–87.

28. Nationalism and bilateralism with the United States in East Asia are often given as reasons for the missing collective identity that is critical for building regional institutions. For example, see Christopher Hemmer and Peter Katzenstein, "Why Is There No NATO in Asia? Collective Identity, Regionalism and Multilateralism," *International Organization* 56 (2002): 575–607.

29. Buzan, "Security Architecture in Asia," 163.

Part III · Policy Implications

CHAPTER 9

A New Order in East Asia?

G. John Ikenberry

EAST ASIA IS A REGION IN TRANSITION—to what, no one is sure, but change is afoot. The old order in East Asia was organized around American military and economic dominance, anchored in the U.S.-Japan alliance; for 50 years it provided stability, security, and open markets as Japan, South Korea, and other Asian countries developed, democratized, and joined the wider modernized world. The worry today is that the new order in Asia will not be orderly at all but rather marked by a return to unstable rivalry among the great powers as China, Japan, and the United States compete for security and influence. In the worst case, East Asia could come to look like Europe in the 1870s, when British hegemony was giving way to power transitions, security dilemmas, military competition, and a struggle for mastery of the West.

This is not a future that the United States and its allies in the region should welcome. Indeed, the challenge is to take advantage of this moment of transition to nudge the region in a different direction—toward something more like Europe of the late 1940s, a moment when the war-weary European states made monumental decisions to build a regional order around multilateral frameworks of cooperation and binding economic and security ties. In East Asia, new grand bargains and regional institutional arrangements are similarly needed if the rapid shifts in power and heightened nationalism are to be channeled in stabilizing and peaceful directions.

The most potent drivers of change in East Asia are the rise of China and the "normalization" of Japan. The rapid growth of China and the spread of its influence across the region is one of the great dramas of the twenty-first century. So, too, is Japan's search for a mature sense of national identity and statehood—and for the traditional rights of sovereignty and self-defense that come with it. Each of these grand developments alone has the potential to jeopardize stable relations in the region, but together they threaten to create vicious circles of antagonism and insecurity.

Other developments in the region are also undermining the old American-led order. The flourishing of democracy and populist politics in South Korea has made it easier for that country's leaders to question its client status and dependence on alliance with the United States. The growth and integration of East Asia's regional economy has also reduced the centrality of American markets and investment and refocused commercial relations on China. Meanwhile, the rise of India and the return of Russia have expanded the geopolitical "space" of Asia and enveloped it in the wider array of Eurasian great power politics. Finally, America's own changing global security priorities and alliance thinking, driven by its war on terror, have created new uncertainties and controversies in the region about Washington's long-term security ties and commitments to the region.

Despite these dramatic changes, the U.S.-Japan alliance remains strong. But increasingly its health and welfare will depend on the building of a new East Asian order that accommodates and softens the impact of a rising China and allows Japan to normalize without triggering new spirals of conflict. The trick will be to hold on to the U.S.-Japan alliance—and the other bilateral security pacts that have formed—while looking for ways to embed them in new layers of regional multilateral arrangements.

Put simply, both China's rise and Japan's normalization need to proceed in tandem with new commitments by both their governments to strengthened regional institutions that bind them to a common vision for an East Asian order. Germany's experience of reintegration and normalization after the Second World War and after unification provides the most relevant model for both China and Japan. And the United States needs to work with the other East Asian nations to create a regional multilateral security organization around which China, Japan, and the United States can make commitments of nonaggression, signal reassurance and restraint, and establish ongoing security dialogues. Such a grouping would not replace America's bilateral security partnerships, but rather would serve as a multilateral vehicle to make them more credible and durable.

In this chapter, I look back at the logic of the old East Asian order and the forces eroding it. Next, I look more closely at the rise of China and the normalization of Japan as developments that are propelling change in the region. Finally, I present the argument that both China and Japan can advance their interests—and the region can be made more stable—if the two countries work to develop a regional security institution that allows them to bind themselves to their neighbors and signal restraint. I argue that the United States, too, has incentives to strengthen the regional security architecture so as to further embed its presence in East Asia.

The Logic of Order in East Asia

There is a widespread view that the postwar East Asian system of economics, politics, and security is not well organized. The contrast with Europe is striking. Europe engineered a stable postwar peace built around a Franco-German accord and layers of regional institutions—the North Atlantic Treaty Organization (NATO), the European Union, the Organization for Security Cooperation in Europe, the Council of Europe, and others. The political movement for a new European constitution has faltered, but the European Union continues to represent a deeply integrated region with an expanding judicial, parliamentary, bureaucratic, and intergovernmental infrastructure. It is now commonplace to call Western Europe a zone of Kantian peace. In contrast, East Asia is seen as "ripe for rivalry."[1] No legally binding, regionwide multilateral institutions exist there. Deep historical antagonisms abound, along with conflicting economic systems, divided and disputed territories, and rapidly shifting power relationships.[2]

Yet, partly by accident and partly by design, a relatively stable and peaceful order did emerge in East Asia over the past half century. It is an order organized around "hard" bilateralism and "soft" multilateralism. At its core is the U.S.-Japan alliance and the wider system of bilateral alliances that connect the United States to Korea, Taiwan, and other Asian countries. Supplementing this security system are a variety of soft regional dialogues, including the (Asia-Pacific Economic Cooperation) APEC, the Association of Southeast Asian Nations (ASEAN) Regional Forum, ASEAN Plus Three, and the Asian Summit.[3] In effect, the security order is built around the American alliance system and the economic order is built around a trans-Pacific trade and investment system, one in which the United States is a major market destination and China is increasingly the low-cost workshop.

Embedded in this East Asian order is a set of grand political bargains between the United States and the countries in the region—bargains that are also embedded in America's relations with Europe. One is the realist bargain, which grows out of America's Cold War grand strategy. The United States provides its European and Asian partners with security protection and access to American markets, technology, and supplies within an open world economy. In return, these countries agree to be reliable partners that provide diplomatic, economic, and logistical support for the United States as it leads the wider international order. Another is a liberal bargain that addresses the uncertainties of American power. East Asian and European states agree to accept American leadership and operate within an agreed-upon political-economic system. In return, the United States opens itself up and binds itself to its partners. In effect, the United States builds an institutionalized coalition of partners and reinforces the stability of these long-term mutually beneficial relations by making itself more "user friendly"—that is, by playing by the rules and creating ongoing political processes with these other states that facilitate consultation and joint decision making. The United States makes its power safe for the world, and in return the world agrees to live within the American system. These bargains date from the 1940s but continue to undergird the order that has arisen since the Cold War.

The system of "hub-and-spokes" alliances has its roots in the early Cold War and in the failure of multilateral security arrangements that were intended to mirror the Atlantic security pact. The U.S.-Japan alliance was intended to deter the expansion of Soviet power and communism more generally in the Asia-Pacific. This Cold War anticommunist goal led the United States to use its occupation of Japan and its military victory in the Pacific to actively shape the region—and it did so more successfully in Northeast Asia than in Southeast Asia. Japan, in turn, has made its bilateral alliance with the United States into the cornerstone of its own postwar regional foreign policy.[4]

From the outset, this bilateral security order has been intertwined with the evolution of regional economic relations. The United States facilitated Japanese economic reconstruction after the war and created markets for Japanese exports, particularly after the closing of China in 1949. The United States actively promoted imports of Japanese goods into the United States during the 1950s to encourage Japanese postwar economic growth and political stability. The United States took the lead in helping Japan find new commercial relations and raw material sources in Southeast Asia to substitute for the loss of Chinese and Korean markets.[5] In effect, Japan and Germany were twin junior partners of the United States during this period, stripped of their military capacities and reorganized as engines of world economic growth. Containment in Asia came to be based on the growth and integration of Japan in the wider noncommunist Asian regional economy—what Secretary of State Dean Acheson called the "great crescent" in referring to the countries arrayed from Japan through Southeast Asia to India. "In East Asia," as the historian Bruce Cumings writes, "American planners envisioned a regional economy driven by revived Japanese industry, with assured continental access to markets and raw materials for its exports."[6] This strategy served to link together threatened noncommunist states along the crescent, create strong economic connections between the United States and Japan, and lessen the importance of European colonial holdings in the area. The United States actively aided Japan in reestablishing a regional economic sphere in Asia, allowing it to prosper and play a regional leadership role within the larger American postwar order. Japanese economic growth, the expansion of regional and world markets, and the fighting of the Cold War went together.

The American security guarantee to its partners in East Asia provided a national security rationale for Japan to open its markets. Free trade helped cement the alliance, and in turn the alliance helped settle economic disputes. The export-oriented development strategies of Japan and the other Asian "tigers" depended on America's willingness to accept imports and huge trade deficits, which alliance ties made politically tolerable. In essence, the postwar order in East Asia has been built according to an American-style hegemonic logic: the United States has exported security and imported goods. It is an order in which the U.S.-Japan alliance, together with the wider hub-and-spokes system of bilateral security ties, has provided the hidden support beams for the wider region.[7]

Over the decades, this American-led system has been quite functional for both the United States and its partners. This is true in at least four respects. First, the hub-and-spokes system of alliances provides the political and geographical foundation for the projection of American influence into the region. With forward bases and security commitments across the region, the United States has established itself as the leading power in East Asia. Second, the bilateral alliances bind the United States to the region, establishing fixed commitments and mechanisms that increase the certainty and predictability of the exercise of American power and reducing worry in the region about American comings and goings. Third, the alliance ties create channels of access for Japan and other security partners to Washington. In effect, the alliances provide institutionalized "voice opportunities" for these countries. Finally, the U.S.-Japan alliance in particular has played a more specific and crucial role: namely, it has allowed Japan to be secure without the necessity of becoming a traditional military power. Japan could be defended while remaining a "civilian power," and this meant that Japan could rebuild and reenter the region without triggering dangerous security dilemmas.[8]

In these ways, the U.S.-Japan alliance and the system of bilateral alliances have been more than defense arrangements; they have also served as a political architecture for the wider system. Through this system, American power has been linked to Japan and rendered more predictable, while

Japan has been able to reassure its neighbors, integrate into the region, and pioneer a civilian pathway to growth and influence. In effect, in the postwar era, if Japan played the role of Germany in East Asia, the United States played the role of France. Just as the Franco-German partnership was the linchpin for the reintegration of Germany into Europe, the U.S.-Japan alliance was the linchpin for Japan's reentry into Asia. China's unspoken support for the U.S.-Japan alliance over the decades reflects the fact that the stabilization and reassurance functions of the alliance were widely appreciated in the region.

Even today, as change erodes aspects of this order, this old logic of order still has its virtues. Indeed, it is hard to envisage a wholly new logic of order for East Asia that is equally functional. It is difficult to imagine a peaceful and workable regional system without these bilateral security underpinnings and the continuing hegemonic presence of the United States. Looking into the future, the challenge will be to adapt this regional order to accommodate the rise of China and the normalization of Japan, but to do so in ways that retain the virtues of the old order.

Caging a Rising China

The rise of China presents a fundamental challenge to this postwar East Asian order. During the Cold War era, China operated largely outside its regional frameworks and bargains. But in the past decade, because of rapid and sustained growth and increasingly activist diplomacy, China has moved to a position squarely inside the region, and its power and influence continue to expand.[9]

China's growing presence in the region has characteristics of a classic "power transition," that is, a moment when a rising state confronts an older and established international or regional order. Such moments are fraught with danger.[10] The rise of post-Bismarck Germany in the late nineteenth century—and the ensuing rivalry among the great powers, along with arms races, instabilities, realignments, and a 30-year war between England and Germany—is the classic case. Germany's ascent began with unification under Bismarck in 1870 and the rapid growth of its economy. In 1870, Britain had a 3 to 1 advantage in economic power over Germany, but by 1903 Germany had pulled ahead of Britain in overall economic and military power. The rise of German power triggered the classic dynamics of a power transition: as Germany unified and grew, so too did its dissatisfactions, demands, and ambitions; and as it grew more powerful, security dilemmas emerged and Germany increasingly appeared as a threat to other great powers in Europe. The result, of course, was a European war.[11]

Of course, not all power transitions generate war or overturn the old order. In the early decades of the twentieth century, Britain ceded power to a rapidly growing America without great conflict or a rupture in relations. Japan's GDP grew from 5 percent of the American GNP in the late 1940s to over 60 percent of its size in the early 1990s without challenging the existing international order. Clearly there are different types of ascent to power and power transitions. Some states (e.g., Japan) have grown rapidly in economic or geopolitical power and, in the end, accommodated themselves to the existing international order. Other great powers (e.g., post-Bismarck Germany) have risen up and indeed sought to challenge the existing order of great powers. Some moments of power transition led to the breakdown of the old order and the establishment of a new global or regional hierarchy of order (e.g., in Britain after 1815 and in America after 1945). Other moments of power transition resulted not in a transformed international order but in more limited adjustments in the regional and global systems (e.g., in Japan and Germany in the postwar era).[12]

Certainly a variety of factors shape the way in which power transitions unfold.[13] The character of a rising state's "dissatisfaction" can vary. This is true in regard to subjective judgments of leaders about their interests and desires for a greater governance role. But there is also variation in the ability of rising states to in fact advance their expanding economic and political goals within an existing international or regional order. Moreover, the actual ability of rising states to experience gains from challenging and overturning the existing order will vary. In the current age, in which China, the United States, and other great powers possess nuclear weapons, the costs and benefits—indeed, the rationality—of hegemonic war are reduced to essentially zero. Likewise, the power transition dynamic is typically seen to play out between the world's dominant state and a rising state. It is seen as a dyadic drama between two states. But the actual power of the leading state is much greater if its power is effectively aggregated with the power of other great powers allied with it. In this sense, a rising state faces not just a lead state but—at least potentially—a wider coalition of status quo great powers arrayed around the hegemonic state. Finally, the character of the international or regional order—and the degree to which it is based on coercion and consent—will matter. It will influence how a rising state calculates its interests and the choices it makes to either integrate with or challenge the order. It will influence the ability of the leading state to aggregate power and to enforce the rules and maintain a stable international order.

The institutional character of the international or regional order can also matter, providing a framework that helps reduce the suspicion or fear that arises during the power transition. Regardless of the intentions of the rising state, its neighbors have reasons to worry about the consequences of adverse shifts in the distribution of power. This is the "security dilemma" problem; a state that is acting in simply defensive ways can trigger fears and defensive responses that, in turn, trigger fears and defensive responses in the first state. The result is a spiral of insecurity and security competition that makes arms races and dangers of war more likely.[14] This is the case even if war itself is removed as a possibility. A regional East Asian security framework can play a role in reducing uncertainty and providing a mechanism through which both China and its neighbors can signal restraint and commitment.

Indeed, as China becomes more powerful, two things are likely to happen. China will want to use its growing capabilities to reshape the rules and institutions of the regional order to better reflect its interests, and it will increasingly be seen as a security threat to other countries in the region. The result will be growing tension, distrust, security dilemmas, and conflict. China presents a formidable and potentially troubling specter— 1.3 billion people, nuclear weapons, 9 percent economic growth, a robust nationalist spirit, and expanding regional aspirations—and it is also a rapidly ascending great power that is emerging largely outside the established regional order.

Accordingly, the current regional order threatens to unravel. East Asian countries will likely find themselves "picking sides." For example, South Korea might increasingly ask itself whether the United States should remain its security patron or whether its long-term future lies in operating within a Chinese-centered regional order. Some countries would flip toward China, and others would flip toward the United States. The United States might find itself increasingly under pressure to hold on to its strategic partners and forward-based positions in the region. The specific scenarios are numerous, but they all include stories about the coming crisis of the old order.

The challenge of the United States is not to block China's entry into the regional order but to help shape its terms, looking for opportunities to strike strategic bargains at various moments along the shifting power trajectories and encroaching geopolitical spheres. The main bargain that the United States will want to strike with China is this: to accommodate a rising China by offering it status and position within the regional order in return for Beijing's accepting and accommodating Washington's core strategic interests, which include remaining a dominant security provider in East Asia.[15]

In striking this strategic bargain, the United States will also want to try to build multilateral institutional arrangements in East Asia that will tie China down and bind it to the wider region. China has already grasped the utility of this strategy in recent years, and it is now actively seeking to reassure and co-opt its neighbors by offering to embed itself in regional institutions such as the ASEAN Plus Three and the Asian Summit. This, of course, is precisely what the United States did in the decades after World War II, building and operating within layers of regional and global economic, political, and security institutions, thereby making itself more predictable and approachable and reducing the incentives that other states would otherwise have to resist or undermine the United States by building countervailing coalitions.

Perhaps more relevant to a rising China is the case of Germany on the eve of unification in 1989. The prospect of a unified—and more powerful—Germany worried the leaders of Britain, France, and Russia. In moving forward with unification, Chancellor Helmut Kohl signaled to his neighbors that if they acquiesced to unification, Germany would redouble its commitment to European integration and the Atlantic security community. German Foreign Minister Hans-Dietrich Genscher articulated the German view in a January 1990 speech: "We want to place the process of German unification in the context of EC [European Community] integration, of the CSCE [Conference on Security and Cooperation in Europe] process, the West-East partnership for stability, the construction of the common European house and the creation of a peaceful European order from the Atlantic to the Urals." Germany's message was clear: to gain acquiescence to its unification and growth in power, Germany was prepared to further bind itself to its neighbors.[16]

Germany, in effect, pursued a strategy that can be called "institutional self-binding," a strategy in which a great power engages in a pattern of institutionalized strategic restraint toward its weaker neighbors in exchange for the latter's collective recognition of the leading state's economic and security interests and leadership. This is also what the United States did after World War II, when it was at the zenith of its power and set out to build an international order that would draw in friendly—but weaker—states in a stable and open American-centered system. The United States sponsored the creation of a wide variety of postwar institutions—economic, political, and security—and agreed to operate within them. Through these institutions the United States bound itself to other states, and they, in turn, agreed to affiliate themselves with the United States.[17]

The challenge for the United States is to encourage China to respond in this same enlightened way. But to do this, China needs an institutional body or mechanism to which it can bind itself. That is, the region needs a formal and articulated regional security organization into which China can integrate. Such an organization need not have the features of a multilateral system of alliances; the countries in the region are not ready for this.

But what is needed is a security organization that has at its center a treaty of nonaggression and mechanisms for periodic consultation. To be sure, there are currently a variety of regional institutional frameworks that already offer China an ability to send signals of restraint and commitment to the region—institutions such as the ASEAN Regional Forum, the Asian Summit, and APEC. But a dedicated regional security organization in Northeast Asia would provide a more explicit institutional setting that would allow a rising China to tie itself to its neighbors.

The United States will want to insist that a new East Asian regional security organization complement rather than supplant its bilateral security alliances. Moreover, the creation of a new East Asian security organization that includes China need not be inconsistent with simultaneous efforts to strengthen ties with America's democratic allies in the region. This is so for two reasons. First, because China's future is so uncertain, the United States will naturally want to hedge China's relations and nurture and reinforce its own relations with democratic states in the region. But also, as Professor Thomas Christensen of Princeton University argues, China's current willingness to pursue an engagement strategy in the region and participate in regional multilateral institutions has been triggered at least in part by Beijing's worries that the United States will seek to contain and counterbalance China. If this is so, the two tracks of American policy will work together, drawing China into a more institutionalized regional order and strengthening the bulwark of the alliances among democratic East Asian states.

Japan—Lost in Transition

As Japan seeks to become a more "normal" great power, it also increasingly poses a challenge to the old East Asian order, and the regional solution to this problem is similar to that for dealing with China. Japan, too, has incentives to bind itself to a regional security order in ways that reduce the worries and security dilemmas that otherwise will emerge.

For more than 50 years, Japan has pursued a strategy of development that has emphasized economic mastery and growth rather than a return to geopolitical prominence. It turned the necessity of the American occupation and the imposition of a constitution mandating peace into a political virtue. Behind the hedge of protection provided by the U.S.-Japanese security treaty, Japan pioneered a "civilian" return to the global political stage. Along the way, it came to celebrate its "peace constitution" and define itself as a civilian great power that would invest in international peace and security under the auspices of the United Nations. It has funded roughly 20 percent of the UN budget, supported international commitments to human security, and been a generous provider of official development assistance.[18]

This distinctive approach to Japanese security and political identity was made possible by the character and organization of the postwar American-centered international order. Both Japan and Germany were reintegrated into the advanced industrial world as "semisovereign" powers; that is, they accepted unprecedented constitutional limits on their military capacity and independence.[19] As such, they became unusually dependent on an array of Western regional and multilateral economic and security institutions. The Western political order in which they were embedded was integral to their stability and functioning. The Christian Democrat Walther Leisler Kiep argued in 1972 that "the German-American alliance . . . is not merely one aspect of modern German history, but a decisive element as a result of its preeminent place in our politics. In effect, it provides a second constitution for our country."[20] The same is certainly true for Japan. More than a few Japanese observers have called the U.S.-Japan alliance an integral part of the Japanese constitution. Western economic and security institutions—the alliance partnerships with America in particular—provide Germany and Japan with a political bulwark of stability that far transcends their more immediate and practical purposes.

By all measures, this distinctive approach to postwar development has been a success, marked by extraordinary material and political advancement. Despite the long economic slump of the 1990s, Japan has followed a dramatic postwar trajectory of economic growth, becoming in the 1980s the second largest economy in the world and enjoying one of the most advanced standards of living. Japan also found a way to shield itself from the suspicions of its neighbors and the burdens of its history. Under the American security umbrella, Japan did not need to rearm or present the region with a "normal" Japan with a traditional great power military identity. The reconstituted Japanese political identity is widely admired. Recent global public opinion polls, for example, have shown that Japan is seen around the world as one of the most admired and respected countries.[21] But this is not the case within Northeast Asia; Japan is still estranged from its own region.[22]

The problem is essentially that Japan has not been able to extinguish the suspicions and grievances that still flicker in China and Korea as a result of its imperial militarist past. While postwar Germany has been able to put the "history issue" to rest, postwar Japan has not. The result is that, 62 years after it surrendered and began its long and peaceful return to the international community, Japan remains isolated and incapable of providing leadership in a region that is quickly being transformed because of the rise of China.

But, to make this problem worse, Japan—with the encouragement of Washington—has embarked on the long path to normalization as a great power. Reform of the Japanese constitution—specifically, amending Article 9, which prohibits the use of force—is at the center of this historic undertaking. In one sense, Japanese normalization is an inevitable process of reclaiming the nation's identity and sovereign rights. This has been an aspiration of Japan for a long time. It has been part of the ruling party's platform since Prime Minister Junichiro Koizumi took office, and Japanese debate about reforming Article 9 dates back to at least the first Iraq war. The debate within establishment circles has been about providing Japan with a legal basis for participation in "collective security" within the framework of the U.S.-Japan alliance and the United Nations. In this narrow sense, there is support in Japan for country's playing a stronger role in UN-sponsored peacekeeping, humanitarian intervention, and conflict prevention. In this cautious approach to regaining sovereign rights, the struggle has been to find a Japanese "third way" between constitutional pacifism and the robust militarization expected of a great power.

This moderate form of normalization is not primarily a response to growing Japanese nationalism. The Japanese scholar Masaru Tamamoto sees the mainstream debate as an issue of "statehood," that is, the ability of Japan to use force in self-defense as an expression and right of state sovereignty. It is a matter of reclaiming the lost sovereignty of the Japanese state rather than a response to swelling public nationalism or patriotic emotion. Tamamoto says:

> Today's dominant political and intellectual voices [in Japan] deem that Japan had ceased to be a state after World War II. The argument is simple: Recovery of statehood means reacquiring the right to use force as an instrument of state policy. In a sense, the rise of such thinking is understandable. After all, Japan is maneuvering between the United States and China, two countries that are extremely sensitive about sovereign statehood, and whose policies are driven by the equation of sovereignty and national security.[23]

Japan's search for a more modest third way toward normalization also recognizes that after the war a Japanese national identity did in fact emerge —a postwar identity organized around democracy, economic achievement, and support for global liberal ideals. Japan has fashioned a role for itself as a unique great power, and it will continue to evolve in that role.

In the meantime, the stakes of normalization have grown. The North Korean nuclear crisis, the rise of China, and America's post–September 11 foreign policy have created pressures within Japan to move faster and further in the direction of a traditional military-capable great power. The administration of President George W. Bush and others in Washington have urged Tokyo to take new steps, appealing to Japan to "step up to the plate" and be a more fully capable ally. Even before September 11, the United States urged Japan to break out of its postwar straitjacket. The influential "Armitage Report," issued in October 2000 by a bipartisan American group of Japanese policy specialists and diplomats, called for Japan to become, in effect, America's Great Britain in Asia.[24] Japan would be a more normal military power but would be tightly tied to the United States in an alliance with a wider regional and global reach than at present. Bush administration officials have spoken of the need for Japan to revise its constitution. Japanese diplomats feel this pressure from Washington, particularly given the Bush administration's seeming ambivalence about fixed and formal alliances.

But the British model for Japanese normalization is not the third way envisaged by Japanese moderates. After all, Britain has nuclear weapons and is constitutionally unfettered from the use of force. If Japan adopted the British model, it would reassert its traditional military rights and capabilities and position itself to deploy forces alongside the United States across the region and around the world.[25]

This sort of normalization would clearly be provocative, and it threatens to generate security competition, arms races, and political instability in East Asia. A more "normal" Japan, defined in this more far-reaching sense, would make the U.S.-Japan alliance a more controversial institution within Asia. For decades, this bilateral alliance has been seen as the linchpin of stability in the region. It now threatens to be the lightning rod of instability. This is not what we should want Japanese normalization to look like in East Asia. Japanese normalization along these lines would continue to antagonize China and Korea, exacerbating and postponing the resolution of Japan's "historical issues" and feeding nationalist passions on all sides.

It is less important for Japan to put itself in a position to field combat troops in far-off places than to help provide global public goods and support aid, trade, and development in troubled parts of the world. Japan should be a "responsible" great power, but it is wrong to equate responsibility with the ability to use force. Will Japan be behaving responsibly if it alters its constitution so that it can more fully join the Bush administration's war on terror, or will it be behaving responsibly if it engages America on its own terms and articulates its own vision of security and international community?

Japan must find a workable formula that allows it to regain its full rights of sovereignty, maintain its security relationship with the United States, and foster stable relations with China. Turning Japan into the Britain of East Asia is not such a formula. A better model, again, is Germany. Just as a rising China should tie its growing power to commitments to strengthened regional security cooperation, so should Japan tie normalization to commitments to a new regional cooperative security organization.

The United States should encourage Japanese Prime Minister Yasuo Fukuda and future leaders to change direction. As a signal to the region that Japan wants to put the "history issue" behind it, Japan should take the lead in calling for talks to lay the groundwork for a new regional security organization, one that would include the United States and be consistent with existing bilateral security alliances. The heart of the new organization might be a treaty of nonaggression among its members, together with formal consultations on defense spending and arms deployments.

The United States should not encourage Japan to renationalize and remilitarize its national security identity so that it can be a full partner in America's war on terror. Rather, the United States should help build an East Asian regional order that can accommodate both a rising China and a Japan that has a sense of its own statehood. The United States has been doing this with regard to Germany within the context of the European Union and NATO. On the other side of the world, the United States and the East Asian countries need to invent regional institutional structures to help both China and Japan continue to redefine their political and security identities without blowing the region apart.

Conclusion: Reinventing American Leadership

The ways in which China and Japan define their security identities and pursue their objectives in East Asia will in part be shaped by the United States. If these countries are to pursue strategies of institutional self-binding, the United States will need to be engaged in the region, reaffirming its alliance ties and playing a constructive role in shaping the regional security architecture. This will itself be a challenge.

Indeed, America's position in East Asia is also in transition. The rise of a unipolar American order after the Cold War has not triggered a global backlash, but it has unsettled relationships worldwide. Asians and Europeans worry about the steadiness of American leadership. Some governments and peoples around the world resent the extent and intrusiveness of American power, markets, and culture. Aside from diffuse hatreds and resentments, the practical reality for many states around the world is that they need the United States more than it needs them—or so it would seem. The political consequences of a unipolar superpower seemed all too obvious. The Bush administration found that it could walk away from treaties and agreements with other countries—on global warming, arms control, trade, business regulation, and so forth—and suffer fewer consequences than its partners. But to successfully conduct a campaign against terrorism, the United States now needs the rest of the world. This is a potential boon to cooperation around the globe. To pursue its objectives—fighting terrorism but also managing the world economy and maintaining stable security relations—the United States will need to rediscover and renew the political bargains upon which its hegemonic leadership is based. East Asia will be a critical location for this process.

Notes

This chapter is an expanded version of G. John Ikenberry, "American Strategy in the New Asia," *The American Interest* 2 (September–October 2006): 89–94.

1. Aaron Friedberg, "Ripe for Rivalry: Prospects for Peace in a Multipolar Asia," *International Security* 18 (1993): 5–33.
2. For an overview of the theoretical debates related to East Asian regional relations, see G. John Ikenberry and Michael Mastanduno, eds., *International Relations Theory and the Asia Pacific* (New York: Columbia University Press, 2003).
3. For recent studies of East Asian regionalism, see Gilbert Rozman, ed., *Northeast Asia's Stunted Regionalism: Bilateral Distrust in the Shadow of Globalization* (New York: Cambridge University Press, 2004); Ellis S. Krauss and T. J. Pempel, *Beyond Bilateralism: U.S.-Japan Relations in the New Asia-Pacific* (Stanford, Calif.: Stanford University Press, 2004); J. J. Suh, Peter J. Katzenstein, and Allen Carlson, eds., *Rethinking Security in East Asia: Identity, Power and Efficiency* (Stanford, Calif.: Stanford University Press, 2004); Edward Lincoln, *East Asian Economic Regionalism* (Washington, D.C.: Brookings Institution, 2004); Muthiah Alagappa, ed., *Asian Security Order: Instrumental and Normative Features* (Stanford, Calif.: Stanford University Press, 2003); and G. John Ikenberry and Takashi Inoguchi, eds., *The Uses of Institutions: The U.S., Japan, and Governance in East Asia* (New York: Palgrave, 2007).
4. See G. John Ikenberry and Takashi Inoguchi, eds., *Reinventing the Alliance: U.S.-Japan Security Partnership in an Era of Change* (New York: Palgrave, 2003). For discussions of the origins and character of the U.S.-Japan alliance, see Michael Schaller, *The American Occupation of Japan: The Origins of the Cold War in Asia* (New York: Oxford University Press, 1985); John Dower, *Embracing Defeat: Japan in the Wake of World War II* (New York: Norton, 2000); and John Swenson-Wright, *Unequal Allies? United States Security and Alliance Policy Toward Japan, 1945–1960* (Stanford, Calif.: Stanford University Press, 2005).
5. Michael Schaller, "Securing the Great Crescent: Occupied Japan and the Origins of Containment in Southeast Asia," *Journal of American History* 69 (September 1982): 392–414.

6. Bruce Cumings, "Japan's Position in the World System," in Andrew Gordon, ed., *Postwar Japan as History* (Berkeley: University of California Press, 1993), 38.

7. For descriptions of this American hegemonic order in Asia, see G. John Ikenberry, "The Future of Liberal Hegemony in East Asia," *Australian Journal of International Affairs* 58 (September 2004): 353–67; Michael Mastanduno, "Incomplete Hegemony: The United States and Security Order in Asia," in Muthiah Alagappa, ed., *Managing Security in Asia* (Stanford, Calif.: Stanford University Press, 2002), 141–70; and Mark Beeson, "American Hegemony and Regionalism: The Rise of East Asia and the End of the Asia-Pacific," *Geopolitics* 11 (Winter 2006): 541–60.

8. For a more extended discussion of this global liberal hegemonic logic, see G. John Ikenberry, *After Victory: Institutions, Strategic Restraint, and the Rebuilding of Order after Major War* (Princeton, N.J.: Princeton University Press, 2001).

9. For a survey of China's activist diplomacy and growing involvement in the region, see David Shambaugh, "China Engages Asia: Reshaping the Regional Order," *International Security* 29 (2004): 64–99; and Evan Medeiros and R. Taylor Fravel, "China's New Diplomacy," *Foreign Affairs* 82 (2003): 22–35.

10. See Robert Gilpin, *War and Change in World Politics* (New York: Cambridge University Press, 1981); and E. H. Carr, *The Twenty Years Crisis, 1919–1939: An Introduction to the Study of International Relations* (New York: Harper and Row, 1964), 208–23.

11. Paul Kennedy, *The Rise and Fall of the Great Powers* (New York: Random House, 1987).

12. For a discussion of variations in the ascents of great powers, see Randall Schweller, "Managing the Rise of Great Powers: History and Theory," in Alastair Iain Johnston and Robert S. Ross, eds., *Engaging China: The Management of an Emerging Great Power* (New York: Routledge, 1999).

13. For a survey of different predictions that international relations theories make about the future of U.S.-China relations, see Aaron Friedberg, "The Future of U.S.-China Relations: Is Conflict Inevitable?" *International Security* 30 (2005): 7–45.

14. On the problem of the security dilemma, see Robert Jervis, "Cooperation under the Security Dilemma," *World Politics* 30 (January 1978): 167–214.

15. See Gerald Segal, "Tying China into the International System," *Survival* 37 (1995): 60–73.

16. See Philip Zelikow and Condoleezza Rice, *Germany Unified and Europe Transformed: A Study in Statecraft* (Cambridge, Mass.: Harvard University Press, 1995).

17. This argument is developed in Ikenberry, *After Victory.*

18. For depictions of the relationship between Japan's security partnership with the United States and its evolving postwar polity, see Richard Samuels, *"Rich Nation, Strong Army": National Security and the Technological Transformation of Japan* (Ithaca, N.Y.: Cornell University Press, 1996), and Michael Green, *Arm-*

ing Japan (New York: Columbia University Press, 1998). For a survey of Japan's developmental strategy, see Chalmers Johnson, *MITI and the Japanese Miracle: The Growth of Japanese Industrial Policy, 1925–1975* (Stanford, Calif.: Stanford University Press, 1982).

19. Peter J. Katzenstein and Yutaka Tsujinaka, " 'Bullying,' 'Buying,' and 'Binding': U.S.-Japanese Transnational Relations and Domestic Structures," in Thomas Risse-Kappen, ed., *Bringing Transnational Relations Back In* (Cambridge: Cambridge University Press, 1995), 79–111.

20. Thomas A. Schwartz, "The United States and Germany after 1945: Alliances, Transnational Relations, and the Legacy of the Cold War," *Diplomatic History* 19 (1995): 55.

21. In a recent BBC poll, Japan was found to be one of the most admired countries. As the report notes: "Japan received very high ratings. Of the 33 countries polled, a remarkable 31 gave a positive rating and 21 of these were a majority. On average 55 percent gave a positive rating and 18 percent a negative one. . . . The two exceptions were China and South Korea, where 71 and 54 percent, respectively, said that Japan is having a negative influence." BBC World Service Poll, reported March 6, 2007, available at http://news.bbc.co.uk/2/shared/bsp/hi/pdfs/06_03_07_perceptions.pdf.

22. Pew Global Attitudes Project, "Publics of Asian Powers Hold Negative Views of One Another," Report, September 21, 2006, available at http://news.bbc.co.uk/2/shared/bsp/hi/pdfs/06_03_07_perceptions.pdf.

23. Masaru Tamamoto, "After the Tsunami: How Japan Can Lead," *Far East Economic Review* 168 (January–February 2005): 10–18. See also Tamamoto, "How Japan Imagines China and Sees Itself," *World Policy Journal* 22 (Winter 2005–6): 55–62.

24. See "The United States and Japan: Advancing toward a Mature Partnership," INSS Special Report (Washington, D.C.: Institute for National Strategic Studies, National Defense University, October 2000). An updated report was released in 2007. See Richard L. Armitage and Joseph S. Nye, *The U.S.-Japan Alliance: Getting Asia Right through 2020* (Washington, D.C.: Center for Strategic and International Studies, February 2007).

25. See G. John Ikenberry and Michael O'Hanlon, "Japan Has Kept Asia Anxious Too Long," *Los Angeles Times,* August 16, 2001.

CHAPTER 10

The Security Architecture in Asia and American Foreign Policy

Francis Fukuyama

IN CONTRAST to the multilateral organizations that were established in Europe after World War II, the security architecture organized in Asia by the United States has been a hub-and-spokes system centered on Washington. This system was designed to meet the security challenges posed by global communism; now that we are well into the second decade after the end of the Cold War, the question naturally arises whether this security architecture is the right one to use in the face of present-day challenges, or whether it needs to be replaced or complemented by other types of institutions. As other contributors to this volume have noted, the number of multilateral regional organizations and initiatives has proliferated over the past several years with relatively little American input, including the Association of Southeast Asian Nations (ASEAN), the ASEAN Regional Forum (ARF), ASEAN Plus Three, the East Asian Summit, and the Chiang Mai Initiative, as well as a host of proposals for yet-to-be-implemented regional trade pacts. Most of these focus on economic issues, but they also have political implications, and often security-related consequences as well. Another multilateral security forum, the Six-Party Talks, emerged with U.S. encouragement to deal with the issue of North Korean nuclear weapons.

Apart from a quiet internal debate within the administration of U.S. President George W. Bush as to how seriously to take the Six-Party Talks, there has been a deafening silence from American policy makers with re-

gard to Asian multilateralism more broadly, a silence that has characterized the administrations of both Bush and President Bill Clinton.[1] It is not
clear, for example, what Washington makes of multilateral institutions like
ASEAN Plus Three that exclude the United States: is this an initiative the
United States opposes, or one that it wants to become part of? The Clinton administration expressed its disapproval of the idea of an Asian Monetary Fund that was floated in the wake of the 1997–98 financial crisis, but
did not oppose the Chiang Mai Initiative or come up with any ideas of its
own for stabilizing monetary systems in future crises. The Bush administration created the Six-Party Talks as a kind of improvisation to help the
nations most affected deal with the North Korean nuclear issue, but has
failed to propose other broader initiatives for regional cooperation.

Silence, along with a renewed commitment to existing political structures like the U.S.-Japan Security Treaty, may be all that is called for under
current circumstances. However, there are several reasons for thinking that
it is worthwhile to at least explore some new approaches.

Limitations of the Hub-and-Spokes System

The old hub-and-spokes system was designed at the beginning of the
Cold War as part of a broader containment strategy directed at several
specific military threats: those posed by the former Soviet Union, China,
North Korea, and North Vietnam and the national liberation movements
they supported. But the Soviet threat has disappeared, and the North Vietnamese won their war. North Korea remains an acute challenge, no longer
because of the conventional balance of power on the peninsula, but because of Pyongyang's nuclear program and its tendency to export military
technology without particular regard for end users. The combination of
nuclear weapons and ballistic missiles means that Japan is under direct nuclear threat from an unstable and erratic regime, which is more frighten-
ing in many respects than the much larger Soviet nuclear threat during the
Cold War.

What is dramatically different about the current situation, however, is
the changed posture of South Korea. Since the election of two left-wing
presidents, Kim Dae-jung and Roh Moo-hyun, and the initiation of Kim's
"sunshine" policy, South Korea has shifted from being a bastion of anti-
communism to seeking reconciliation and ultimate unification with North
Korea. This shift reflects a very deep generational change in attitudes among
Koreans; younger people in the South are increasingly nationalistic and
anti-American. Indeed, America and its military posture on the peninsula
are frequently blamed for prolonging Korea's political division. Despite

China's role as a supporter of the North, South Korean–Chinese relations have warmed considerably. Thus, in a curious way both the United States and Japan feel themselves directly threatened by North Korea in a way that South Korea does not—a reversal of the situation during the Cold War.

The South Korean spoke of the wheel is thus slowly rotting away. While elites in both South Korea and the United States have sought to keep their relationship on an even keel (for example, by Seoul's dispatch of troops to Iraq), the relationship has been described as a loveless marriage. It is entirely possible to imagine a spiral of misunderstanding emerging as Koreans blame the United States for excessive belligerence and the United States reacts to what it perceives as Korean ingratitude.

A second reason for thinking that the hub-and-spokes system may not be adequate at the present moment has to do with rising nationalism in China, Japan, and Korea and the need for these countries to be able to better deal with each other directly on issues related to history and national self-esteem. The potential for misunderstanding and conflict between South Korea, China, and Japan in the coming years is substantial, but may be mitigated if there are multiple avenues of communication between them.

Several recent incidents illustrate these latent tensions. Despite burgeoning bilateral trade between China and South Korea, relations between the two countries became strained in 2004 due to work by government-sponsored Chinese researchers who asserted that the ancient kingdom of Goguryeo, spanning the Chinese–North Korean border, was under Chinese dominion. The Koreans, by contrast, asserted that Goguryeo was 100 percent Korean, and the ensuing fight had to be papered over in a five-point accord negotiated by the countries' respective foreign ministries. China's motives for allowing publication of this article are unclear: the Chinese have made similar claims about the centrality of China in the history of other countries on their border, in line with rising Chinese nationalism. Allowing the article to be published was also possibly a reaction to loose talk in South Korea about a "greater Korea" that would include not just North and South Korea but the two to three million Koreans currently living in Manchuria.

Chinese-Korean distrust pales in comparison to the downward spiral in Chinese-Japanese relations since 2001, which began with Japanese Prime Minister Junichiro Koizumi's decision to visit each year the Yasukuni Shrine, where war dead are entombed, something that had last been done publicly in 1985 by Prime Minister Yasuhiro Nakasone.[2] At this point, it remains something of an enigma why China, which has generally bent over backward to persuade other countries in East Asia of its peaceful intentions, ratcheted up tensions with Japan during this period. At an August 2004 Asian Cup soccer game in Beijing, Chinese fans screamed "Kill! Kill! Kill!"

at the winning Japanese players and forced the team to leave China prematurely. This coincided with a petition campaign, led by younger, well-educated Chinese, to protest the idea of a Japanese seat on the United Nations Security Council, a drive that reportedly yielded over 44 million signatures across China.[3] In April 2005, the Chinese police stood by while anti-Japanese demonstrators protesting the revision of Japanese history books to soften the account of the Japanese occupation of China attacked the Japanese embassy in Beijing. As David Hale points out in his chapter, positive Japanese feelings about China were in decline in the decade between 1995 and 2005, found in only a third of the population. Although Koizumi's successor, Shinzo Abe, took steps to mend relations with China, the underlying Japanese failure to confront historical issues guarantees that they will continue to be irritants in Tokyo's relations with Beijing.

Underlying these popular emotions is a structural rivalry. Although the Japanese economy is currently larger than China's, the handwriting is clearly on the wall with regard to their ultimate relative positions. Japan's workforce, already only a tenth the size of China's, has been shrinking in absolute numbers, while China's continues to grow; barring major instability in China, it seems to be only a matter of time before that country will displace Japan as Asia's predominant power. The Chinese have also been irritated at Japan's increasing closeness both to Taiwan and to the United States and at the greater degree of military collaboration between Japan and the United States on issues such as missile defense. The two countries also have traditional territorial issues over oil drilling in the East China Sea, where potentially large economic interests are at stake.

Enmity between China and Japan has been mutually reinforcing. Since the revelation of prime ministerial visits to the Yasukuni Shrine in the 1980s, the Chinese government has traditionally used those visits and other manifestations of Japanese nationalism to make political demands of Tokyo; in the case of the signature campaign and embassy demonstrations, it apparently sought to use popular anti-Japanese feelings to turn up the heat on outstanding diplomatic issues like Japan's Security Council seat and the East China Sea dispute. But much of the anti-Japanese emotion in China is spontaneous, and in that instance it quickly got beyond the Chinese leadership's control. In sharp contrast to its skillful management of relations with ASEAN, China has deeply antagonized Japan, its largest Asian trade and investment partner in Asia. More important for the future, it has stimulated significant growth in Japanese nationalism and anti-Chinese feeling, thereby provoking the very things it wanted to prevent.

Then there are Japanese–South Korean relations. Like the Chinese, the Koreans have reacted very negatively to Koizumi's Yasukuni Shrine visits and to the textbook revisions. To an even greater degree than the United

States, Japan has issues with North Korea, concerning not just Pyongyang's nuclear weapons that can target Japan, but also the North Korean abductions of Japanese citizens that were revealed during Koizumi's September 2002 visit. The South Koreans, by contrast, have been seeking warmer relations with the North and find Japan's position not helpful to eventual reconciliation. In addition, Korea's growing economic and military weight, while less than that of China, remains a concern. In the mid-1990s, when doing research in Tokyo, I was told by a number of officers in the Japanese Self-Defense forces that in the event of Korean unification, the combined militaries of North and South Korea would be close to 10 times the size of Japan's armed forces. If Korean troop strength were not reduced dramatically at that point, they said, Japan would have to interpret this as a decision aimed against Japan and take appropriate defensive measures. Today, there is the added factor of nuclear weapons and what South Korea would do if it assumed joint possession of a North Korean bomb. In a recent Tokyo Shimbun poll, 80 Japanese Diet members said publicly that Japan should consider nuclearization in light of the North Korean threat. The remarks by former prime minister Abe in March 2007 denying that Korean "comfort women" had been coerced into prostitution by the Japanese army undercut his earlier efforts to mend fences with Seoul.

A final reason for considering a multilateral framework for Asia has to do with the rise of China as an economic power, its eventual rise as a military power, and the role of China within Asia. The hub-and-spokes system was designed to contain communism, but containment is not the best way to think about how the United States and other Asian countries should deal with China's rise.

China poses some new challenges for U.S. foreign policy precisely because it is complex and multidimensional in a way that the old communist threat was not. Great power rivals of the United States in the twentieth century, such as Nazi Germany and the former Soviet Union, constituted adversaries that were territorially aggressive, had unlimited aims, and were willing to use force to achieve their international ambitions. China is a different kind of power.[4] In many ways, it is playing by Western rules: its growth is powered by market capitalism, it has begun to engage international institutions like the United Nations and the World Trade Organization, and it presumably does not have unlimited ideological or territorial ambitions.[5] There is also a large area of shared interest between China and potential strategic competitors like the United States and Japan in terms of trade and investment interdependence.

If we assume that China will remain on its current economic and military growth path over the next two decades, surpassing Japan in absolute GDP and developing power capabilities that could challenge U.S. military predominance in Asia, what will Chinese goals be, and to what extent will Chinese ambitions be compatible with U.S. interests? It is certainly easy to imagine scenarios in which U.S.-Chinese conflict might occur, such as an unprovoked Chinese effort to conquer Taiwan or military aggression against other neighbors such as Japan or Korea. But is it also possible to imagine the United States accommodating a rising China, much as Britain accommodated a rising United States at the beginning of the twentieth century? The British case, after all, is the most notable recent example of a major power shift that did not produce a conflict between great powers.[6]

Even raising the British precedent suggests limits to the analogy. The United States and Britain shared a common ethnicity, culture, and historical tradition; the latter could look with equanimity on the growth of U.S. power because it saw America as broadly supportive of its global interests. China might approach a status something like this if it underwent a democratic revolution and became a developed liberal democracy, which is what many observers have been hoping for as the solution to the rising China problem. But even a democratic China would be quite different from the United States culturally, and it would likely be nationalistic in many ways. In any event, we cannot count on democratic change. We need to plan strategically for dealing with a rising China that will continue to be communist, authoritarian, and nationalistic.[7] What will Chinese ambitions be in that case?

The first answer is not simply that we do not know, but that the Chinese themselves do not know. There is a plurality of views within China. Part of Chinese society is highly Westernized and seeks to integrate into the broader East Asian and world communities, part is highly nationalistic, and ideology continues to drive the Chinese Communist Party, whose legitimacy remains contested. Many observers have pointed out that whatever a country's ambitions are at a given point, they change and become more expansive with increasing national power. But economic growth will strengthen other voices in the country as well, and it is not possible to predict how the resulting political struggle will turn out.

China thus occupies an ambiguous position: it is a potential peer competitor that may one day challenge the American position in Asia and other U.S. interests around the world (e.g., access to oil), as well as the positions of U.S. allies like Japan, but at the same time it is an important economic partner whose willingness to buy U.S. Treasury securities has allowed the United States the luxury of both high consumption and low interest rates. This means that any effort to substitute China for the former Soviet Union in the Cold War framework will simply not work. The use of the term *containment* with regard to China is particularly unhelpful. The Soviet Union was the center of a global communist movement that sought to use local communist and fellow traveler organizations to spread Soviet influence and ultimately accomplish pro-communist "regime change." In that context, containment meant stopping local communist forces, deterring the direct use of force, and balancing Soviet efforts to gain influence through arms supplies and aid.

None of this applies to contemporary China. China is not trying to spread its own way of life around the world; if anything, it is promoting a strict respect for sovereignty that would leave in place whatever local institutions exist among the countries it deals with. China's rise is powered by its economic growth and by its acquisition of military capabilities; the United States can do nothing to prevent either of these and, in the case of economic growth, has a positive interest in seeing it continue.

China is presumably seeking to recover a respect and status as a great power that it once enjoyed. Some have suggested that China would like to re-create something like the old imperial system in East Asia, in which surrounding countries were not absorbed into China directly, but stood in a relationship of deference to Beijing. Clearly, China would like to shape international institutions and the broader environment in ways that promote its national interests (e.g., by not including human rights as a criterion for lending, trade, or intervention). The United States may seek to contest these objectives or deny China these goals, but *containment* is simply the wrong word to use to describe a policy designed to deal with the rise of a country that will look much more like a traditional great power than like the head of an ideologically driven movement.

If the challenge that China presents to the international system is more like that of a unified Germany after 1871 than like that of Nazi Germany or the former Soviet Union, one clear objective of American policy should be to prevent the rise of a hostile or expansionist China from becoming a self-fulfilling prophecy. Britain and France interpreted the challenge posed by Wilhelmine Germany as a strategic threat and built an Entente to contain it. After Bismarck, Germany did much to contribute to the perceived threat by building a blue-water navy and seeking a "place in the sun" in Africa, but remained a very different kind of great power than the Nazi regime that later emerged. The failure of the European state system to appropriately handle a rising Germany resulted in a conflict that was a disaster for everyone concerned and undermined European civilization itself.

The Evolution of American Policy in Asia

The hub-and-spokes security system that emerged in Asia after the Second World War differed greatly from the one that formed in Europe, where the European Union, the North Atlantic Treaty Organization (NATO), and smaller groups like the Organization for Cooperation and Security in Europe and the Council of Europe took on responsibilities for guaranteeing the continent's security against the Soviet threat.[8] In his chapter of this book, Bruce Cumings suggests that the Asian system reflected a deliberate unilateralist choice on the part of American policy makers, who sought to maximize their freedom of action by dealing with countries on a bilateral basis.[9] But this begs the question of why Washington did not attempt something similar in Europe.

The answer, of course, is that multilateral institutions were preferred by the Europeans themselves and arose out of a substantial degree of common interest and commitment on their part. The European Coal and Steel Community, which was the nucleus of what later became the European Union, was a Franco-German initiative that received American blessing only after the fact. The NATO alliance was shaped more deliberately by Washington and was multilateral from the start because of the reality of the tripartite occupation of West Germany. These institutions were consolidated in later years because they built on a common culture and a shared experience of the twentieth century that promoted collective action. It was the Europeans themselves who sought a "postnational" multilateral structure in which member states would cede to the collective (the European Union) important elements of sovereignty, such as control over their own currency.

Nothing like this common consciousness existed in East Asia. The growing ideological divide prevented cooperation between communist and noncommunist nations in Asia of the type that occurred in Europe, but the noncommunist parts of the region were also divided by history and culture in ways that the West Europeans were not. Unlike the pooling of sovereignty achieved by embedding West Germany in NATO and the European Union, the United States took on this function by itself through the imposition on Tokyo of a constitution mandating peace and the substitution of its own military forces for those of Japan. It is not clear that the United States actually preferred the hub-and-spokes structure over a multilateral one; the administration of President Dwight Eisenhower tried to establish a Southeast Asia Treaty Organization modeled on NATO, but it failed for lack of regional enthusiasm.

Multilateralism took root in Asia with the establishment of ASEAN in 1967 and the 1977 creation of the ASEAN Post Ministerial Conference (PMC), which opened the forum up to the participation of the United States, Japan, and other countries outside of Southeast Asia. In 1994, ASEAN also spawned the ARF, which was meant to deal with security issues. As Cheng-Chwee Kuik indicates in his chapter, China was invited to join the ARF but was initially suspicious and aloof; only later did it come to embrace the forum as a diplomatic tool by which it could reassure its neighbors of its intentions.

It was at an ASEAN PMC in 1989 that Malaysian Prime Minister Mohamad Mahathir first proposed an East Asian Economic Caucus (EAEC) that would exclude the United States and other "white" powers from the "Asian club." The American reaction was quick and decisive: Secretary of State James Baker made clear that the United States was opposed to the formation of an EAEC, and strongly urged Japan to use its influence as a member of the Asian club to kill the idea. The United States and Australia strongly pushed APEC as a more inclusive alternative, and to this day it remains the primary multilateral anchor of U.S. influence in the region.

Many of the more recent proposals for East Asian multilateral institutions have been focused on economic issues and have stemmed from the 1997–98 Asian economic crisis. Many countries in East Asia viewed the United States and U.S.-influenced international institutions like the International Monetary Fund and the World Bank as exploiting the crisis to push a pro-market agenda that would benefit American interests. When Japan proposed an Asian Monetary Fund, Washington summarily rejected the idea, but offered nothing in its place to act as an institutional coordinating mechanism that could mitigate a future crisis. As a result, countries in the region have been proceeding on their own to build some new multilateral organizations and initiatives. The United States has been largely indifferent to this process. These have included the Chiang Mai Initiative, which allows central banks from 13 participating countries to swap currency reserves in the event of a speculative attack, and the ASEAN Plus Three forum, which links ASEAN member states with China, Japan, and Korea. At the ASEAN summit meeting in Vientiane, Laos, in December 2004, the organization decided to hold an East Asian Summit in 2005 in Kuala Lumpur that would be based on the membership of the ASEAN Plus Three group, but it subsequently came to include Australia and India.

In sharp contrast to U.S. treatment of Mahathir's proposal for an EAEC, the United States has taken a "wait and see" attitude toward the new multilateral forums of which it is not a member, namely ASEAN Plus Three and the East Asian Summit. It has neither made a principled argument that it deserves to be part of any East Asian grouping nor tried to deliberately undermine these initiatives. It is not clear whether this ambiguity stems from a well-thought-out long-term strategy or from a failure on the part of senior policy makers to focus on Asian issues at a time of preoccupation with terrorism and the Middle East.

Northeast Asia, by contrast, has been the subject of a great deal more attention on the part of the Bush administration, whose evolving policy toward that region has been more coherent. The administration came into office determined to reverse the Clinton administration's nomination of China as a "strategic partner" at the expense of traditional allies like Japan. The so-called Armitage-Nye Report,[10] written in 2000, served as a blueprint for the policy actually pursued by the Bush administration, which deliberately upgraded Japan's status and deepened military cooperation between the two allies. Japan sent troops in support of the American intervention in Iraq, collaborated on missile defense, and settled outstanding bilateral issues such as Okinawa basing of U.S. forces. Upgrading the military components of the U.S.-Japan relationship fit into a larger plan pushed by the Pentagon to invigorate a series of bilateral relationships with countries on China's periphery, including India, Mongolia, Singapore, Taiwan, and Vietnam.

As a result of its efforts to prevent North Korea from obtaining nuclear weapons, the Bush administration stumbled into a new Asian multilateral framework in the form of the ongoing Six-Party Talks on Korean security, which involve the United States, North and South Korea, Japan, China, and Russia. This happened because Pyongyang, in the wake of the collapse of the 1994 Agreed Framework, insisted on bilateral negotiations with the United States on the future of its nuclear programs. Washington correctly saw this as an effort to divide it from its South Korean ally and insisted on a multilateral framework for the talks. Over time, another important motive emerged as well: only China, with its ongoing economic ties to North Korea, had the leverage to bring the latter to the bargaining table. Indeed, China was able to strong-arm Pyongyang into accepting the six-party format by briefly cutting off its energy supplies.

The Bush administration's policy toward China continues to be a subject of internal debate in its second term. Former deputy secretary of state Robert Zoellick sought to define America's attitude toward China not in terms of a threat, but by taking at face value China's claims of seeking a "peaceful rise."[11] The Pentagon, by contrast, tends to share Japan's more alarmist view of long-term Chinese intentions, as indicated by remarks made by former secretary of defense Donald Rumsfeld in Singapore in June 2005, when he raised questions about the motives behind China's defense buildup.[12] It is not clear which of these views will ultimately predominate as the administration completes its second term.

The Future of the U.S.-Japan Alliance

The U.S.-Japan relationship had become extraordinarily close by the second term of the Bush administration, and appropriately so. Apart from being a long-time U.S. ally, Japan is the oldest developed democracy in East Asia, a country that shares many American values and interests. Putting Japan and China on an equal footing, or even giving priority to China, as the Clinton administration had seemed ready to do, sent a bad signal to all American allies and was not conducive to the region's overall stability.

Reassuring a traditional ally like Japan is particularly important at the present moment, because Japan feels unusually isolated and vulnerable. Whatever provocation the visits to the Yasukuni Shrine by Prime Minister Koizumi may have provided China and South Korea, the fact remains that China dramatically overreacted to signs of rising Japanese nationalism, and it made the situation much worse by its tacit encouragement of popular anti-Japanese feeling. In 1994, a previous Japanese prime minister, Tomiichi Murayama, had clearly apologized for Japan's aggression against China—an apology that was repeated in 2005 by Koizumi—and it is reasonable to ask what further steps the Japanese government can be expected to take. The significance of the history textbook revisions protested by China and Korea was greatly exaggerated, and the news of the revisions was passed around as an established fact rather than as an issue to be investigated. Japan's security problems with China and North Korea are real, and the purpose of the U.S.-Japan Security Treaty, concluded in 1951 to cement U.S.-Japanese cooperation in the Cold War, was precisely to backstop Japan against whatever new threats might appear on the horizon.

In light of all that I have said, the current situation poses some unusual challenges given the current climate of rising nationalism in Northeast Asia, in ways that suggest that the bilateral framework may not be adequate in the coming years as a way of managing U.S. strategic interests in Northeast Asia. The issue that promises to be the most neuralgic is the intention of the Japanese Liberal Democratic Party (LDP) to revise Article 9 of the postwar Japanese constitution, written by Americans and imposed on Japan after the Pacific War. The intention to move Japan away from its dependence on U.S. military power to a more normal type of strategic alliance was signaled by former prime ministers Koizumi and Abe. Article 9 forbids the country to make war or maintain a military (something Japan has observed in the breach by calling its military "self-defense forces"). Underlying this intention is an important shift in Japanese domestic politics indicated by a collapse of the left (with socialists and communists, formerly 14 percent of the population, falling to 3 percent by 2005). The idea of Japan's becoming a "normal" country with sovereign authority over its own security policy is an old idea, one that was most closely associated with LDP renegade Ichiro Ozawa. The United States has been on record for a long time as supporting a change in the 1949 constitution's strictures against Japan's maintaining military forces. This stance dates back at least to the last decade of the Cold War, when the administration of President Ronald Reagan pushed Japan to take on greater responsibilities for its own defense. After the Cold War, and particularly after Japan's embarrassment at not being able to supply peacekeeping troops in support of the 1991 Gulf War, participation in internationally sanctioned humanitarian interventions became the chief justification for a more robust Japanese defense posture.[13] The 2000 Armitage-Nye Report reiterated the long-standing American support for revision of Article 9 in the following terms:

> Japan's prohibition against collective self-defense is a constraint on alliance cooperation. Lifting this prohibition would allow for closer and more efficient security cooperation. This is a decision that only the Japanese people can make. The United States has respected the domestic decisions that form the character of Japanese security policies and should continue to do so. But Washington must make clear that it welcomes a Japan that is willing to make a greater contribution and to become a more equal alliance partner.[14]

The report went on to argue, following Ozawa's lead, that the U.S.-Japan relationship ought to be modeled on the special relationship between the United States and Britain.

The United States has thus committed itself to supporting a Japanese revision of Article 9 in the context of increasingly vitriolic relations between Japan on the one side and China and Korea on the other. As the Armitage-Nye Report states, China should not be allowed to veto measures that Japan thinks are necessary for its own self-defense. On the other hand, Japanese behavior is to some extent responsible for exacerbating the hostile reactions of its neighbors, and Washington has an interest in making sure that these relations do not deteriorate further.

Former prime minister Koizumi had a number of legitimate reasons for wanting to visit the Yasukuni Shrine. It memorializes the spirits not just of people the United States and some of Japan's neighbors regard as war criminals, but all members of the Japanese military who have served their country since the birth of modern Japan.[15] The motives of Koizumi and members of the generation of Japanese who did not live through the Pacific War may be compared to those of former German Chancellor Gerhard Schröder and many younger Germans, who watched their parents suppress their feelings of national pride. These younger Japanese feel that Japan has apologized sufficiently for the past, that in any case they were not responsible for whatever atrocities were committed in the past, and that Japan and its neighbors need to move beyond the endless rehashing of old historical issues.

Japan's problem, and the reason that it has never been able to achieve the degree of reconciliation with its neighbors that Germany has achieved, is that there are proportionately more Japanese than Germans who not only believe their country has apologized sufficiently, but think that their country did not have much to apologize for in the first place.[16] This type of nationalist does not constitute anything like a majority of the Japanese public, but it does constitute much less of a fringe group than Germany's neo-Nazis, and this group is one that has been growing rapidly. Japan, unlike China, is a democratic country and cannot prevent its citizens from expressing their opinions. On the other hand, it is not unreasonable for Japan's neighbors to voice concerns about the nationalism of a significant minority of Japanese.

Koizumi's stunning victory in the lower house elections in September 2005 gave the LDP a solid legislative majority and a mandate to move ahead with constitutional revision. His successor, Shinzo Abe, who would be forced to step down after less than a year in office, made the revision of Article 9 an explicit goal to be accomplished in six years.

Although Abe was replaced by the less nationalistic Prime Minister Yasuo Fukuda in October 2007, it is not clear that revision of the constitution is off the table for good, and it is at least worth thinking through the logic of strong American support for revision of Article 9 at the present time. Washington has supported this because it needs not only Japan's resources, but Japan's active support for its strategic position, from overall deterrence to peacekeeping and nation-building. On the other hand, the basic premise of the entire U.S.-Japan relationship was originally that the United States would assume certain functions of a sovereign Japan (including nuclear deterrence) in Japan's place. The presence of the American Seventh Fleet in the Eastern Pacific, as well as the U.S. posture throughout the region as a nuclear force, has been legitimated by the fact that other Asian countries trust the United States with military power more than they trust Japan. This greater trust for the United States has been the case, by and large, in China as well. If Japan returns to being a fully sovereign country like Britain, the justification for the presence of a large American force in Asia will change.

Germany, too, has been regaining sovereignty much as Japan has. It has reduced the number of foreign troops on its soil and has sent German military units out to perform peacekeeping duties in the Balkans and in Afghanistan. But German sovereignty remains encased in regional multilateral institutions—NATO and the European Union—that do not have counterparts in East Asia.

This suggests a final reason why some type of multilateral framework might be useful as a supplement to the existing U.S.-Japan bilateral relationship. Revision of Article 9 should not in theory threaten Japan's neighbors, but it will be very controversial in Beijing, Seoul, and other capitals and could be a source of enormous misunderstanding. It is an initiative that would be best undertaken with careful planning and good communication all the way around rather than as a unilateral move by Tokyo with silent acquiescence on the part of Washington. A multilateral security framework facilitating better communications between the major players in Northeast Asia would at least provide a forum to prepare the way for Japan's normalization.

It is very important to underscore the fact that any multilateral framework would complement and not substitute for the bilateral U.S.-Japan relationship. Japan feels vulnerable and isolated, with the United States as its only reliable friend. America can have influence only if it stands by Japan and addresses the fundamental sources of its insecurity. The Bush administration has done an excellent job of reassuring Japan and building trust in Tokyo; this is not an asset to be squandered lightly. An insecure Japan is far more likely to take matters into its own hands and remilitarize in ways that other Asian countries will find intensely threatening.

Alternative Approaches

There are several alternative approaches the United States can take in dealing with the security architecture in Asia. Each has pluses and minuses, and none will fully guarantee stability in the region.

Option 1: Maintain the current bilateral system and oppose the formation of new multilateral organizations that do not include the United States. This is essentially the position of Richard Armitage, articulated both before and after his tenure as deputy secretary of state and largely put into practice by the Bush administration. Under this option, the United States would continue to emphasize traditional bilateral ties with its Asian allies, particularly Japan. The United States would use its influence to block the formation of new regional multilateral institutions like ASEAN Plus Three that do not include the United States, either by seeking to stop them outright, as it did with Mahathir's EAEC, or by diluting them through expansion of their membership to include more countries friendly to the United States.

A further extension of this policy, which has been promoted by the Bush Defense Department, is to enhance bilateral military ties not just with existing allies, but with whatever other countries are willing to collaborate with the United States on security matters. Washington has significantly upgraded its ties with India by accepting its status as a state with nuclear weapons, provided assistance to Mongolia and other countries on China's periphery in Central Asia, and quietly worked on security issues with Singapore.

This policy, in a sense, represents a renewal of the hub-and-spokes system, this time with the implicit intent of containing China. There are two possible dangers here. The first is the danger, referred to earlier, of creating a self-fulfilling prophecy in which the Chinese will see themselves ringed by an American containment barrier and thus locked into an increasingly hostile relationship with the United States. A subsidiary danger is that, in the context of a Japanese revision of Article 9, the United States will be seen not simply as reassuring a traditional ally but as supporting Japan's reemergence as a great power with an increasingly nationalistic agenda. This may drive South Korea further into an alignment with China, and might isolate the United States and Japan from other countries in the region that will seek to jump on the Chinese bandwagon with rather than balance China.

Japan has, in any event, been moving to implement its own version of a hub-and-spokes system, tying itself more closely to countries that might balance China under the rubric of a "values-based" foreign policy. In March 2007 it concluded a defense cooperation agreement with Australia that calls for partnership "on disaster relief, border security and fighting terrorism."[17] It has also strengthened its ties with India by agreeing to enhanced cooperation on maritime security through joint naval exercises. Japan is in effect trying to connect the ends of the spokes to one another, creating a "virtual" multilateral framework through interlocking bilateral deals.

If China's ambitions are more settled and expansionist than portrayed in our earlier discussion, the United States and Japan have little to gain by seeking to calm Chinese anxieties. In this case, the challenge would be to construct political relationships among states that wanted to balance Chinese power, of which the U.S.-Japan relationship would be the core. However, new multilateral groupings risk being dominated by China or being used by China as a means of legitimating its role and influence in Asia even as it seeks a hegemonic position there.

Option 2: Lay the foundations for a multilateral containment barrier against China. A number of observers have suggested that the United States foster in Asia a multilateral security alliance modeled on NATO that would include the United States, Japan, Australia, India, and other democracies.[18] The problem with this approach is that, with the possible exception of Japan, no other nation in the region (including otherwise close allies like Australia) would sign on to such an alliance. All states in Asia have close economic ties with China and, for the reasons described earlier, do not want to provoke China or to see the region polarized into pro- and anti-China camps. This is particularly true among the ASEAN states, which are most vulnerable to China and at the same time dependent on it.

There is a more sophisticated version of this strategy that might have a better chance of gaining adherents, one that starts with economics rather than security.[19] At the core would be an East Asian Community modeled very loosely on the European Union in its early days. This could start with a free trade agreement (FTA) between the United States, Japan, and whatever other countries initially wanted to join. Rather than being yet another of the proliferating FTAs described in the chapters by John Ravenhill and David Hale, however, this one would incorporate as criteria for membership certain elements of good governance—for instance, rule of law, transparency, government accountability, and so on. Membership in this FTA would provide access to the first and second largest economies in the world, which would constitute an enormous incentive for joining. Unlike the European Union, an East Asian Community would not set ambitious goals like the creation of a common currency or broad harmonization of rules; rather, it would harmonize rules in areas directly linked to trade promotion and economic integration.

The rationale for an East Asian Community would be entirely economic at the outset: it would be a vehicle for promoting governance and rule of law over the world's most economically dynamic region. Membership would effectively be limited to democracies, though democracy would not have to be an explicit criterion for membership. Such a community would serve as the nucleus for a democratic alliance in Asia, much as the European Union anchors democracy in Europe. It would not be directed against China; indeed, from the outset China would be urged to meet the community's membership criteria and join. But the community would also be a hedge: by providing a multilateral forum through which democratic countries in the region could talk to each other and integrate, it would create a ready-made political platform for cooperation in security matters if that became necessary one day.

The downside of such a community is to be found in domestic American politics. Although a U.S.-Japan FTA has been discussed for many years now, there are formidable political obstacles to winning the approval of Congress to form one. Bilateral U.S.-Japan trade issues have not been irritants in the relationship recently as they were in the 1980s, but they are still latent, and would likely emerge as obstacles to approval of an FTA. Moreover, the open-ended invitation to join the community would involve restrictions on U.S. sovereignty that would potentially be controversial in Congress.

Option 3: Create a new five-power organization based on the Six-Party Talks. As a result of U.S. efforts to prevent North Korea from obtaining nuclear weapons, the United States has stumbled into a new Asian multilateral framework in the form of the ongoing Six-Party Talks on Korean security involving the United States, North and South Korea, Japan, China, and Russia.[20] Through five rounds of negotiations, by the fall of 2007 the Six-Party Talks appeared to be making some progress toward the objective of forcing North Korea to accept constraints on its nuclear program. Whether or not they succeed in meeting the goal of nuclear disarmament of Pyongyang, an ongoing five-power security dialogue similar to that of the Organization for Cooperation and Security in Europe would be useful as a communications channel.

An important obstacle to creating a permanent five-power organization is North Korea itself, which really does not belong in any civilized community of nations given its human rights and security records. Pressing ahead too rapidly to convert a narrowly focused six-party negotiation into a permanent five-power organization might undermine the current talks. The trick would be to isolate Pyongyang within the six-party format and help the other five powers to become comfortable in dealing with one another over the long term, perhaps initially as a separate informal caucus within the framework of the Six-Party Talks.

China, too, has been reluctant to extend the mandate of the Six-Party Talks or to engage in organizations that may force it to open up its security decision-making process to outsiders. But this is precisely why such an organization would be valuable in the long run. For example, if all members were asked to lay out five-year defense spending plans and justify them, it would force an articulation of fears and force direct discussion of goals among all parties. Given the outstanding issues among China, Japan, and South Korea, it is important that they be able to talk to each other directly rather than relaying messages through Washington.

Option 4: Try to revitalize existing multilateral forums like APEC or the ARF in which the United States already participates. These can serve as alternatives both to ASEAN Plus Three on the one hand and to strict bilateralism on the other. Part of APEC's original rationale was to serve as an alternative to Mahathir's proposed EAEC, and it still serves as such by providing a more inclusive form of East Asian multilateralism. Unlike APEC, the ARF deals explicitly with security matters, and China has now decided that participation in it is useful to its diplomatic purposes. Thus, there is already a forum for dealing with issues like Japan's normalization.

The problem with these forums is that they are too large and have mandates too diffuse to allow them to be useful in any kind of concrete discussions of security. The ARF would be completely incapable of dealing with an important security issue like Taiwan. A five-power organization would not be able to diffuse a Taiwan crisis either, but its smaller membership and Northeast Asian focus would give the United States and Japan proportionately greater weight than they have in either APEC or the ARF.

Option 5: Encourage existing trends toward Asian multilateralism as a means of integrating Japan into Asia. A completely different approach to multilateralism is the one suggested by Kazuhiko Togo in his chapter, which is for the United States to actually encourage Japanese participation in ASEAN Plus Three as a way of bridging current differences between Japan and its Asian neighbors. Japan has always had a schizophrenic view of itself as alternately an Asian and a Western power, a division that is mirrored in the Foreign Ministry itself. The critics of China in Japan today correspond to those who would like to see Japan as a Western power and an outlier in Asia.

The United States has typically worried that Japan might shift to a pro-Asian stance, paying more heed to Beijing than to Washington. But in the current climate of enmity between Japan and its nearest neighbors, an effort to "re-Asianize" Japan might have the salutary effect of reassuring China and Korea about Japanese intentions. In this kind of scenario, Japan itself would take responsibility for managing a revision of Article 9 in the context of ASEAN Plus Three, and the United States would follow the process at a distance. ASEAN Plus Three would thus be regarded not as an alternative to a U.S.-centric security system, but rather as a complement to it, one that would provide multiple forms of connection among Asian powers and would prevent the region from polarizing into pro- and anti-Chinese camps. The United States would have to be concerned only that such a regional grouping did not take on an anti-American cast; but with Japan in the group, the likelihood of this happening would be slight.

Conclusion: Structuring Future Choices for Asia

The options for American policy I have sketched appear to represent major strategic choices between multilateral and bilateral frameworks, between pro- and anti-Chinese postures, and between U.S. inclusion from Asian affairs and its exclusion. But these choices are a bit less stark than they may at first appear, because it would be possible to combine them in different ways. Economic regionalism like that seen in ASEAN Plus Three is less threatening to U.S. interests (and those of other powers not included) in the context of a global World Trade Organization. As noted earlier, all of the alternative multilateral approaches ought to be seen as complements to and not substitutes for the existing bilateral relationships, particularly the U.S.-Japan Security Treaty. If Chinese-Japanese enmity makes a deepening U.S.-Japan alliance seem threatening to China, it could be balanced by greater Japanese attention to and participation in ASEAN Plus Three.

Since the attacks of September 11, 2001, the United States has been tremendously preoccupied with the Middle East, especially Iraq, and with the global war on terrorism. In the long run, however, there are good reasons for thinking that classic interstate competition in Asia, particularly Northeast Asia, will become America's greatest long-term strategic challenge. As John Ikenberry notes in his chapter, it would be best for Washington to start thinking now about institutions that might better shape the incentives of the region's players now, ahead of the time when changes in the regional balance of power will make existing arrangements clearly obsolete.

Notes

1. Early on, the Clinton administration was more receptive to multilateral organizations such as the Asia-Pacific Economic Cooperation (APEC) and the ARF, as well to the Track 2 North East Asia Cooperation Dialogue.
2. The shrine was visited privately by Prime Ministers Kiichi Miyazawa and Ryogo Hashimoto in 1992 and 1996, respectively.
3. See Joseph Kahn, "If 22 Million Chinese Prevail at UN, Japan Won't," *New York Times,* April 1, 2005, and Minxin Pei and Michael Swaine, *Simmering Fire in Asia: Averting Sino-Japanese Strategic Conflict* (Washington, D.C.: Carnegie Endowment for International Peace, 2005).
4. Evan S. Medeiros and M. Taylor Fravel, "China's New Diplomacy," *Foreign Affairs* 82 (2003): 22–35.
5. On China's use of multilateralism, see the chapter in this volume by Cheng-Chwee Kuik; see also his article "Multilateralism in China's ASEAN Policy: Its Evolution, Characteristics, and Aspiration," *Contemporary Southeast Asia* 27 (2005): 102–22.
6. On this subject, see Aaron L. Friedberg, "Ripe for Rivalry: Prospects for Peace in a Multipolar Asia," *International Security* 18 (1993): 5–33, and "The Struggle for Mastery in Asia," *Commentary* 108 (2000): 17–26.
7. We might also want to plan against a fragmenting or collapsing China, which will pose a very different set of challenges.
8. Peter Katzenstein and Christopher Hemmer argue that the United States found itself better able to identify with a North Atlantic cultural community, but not with any comparable grouping in Asia. See their article "Why Is There No NATO in Asia? Collective Identities, Regionalism, and the Origins of Multilateralism," *International Organization* 56 (2002): 575–88.
9. The one clear case in which unilateralism was the result of an American choice rather than a product of regional realities was General Douglas MacArthur's decision to exclude the other members of the wartime coalition, particularly the Soviet Union, from any active role in the occupation of Japan. But even

this decision was brought on by local events: unlike Germany, Japan was occupied by the Americans alone.

10. *The United States and Japan: Advancing toward a Mature Partnership* (Washington, D.C.: National Defense University, Institute for National Strategic Studies, October 2000).

11. Robert Zoellick, "Whither China: From Membership to Responsibility?" remarks made to the National Committee on United States–China Relations,
New York, September 21, 2005.

12. Donald Rumsfeld, remarks made at the International Institute for Strategic
Studies, Singapore, June 4, 2005.

13. See Francis Fukuyama and Kongdan Oh, *The US-Japan Security Relationship
after the Cold War*, MR-283-USDP (Santa Monica, Calif.: RAND Corporation,
1993).

14. *The United States and Japan.*

15. Ronald Reagan was severely criticized for visiting Bitburg Cemetery with German Chancellor Helmut Kohl in 1984 on the grounds that a number of Waf-
fen SS officers were buried there. Kohl and other Germans argued, much as did
the Japanese, that these were a small minority and that the bulk of the dead
buried there were ordinary Germans who had not committed war crimes.

16. On the comparison between Japan and Germany with regard to historical
memory, see Ian Buruma, *The Wages of Guilt: Memories of War in Germany and
Japan* (New York: Farrar, Straus and Giroux, 1994).

17. "Japan and Australia Sign Defense Pact," *Christian Science Monitor,* March 14,
2007.

18. See, for example, Ellen Bork and Gary Schmitt, "A NATO for Asia," *Weekly
Standard,* December 11, 2006.

19. For a version of this, see Sherman Katz and Devin Stewart, "Securing America's Presence in the East Asian Order" (Washington, D.C.: Center for Strategic and International Studies, November 1, 2005).

20. For a fuller discussion of this option, see Francis Fukuyama, "Re-envisioning
Asia," *Foreign Affairs* 84 (2005): 75–87.

Conclusion

Kent E. Calder and Francis Fukuyama

THE DEEPENING ECONOMIC INTEGRATION in East Asia over the past two decades has clearly been one of the epic developments of our time, with fateful implications for the future configuration of global affairs. The region already generates well over 20 percent of global GDP and is growing much more rapidly than either Europe or North America, the other major centers of global political-economic power. The chances are good that East Asia, with well over a third of the world's population—a share that is also steadily growing—together with impressive levels of education, health, bureaucratic competence, political stability, and organizational efficiency, will continue to experience rapid and sustained growth for many years to come.

In finance, where the dividends of past economic success become palpable, East Asia's potential influence is latent, but undeniable. With China and Japan, now incontestably the largest creditors on earth, holding well over U.S.$2 trillion in foreign exchange reserves between them, the region possesses two-thirds of all the foreign exchange reserves on earth. Its financial decisions have the potential to shake capital markets everywhere in the world.

Asia's influence in the political-military dimension is also becoming ever more substantial. Several nations of the region—China, India, Japan, and South Korea, in particular—already have sophisticated levels of defense technology, with their competence in microelectronics, missile guidance systems, defense communications, and software development especially notable. With North Korea's nuclear, chemical, and biological programs continuing in the wake of an actual nuclear test in 2006, and with nearby Japan's manifest capacity to go nuclear unquestioned by specialists, the dark shadow cast by weapons of mass destruction is deepening as well.

As Asia's economic and technological sophistication rise, that dynamic region's capabilities and intentions become ever more consequential on the global scene. Yet, at this critical juncture, both the regional political scene and the domestic systems of key nations in East Asia are in the throes of major transition. As Francis Fukuyama and Cheng-Chwee Kuik point out in this volume, China is rapidly rising as a regional power, growing more multilateral in its orientation, and this development poses far-reaching consequences for intra-Asian affairs. Japan is reorienting its security policies, and considering the revision of its constitution, to become a more "normal" nation, with less inhibited defense capabilities. Korea is in transition. And India, now with nuclear weapons, is becoming increasingly activist in regional matters.

Given the rapid pace of political-economic change in an East Asian region of major global strategic importance, it is time for international relations generalists to combine with regional specialists to think about creative, insightful ways of stabilizing the region's political-economic architecture. That has been the premise behind this volume. Fukuyama has succinctly presented the central argument for reconsidering multilateralism, in particular, stressing (1) the limits to the traditional "hub-and-spokes" organization of the region, including the deterioration in U.S.-Korea relations and rising nationalism within Asia; (2) the rise of China as an economic power; and (3) the need for a forum for easing the "normalization" of Japan's security role in the region. Calder has noted that multilateralism does have more of a history in Asia than is often appreciated, and has recently taken on important manifestations such as the Six-Party Talks. John Ikenberry stresses the positive role that multilateralism has played in mediating "power transitions elsewhere in the world, including Europe," and argues that it could also play such a mediating role in twenty-first-century East Asia.

Across the preceding pages we have explored several dimensions of Asian multilateralism: its nature and origins, the broader economic and social constraints on its operation, and its future prospects in light of those constraints. In our assessment of recent Asian political-economic developments with respect to regionalism, we have focused on the evolution of Northeast Asian approaches. We have given special attention to developments in China, Japan, and South Korea, which together have around 70 percent of the population and GDP of the entire region and the most convoluted security circumstances, giving rise to lingering uncertainties on the Korean peninsula, in the Taiwan Straits, and regarding Sino-Japanese policies and mutual relationships. The interaction of the Northeast Asian nations, both with one another and with the Indian subcontinent, clearly poses the most serious long-term security issues that Asia confronts.

One central preoccupation throughout this volume has been cataloging and understanding the recent profile of Asian regionalism. At the same time, however, we have also been critically interested in the implications of regionalist trends for American foreign policy, and in how the United States can help configure the emerging regional framework in a manner consistent with its own national interests. Whether the nations of Asia can cohere with one another, and how the United States will relate to their prospective union, are matters of priority concern for future American foreign policy, just as the evolution of the European Union has been of concern in Washington.

Taken together, the chapters of this volume clearly show the importance of an interdisciplinary approach to Asian regional integration. A historical understanding is critical, as Calder and Bruce Cumings suggest, because it clarifies the embedded institutional constraints that limit what policy makers of any nation can achieve in reconfiguring regional affairs. It also helps make clear the discontinuities in individual national approaches to regional integration, such as China's historic shift toward multilateralism during the late 1990s, which Kuik chronicles in detail. History also clarifies the causal dynamics at those fateful, catalytic turning points, many of them deep in the past, that have ultimately created the contours of regional relations prevailing even today.

Historical understanding thus tempers our natural inclination, however facile, to assume that problems can be readily resolved if only people of good will have the determination and courage to do so. The "dead hand of the past," as Karl Marx put it, lies heavy on current realities in the form of established institutions and consciousness, complicating the process of change. For precisely this reason, history also suggests to us the critical importance of those unusual periods when institutional constraints are relaxed, amid the fluidity of a "critical juncture." The Korean War, China's economic opening during the late 1970s, and the 1997–98 Asian financial crisis have all had powerful impacts on the prospects for and the profile of East Asian regionalism, as several of our authors make clear.

These authors also suggest the importance of economics to a full and balanced understanding of regionalism. As Daniel Rosen points out, Asian regionalist institutions are necessarily embedded in a broader, preexisting global economic system that functions efficiently to solve many of the major concerns of the constituent nations and private firms. This embedding factor is highly important, he strongly argues, in the case of China in particular. China, he suggests, has a far greater need for sophisticated global financial markets, already established in New York and London, and of Western technology and management, than Asia might provide locally. To the extent that global institutions effectively address the concerns of Asian nations, the incentives for effective and dynamic regional integration are significantly reduced, Rosen argues.

Rosen's observations about the primacy of global institutions, and their economic utility, provide useful context for the anomaly that John Ravenhill painstakingly describes: a recent proliferation in Asia of bilateral free trade agreements (FTAs) of doubtful economic utility, despite the high priority that regional leaders typically assign to economic growth. If the utility of such agreements is low, one might wonder why nations devote so much political capital to negotiating and observing them.

Ravenhill suggests that the answers lie in diplomacy and domestic politics rather than in economics. Most of the early East Asian FTAs, he notes, were concluded with relatively insignificant trading partners—a pattern in contrast to patterns in other parts of the world. Examined in detail, this unusual Asian behavior appears to have four motives: (1) fewer domestic political costs for Asian governments in such incrementalism; (2) benefits for narrow but powerful export constituencies, such as the auto sectors in Japan and South Korea; (3) a desire to create catalysts for domestic reform; and (4) diplomatic reassurance, as in China's FTA with the Association of Southeast Asian Nations (ASEAN). In an important contribution to our understanding of subnational determinants of regionalism, Ravenhill concludes that Asia's bilateral FTAs are a political-economic exercise in negotiated protectionism, unlikely to lead to multilateralism. Like Rosen, he is skeptical of the potential for coherent, exclusivist Asian institutions due to their apparent economic irrationality in a world of global interdependence.

Economics, like history, also gives us useful insights into the positive forces that drive the system of regional relations in Asia. David Hale, for example, argues that Asia's rising economic interdependence—and especially China's rapidly rising interdependence with the broader world—is inhibiting the policy radicalism that had been so strongly expressed in the Maoist years. The simple fact that the world absorbs fully *half* of China's manufacturing output—and that rising manufacturing employment allows China to absorb the rapid, destabilizing drift of migrant workers to its cities—forces the People's Republic of China (PRC) to be quite pragmatic in international economic affairs. Several authors also note that economic forces—especially the vast accumulation of foreign exchange reserves in

Asia and the region's lack of domestic energy resources—do create special incentives for regional coordination in finance and energy that do not exist in trade.

How Much Potential Is There for Asian Multilateralism?

The central focus of this volume, of course, has been on East Asian multilateralism, in both its security and its economic dimensions. Fukuyama has posited multilateralism as a crucial future stabilizer for international relations in this strategic corner of the world. What prospects do our other authors see for this to materialize?

Calder, Cumings, and Ikenberry all point, first of all, to the "organization gap" that has been the embedded historical heritage of East Asia in its relations with the modern world since World War II. Although we disagree marginally about the extent to which Washington initially desired unilateralism, we all note the hub-and-spokes system of unequal bilateral relationships radiating from Washington as the crucial defining feature of the traditional East Asian institutional landscape. We see it as the necessary, if inhibiting, point of departure for any future efforts at coherent regional organization.

In his detailed study of bilateral trade agreements in Asia and their relationship to multilateralism, Ravenhill clearly documents both the embedded organization gap and the recent momentum of regional efforts to overcome it. For example, he notes that in 2000 East Asia, and the Asia-Pacific region more broadly, were significantly underrepresented in the "rush to regionalism," with China, Japan, Korea, and Taiwan "alone among the world's large economies in not having negotiated a preferential trade arrangement (PTA)." He further notes, however, that in half a decade this embedded pattern has sharply shifted, with East Asia becoming the world's most active region for the negotiation of PTAs. ASEAN, China, Japan, South Korea, and even Taiwan are implementing major bilateral and minilateral FTAs, with numerous additional projects also under negotiation.

Calder, Hale, Kuik, and Sook-Jong Lee also note a recent discontinuous acceleration of East Asian regionalist economic arrangements, especially relating to finance, energy, and infrastructure. Most chronologically trace this new intensification of regionalist activity to the aftermath of the Asian financial crisis, when the region was badly shaken by its inability to respond coherently to the powerful economic downdrafts that the crisis provoked. Several also note, however, that before the crisis economic integration had been growing, thus deepening the felt need for collective action to stabilize regional affairs once the financial crisis hit. Kuik also notes the shift since the end of the Cold War in China's regional security circumstances, which has made it more proactive in seeking intraregional partners, as another important factor in triggering the recent regional quest for new institutional forms.

The North Korean nuclear crisis also led, in the spring of 2005, to markedly intensified multilateral interactions on security matters, as we noted in the introduction to this volume. Despite the 2006 nuclear tests by the North—or perhaps because of them—there has been some progress toward capping the North Korean nuclear program. A network of human ties among negotiators from China, Japan, the two Koreas, Russia, and the United States has also begun to evolve that may be useful in mediating future issues of broader import.

To say that there is an accelerated quest in East Asia for regionalist institutional vehicles is not necessarily to say, however, that these new organizational forms are either substantive or necessarily enduring. We noted in the introduction that many past innovations in regional organization, such as Maphilindo, the Asia and Pacific Council (ASPAC), and the Southeast Asia Treaty Organization, were diplomatic vehicles, with little broader substance, that disappeared when their original rationale became superfluous. For example, several regional bodies established during the 1950s and the 1960s to contain China collapsed following the 1970–72 overtures to the PRC by President Richard Nixon and Secretary of State Henry Kissinger and the fall of Saigon in 1975.

Rosen cautions, as suggested earlier, that the embedded global economic context of regionalism forces East Asia, especially China, into such heavy reliance on global trade, as well as financial markets, that full-fledged regionalism is impossible in the short run. Hale notes, in a similar vein, that 57 percent of China's exports are currently generated by foreign firms, that the PRC's ratio of exports to GDP is triple the levels common in the Group of 7, and that a large share of these exports goes to nations outside of Asia. Under such circumstances, he maintains, exclusivist regionalism is impossible. Ravenhill, looking more narrowly at FTAs, concurs.

Is This the Twilight of the San Francisco System?

Is Asian regionalism, then, merely an evanescent matter of bombast, smoke, and mirrors, posing little challenge to the remarkably durable "San Francisco" system of hub-and-spokes relations that has persisted for half a century and more? Is there anything in the present whirlwind of rhetoric and organizations that is likely to endure? And are changes under way that are likely to be of strategic significance for future trans-Pacific relations?

Most of our authors stress that whatever Asian regionalist institutions will ultimately emerge cannot easily be exclusivist. As Hale, Ravenhill, and Rosen all note, Asian trade and investment are simply too deeply linked to the broader world to be exclusive. Critically, this interdependence is especially pronounced in the case of China, the country with the most powerful geopolitical incentives for a regionalism excluding the United States, its prospective future rival.

The one economically plausible basis for an exclusivist regionalism could flow from an entente between China and Japan. Together, the two Asian giants comprise a fifth of global GDP, with highly complementary strengths in finance, labor, resources, and manufacturing. Yet mutual political animosities, including both strategic apprehensions and painfully divergent approaches to history, make an entente between these great powers very difficult.

Even if totally exclusivist regionalism is unlikely, some form of deeper Asian community than exists at present—excluding the United States in some dimensions—could well be in the cards. With respect to the future, Kazuhiko Togo registers an important cautionary note often lost on American skeptics of Asian regionalism. Although Togo is a political realist and long-time personal supporter of the U.S.-Japan alliance, he argues that for Japanese—not to mention Chinese, Koreans, and other Asians less intimately linked to Washington—Asian identity is an important personal consideration that makes *some* form of intra-Asian, as opposed to trans-Pacific, regional organization desirable, even when the symbolic elements outweigh the practical. Japan's security, he argues, is best ensured when geopolitical power, economic efficiency, and a search for identity (in Asia) are all harmonized with one another.

In a world where the West has many of its own exclusivist regional bodies and initiatives, such as the European Union and the North American Free Trade Agreement, equity considerations reinforce this point. It is thus narrow-sighted to view initiatives such as the nascent East Asian Summit in terms of their concrete achievements alone. Even when they do not function efficiently—indeed, sometimes precisely *because* they do not function efficiently—exclusivist regional bodies may be useful in giving Asia a positive, if limited, sense of community and identity.

Within the context of a broader system architecture that *also* includes a role for global bodies like the World Trade Organization (WTO) and the International Monetary Fund, Asia-only multilateral organizations may also make domestic political sense in several Asian nations apart from Japan. Lee notes that in South Korea the administrations of both Kim Dae-jung and Roh Moo-hyun (1998–2008) were enthusiastic about such exclusivism in forms such as the ASEAN Plus Three summits. As Kuik points out, China has also found regionalism congenial geopolitically as long as it can simultaneously maintain broader global multilateral affiliations, such as China's WTO membership.

Beyond issues of symbolism and identity, the significance of emerging Asian regionalist profiles—and indeed the very shape of Asian regionalism itself—will critically depend on the causal "forces that drive the system." Our authors have identified at least six positive determinants of future patterns of regional organization, and at least two additional potential catalysts whose impact will likely increase. Due to their prospective importance in shaping the future of a crucial global region, the forces our authors have identified are worth summarizing here.

In the view of virtually all our authors, the most fundamental future determinant of patterns of Asian regional organization is likely to be *economic change.* Concretely, the rising economic importance of the PRC, along with its deepening reorientation toward neighboring areas, especially Korea, Taiwan, and ASEAN, and its relative distancing from the United States, could give fresh incentives to regionalism. As Hale points out, China already consumes 44 percent of Hong Kong's exports, 37 percent of Taiwan's, 22 percent of Korea's, and 13 percent of Japan's. South Korea invested over U.S.$6 billion in China during 2005. Transnational production networks, fueled by intraregional foreign investment, are institutionalizing these relationships still further. And foreign exchange shifts, which almost inevitably will increase the value of the Chinese renminbi, would likely further intensify this China-centric character of recent Asian trading patterns.

American unilateralism has been a major determinant of Asian regionalist profiles in the past, as Cumings observes. He points out that U.S. opposition to Asian multilateralism in the early 1990s was a central reason for the failure of Malaysian Prime Minister Mohamad Mahathir's East Asian Economic Caucus concept. No doubt American influence will continue to be significant in future profiles of Asian regionalism, but likely in new and more subtle ways, as the configuration of the 2005 Kuala Lumpur East Asia Summit suggests. Although this major Asian regional summit was held without U.S. participation, it was configured in such a way, with the presence of American protégés such as Australia, India, and New Zealand, as to limit the geopolitical challenge presented to Washington's interests.

Interpersonal networks are a third important force that is quietly shaping long-term prospects for Asian regionalism. During the 1997–98 Asian financial crisis, the *lack* of such networks was an important force impeding Chinese and other Asian cooperation with Japan's regionalist Asian Monetary Fund initiative, as Calder points out. Today the interaction of both policy makers and epistemic communities in such areas as finance, energy, and transportation is much more intense, as Cumings, Hale, and other authors suggest, making the communication gaps and policy coordination difficulties that greatly intensified the 1997–98 crisis increasingly unlikely in the future.

Domestic interests are inevitably influencing Asian regionalist profiles, as Kuik and Ravenhill note. They are likely to do so decisively in the future as well, building on a broadly held sense in Asia that Asians deserve the same rights to two-tiered regionalist and globalist architecture that Europe and North America enjoy. Cross-nationally, the most prominent and interesting new domestic political change is the rise of powerful and prominent Northeast Asian automotive and electronics industries, centered especially in Japan and South Korea. These sectors have an anti-protectionist bias and are becoming catalysts for FTAs, albeit with a disturbing "negotiated protectionism" undertone. Sometimes, as Ravenhill points out, these are transregional arrangements, such as between Japan and Mexico or Korea and Chile. Yet, by creating precedents and sensitizing consumers, they potentially prepare the ground for a move away from the agriculturally oriented protectionism of the past. Such an evolution may also have important economic consequences for regional trading ties with closer neighbors.

Political-economic crisis, as Calder and Hale both observe, can be an especially powerful catalyst for new initiatives in regional organization. Indeed, it was the Asian financial crisis that produced the most dynamic, often discontinuous changes in recent years in profiles of regional organization, many of them unexpected before the crisis exploded. As Calder suggests, in the future a "Chiang Mai model," whereby crisis produces discontinuous leaps in regional institution-building founded on preestablished patterns of economic interdependence, could represent an important paradigm for how East Asian regional integration may proceed. This creative, if volatile, dialectic between ideas and economic interdependence may yet bring Asia closer to Europe's eclectic profile of national and regional community than most analysts have foreseen.

Political leadership has also been an important catalyst in determining patterns of regional integration, both in crisis situations and in instances of more incremental policy innovation. As Lee points out, President Kim Dae-jung of South Korea represents a striking case in point. During the Asian financial crisis, Kim proposed trilateral Korea-China-Japan summits within the ASEAN Plus Three framework, as well as establishment of the East Asia Vision Group, and both proved to be important policy innovations. Kim's successor, Roh Moo-hyun, also accelerated Korea's regionalist orientation with an enhanced Northeast Asia emphasis, as Lee also observes.

New catalysts for regional integration—only indirectly linked to regionalist diplomatic strategies—could potentially emerge in the foreseeable future. Some analysts point to "infraregionalism"—the advent of large-scale infrastructure projects such as airports, ports, and pipelines—which could be important in integrating the region. Incheon International Airport near Seoul, the Busan port in Southeast Korea, and the Kaesong Special Economic Zone just north of the demilitarized zone, already in progress, are prospective cases in point. Others, such as a Northeast Asian regional electric power grid, could follow major progress in the denuclearization of North Korea.

Infraregionalism, it might be added, has the distinct political advantage of being feasible without creating an overarching legal or regulatory framework. It has the additional virtue, from the standpoint of regional integration, of creating policy coordination pressures in its wake. For example, if airports and pipelines are built, thinking about transport, energy, and tax policy planning will need to follow. Given the importance of construction in the domestic political systems of Japan, Korea, Taiwan, and increasingly China as well, infraregionalism may thus arguably be, despite the enormous financial costs and risks involved, an important future vehicle, through a spillover dynamic, for deepening political-economic integration among nations of the region, especially within Northeast Asia.

A final potential force for deepening integration in East Asia identified by our authors is national political transformation. Cumings notes, for example, that political change on the Korean peninsula could potentially be an enormous catalyst for regional integration, although the prospective profile is uncertain. After all, Korea is quite literally the hub of the Northeast Asian region, bordering on both China and Russia while also lying directly adjacent to Japan. Korea's unification, or even a limited relaxation of economic relations between North and South Korea, could substantially enhance and accelerate integration in the region more generally.

Fukuyama and Ikenberry both note that China and Japan also stand on the verge of potentially fateful transformation. China is evolving internationally into a power of major global importance, even as it is undergoing historic domestic changes. Japan is also seeking to recover a lost sense of nationhood, in ways that could intensify regional security dilemmas. Both see multilateralism, with major American involvement that does not undermine the U.S.-Japan alliance, as crucial to easing the historic "power transition" under way in Northeast Asia.

Calder, Cumings, and Fukuyama all see the dynamics of the Six-Party Talks on the North Korean nuclear issue as a prototype for how East Asian integration might productively proceed in the future, and for the sort of soft-institutional configuration that might accompany it, provided that the nuclear problem is resolved. The concrete dynamic, in the view of Cumings, is "Chinese diplomatic muscle, regional interaction, and American acquiescence," although others present Washington's nuclear stance in a more positive vein, as crucial to long-term regional stability. Ikenberry emphasizes that some new security institutions may be needed, possibly supplemented by treaties of nonaggression and regular consultation mechanisms, as a vehicle through which China and Japan, in particular, can bind themselves so as to ease incipient security dilemmas. One concrete organizational vehicle for deeper regional coordination, Fukuyama suggests, could be a "five-power organization" consisting of China, Japan, the two Koreas (as one), Russia, and the United States. Regardless of how it is conceived institutionally, this constellation of forces, catalyzed by a political-military crisis, seems likely to play a major role in determining the configuration of East Asia's future.

What Are the Policy Implications for the Pacific's Future?

Our authors are unanimous in recognizing, as Hale puts it, that "there are new forces at play in East Asia," and that these make new thinking about institutional infrastructure in the region imperative. Three major trends are most often identified: rising intraregional economic interdependence, with its attendant regulatory imperatives; the rise of China; and the political-military transformation of Japan. Together, these are seen as necessitating some modification of the hub-and-spokes framework that has prevailed for half a century. Although such modification may produce some short-run reduction in American regional leverage as the "spokes" of the Washington-centric wheel begin talking with one another more systematically, it should also, in the view of most of our authors, give some greater legitimacy to American policy in the region than would rigid U.S. insistence on maintaining the hub-and-spokes framework itself.

Contrary to the common conception, American policy has *not* been static, Hale also argues. Washington, he notes, has successfully negotiated FTAs with Australia and Singapore and has proactively pursued such talks with South Korea as well. The United States also supported the notion of the Six-Party Talks, with American representative Christopher Hill, in close cooperation with China and Japan, playing a key role in negotiating the September 2005 Beijing agreement by which North Korea committed to ultimately abandon its nuclear program, along with subsequent agreements to close and dismantle facilities such as Yongbyon, albeit subject to economic, security, and monitoring provisions still to be fully tested.

Although some success stories have been cited, many of our authors have pointed to the long-time passivity, or the "deafening silence," of American policy on the issue of Asian multilateralism, and to the perverse consequences of this neglect. Fukuyama, Ikenberry, Togo, and others note the importance of the U.S.-Japan alliance to regional stability, especially on delicate and explosive deterrence questions such as those relating to North Korea and the Taiwan Straits. Yet they also observe that there are impending issues, such as the need to cope with the rise of China, a possible collapse of North Korea, and a conceivable remilitarization of Japan, on which the existence of a residual multilateral framework could also be highly important, and the bilateral alliance framework alone inadequate. Multilateralism could thus usefully promote the very regional stability that is the central objective of American policy, provided that credible bilateral alliances also remain to ensure deterrence.

As Fukuyama points out, the United States has "stumbled" into multilateralism in East Asia due to its desire to counter North Korean insistence on bilateralism in the nuclear negotiations, coupled with Washington's desire to exploit Chinese leverage in dealing with the North. It is crucial now, as our authors agree, to more systematically build on that seemingly accidental development. A five-power organization and a revitalized ASEAN Regional Forum, possibly supplemented by nonaggression treaties and strategic dialogues, are but two of the possibilities. We hope that this volume, with both its candid assessment of where East Asian regionalism stands today and its more far-sighted analysis of the forces driving future configurations, will provide a useful tool for both policy makers and general readers in assessing the profile of an Asian regional future with crucial implications, for the United States and for the broader world.

Contributors

Kent E. Calder is director of the Edwin O. Reischauer Center for East Asian Studies and Reischauer Professor of East Asian Studies at the Paul H. Nitze School of Advanced International Studies (SAIS) of the Johns Hopkins University. He was formerly a tenured professor at Princeton University and has held the Japan Chair at the Center for Strategic and International Studies. He was also previously a lecturer in the Department of Government at Harvard University, where he served as the first executive director of the Harvard University Program on U.S.-Japan Relations. Calder has also been special adviser to the U.S. ambassador to Japan and special adviser to the assistant secretary of state for East Asia and Pacific affairs. His books include *Pacific Defense: Arms, Energy, and America's Future in Asia; Crisis and Compensation: Public Policy and Political Stability in Japan; Strategic Capitalism: Private Business and Public Purpose in Japanese Industrial Finance; Embattled Garrisons: Comparative Base Politics and American Globalism;* and *The East Asia Edge.* He is a former associate editor of *World Politics* and currently a member of the editorial board of *Asian Security.*

Bruce Cumings researches and teaches at the University of Chicago on 20th-century international history, U.S.–East Asian relations, East Asian political economy, modern Korean history, and American foreign relations. He is interested in the multiplicity of ways that conceptions, metaphors, and discourses are related to political economy and material forms of production and to relations between East and West. His publications include *The Origins of the Korean War, War and Television, Korea's Place in the Sun: A Modern History,* and *Parallax Visions: American–East Asian Relations at the End of the Century.*

Francis Fukuyama is the Bernard L. Schwartz Professor of International Political Economy at the Paul H. Nitze School of Advanced International Studies (SAIS) of the Johns Hopkins University. He is also director of the International Development program at SAIS. He has written on issues of democratization and international political economy. His books include *The End of History and the Last Man, Trust: The Social Virtues and the Creation of Prosperity, The Great Disruption: Human Nature and the Reconstitution of Social Order, Our Posthuman Future: Consequences of the Biotechnology Revolution, State-Building: Governance and World Order in the 21st Century,* and *America at the Crossroads: Power and the Neoconservative Legacy.* He has worked at the RAND Corporation and at the U.S. Department of State, with expertise in Middle East affairs and European political-military affairs. From 1996 to 2000, he was Omer I. and Nancy Hirst Professor of Public Policy at the School of Public Policy of George Mason University.

David Hale, a global economist, is founder of the Chicago-based Hale Advisors, LLC, and serves as chairman of the board of China Online, LLC, a service provider for business and economic news about China. Before launching his own firm, he was the global chief economist for the Zurich Financial Services Group, where he advised the group's fund management and insurance operations on the economic outlook and a wide range of public policy issues. Previously he was chief economist at Kemper Corporation. His articles have appeared in such publications as the *Wall Street Journal, Far Eastern Economic Review, Financial Times, New York Times, Nihon Kezai Shimbun, Financial Analyst Journal, Harvard Business Review,* and *Foreign Policy.*

G. John Ikenberry is the Albert G. Milbank Professor of Politics and International Affairs at Princeton University in the Department of Politics and the Woodrow Wilson School. He has also taught at Georgetown University and the University of Pennsylvania and has been affiliated with the Carnegie Endowment for International Peace and the Brookings Institution. His books include *After Victory: Institutions, Strategic Restraint, and the Rebuilding of Order after Major Wars; State Power and the World Economy; Reasons of State: Oil Politics and the Capacities of American Government;* and *The State and American Foreign Economic Policy.* His edited volumes include *New Thinking in International Relations, U.S. Democracy Promotion: Impulses, Strategies, and Impacts, International Relations Theory and the Asia-Pacific,* and *American Unrivaled: The Future of the Balance of Power.*

Cheng-Chwee Kuik is a doctoral candidate in the Southeast Asia Studies program at the Paul H. Nitze School of Advanced International Studies (SAIS) of the Johns Hopkins University and is concurrently a lecturer in the Program in Strategic Studies and International Relations, Universiti Kebangsaan Malaysia (UKM).

Sook-Jong Lee is a professor in the Graduate School of Governance, Sung Kyun Kwan University in Seoul, and a former senior research fellow at the Sejong Institute. She has taught at the Paul H. Nitze School of Advanced International Studies (SAIS) of the Johns Hopkins University and has been a visiting fellow at the Brookings Institution's Center for Northeast Asian Policy Studies. She researches and writes on the political economies of Korea and Japan and on their civil society and governance.

John Ravenhill has been on the faculty of the University of Sydney, the University of Virginia, the International University of Japan, the Institute of Defence and Strategic Studies at Nanyang Technological University in Singapore, and the University of California, Berkeley. His recent books include *Global Political Economy, Asia Pacific Economic Cooperation: The Construction of Pacific Rim Regionalism, The Asian Financial Crisis and the Architecture of Global Finance,* and *The National Interest in a Global Era: Australia in World Affairs.* His articles have appeared in many of the leading international relations journals, including *World Politics, International Organization, World Policy Journal, World Development,* and *International Affairs,* and he is on the editorial boards of *Pacific Affairs, International Relations, International Relations of the Asia-Pacific,* and *Global Economic Review.* His research interests center on global political economy, especially the fields of trade and production, and on Australian foreign policy.

Daniel H. Rosen is an economic adviser specializing in China's commercial development, and he writes and speaks extensively on U.S.-China economic relations. He is the principal of China Strategic Advisory, a specialized practice that helps senior executives and directors analyze and understand commercial, economic, and policy trends in Greater China. He is also an adjunct associate professor at Columbia University and a visiting fellow with the Institute for International Economics (IIE) in Washington, D.C. He has written books on changes in China's agrobusinesses sector and on U.S.-Taiwan trade dynamics.

Kazuhiko Togo is a visiting professor at Seoul National University (fall 2007). In 1968 he joined the Foreign Ministry of Japan, where he worked extensively on Soviet/Russian affairs, as well as on Europe, America, international law, and economics, and served as Japan's ambassador to the Netherlands before retiring in 2002. In 1995 he began teaching at universities in Moscow and Tokyo, and after retirement taught at Leiden, Princeton, Tansui (Taiwan), and Santa Barbara. His recent publications include *Japan's Foreign Policy 1945–2003: The Quest for a Proactive Policy* and *The Inside Story of the Negotiations on the Northern Treaty: Five Lost Windows of Opportunity* (in Japanese). His edited volumes include *Russian Strategic Thought toward Asia* and *Japanese Strategic Thought toward Asia*.

Index

Abe, Shinzo, 49; Article 9 amendment debate and, 244, 246; foreign policy issues and, 65–66, 181, 184, 188
ACFTA. *See* ASEAN-China Free Trade Area
Acheson, Dean, 20, 43, 46, 220
ADB. *See* Asian Development Bank
agriculture, exclusions from free trade agreements, 92–93, 99
Albright, Madeleine, 51
alliances. *See* hub-and-spokes security relationships; security architecture
AMF. *See* Asian Monetary Fund
ANZCERTA. *See* Australia New Zealand Closer Economic Relations Trade Agreement
APEC. *See* Asia-Pacific Economic Cooperation
APT. *See* ASEAN Plus Three
Arai, Toshiaki, 177–78
ARF. *See* ASEAN Regional Forum
Armitage, Richard, 52–53, 175, 247
Armitage report, 52–53, 243, 245
ASEAN. *See* Association of Southeast Asian Nations
ASEAN-China Free Trade Area (ACFTA), 72–73, 127; Framework Agreement on

Economic Cooperation, 212n16; proposal for, 33, 58, 61, 81, 96, 110, 173, 204
ASEAN Institutes of Strategic and International Studies (ASEAN-ISIS), 168–69
ASEAN Plus Three (APT), 34, 242, 251; Chinese policies toward, 110, 121, 175, 176; East Asian Community discussions of, 172–76; establishment of, 8, 172–73, 201; financial cooperation of members of, 8, 32, 59, 64, 96; financial crisis and, 30, 85, 201–2; Japan-South Korea-China meetings, 173, 201, 263; mission of, 96, 110; regional cooperation issues and, 96, 147, 173; South Korean participation in, 201–2, 204; summit meetings of, 32, 118, 172–73, 174, 204
ASEAN Regional Forum (ARF), 171, 250, 266; Chinese membership of, 66–67, 241–42; Chinese participation in, 110, 119, 122, 125, 132, 171, 250; development of, 168, 171–72; establishment of, 170, 201, 241; intentions of members of, 47, 211n7; Japan's participation in, 168–72, 187; members of, 66; mission of, 66, 187; Northeast Asia Security Dialogue proposal, 199

• *271* •

Panama, free trade agreement with Taiwan, 80, 89
pan-Asianism, 4, 5, 20
Park Chung-hee, 7
Paulson, Henry, 75
PECC. *See* Pacific Economic Cooperation Council
Pempel, T. J., 207
People's Republic of China. *See* China
Perry, William, 50, 53
Philippines: multilateral initiatives proposed by, 5, 20, 21, 23; relations with United States, 6, 19, 20; trade with China, 62
Poling, Daniel, 20
popular culture, 48
positional goods, free trade agreements as, 87–88, 96, 97
Powell, Colin, 52, 53, 185
power maximization, as goal of Chinese multilateralism, 112, 120, 122, 130
power transitions, 222–24, 239
preferential trade agreements (PTAs), 79, 80, 91–93. *See also* free trade agreements

Qian Qichen, 125
Quirino, Elpidio, 5, 20

Rato, Rodrigo de, 158
raw materials and energy, Chinese imports of, 61–62, 67, 73–75, 127, 154–55, 156, 157, 159–62
Reagan, Ronald, 52, 53, 116, 245, 253n15
regime preservation, goals of Chinese Communist Party, 112, 122–28, 130–31, 132
regionalism: "domino" theory of, 83, 89; sub-, 6–7. *See also* multilateralism, East Asian; Northeast Asian regionalism; Southeast Asia
Republic of China. *See* Taiwan
Rhee, Syngman, 5, 17, 21
Rice, Condoleezza, 70
Roh Moo-hyun, 47; foreign policy of, 41, 204, 235; regionalist policies of, 205–8, 209, 261, 263
Roh Tae-woo, 199
Romulo, Carlos, 5, 18, 20
Rostow, W. W., 46
Rozman, Gilbert, 181
Rubin, Robert, 49
rules of origin, 87
Rumsfeld, Donald, 54, 243

Rupp, Kevin, 72
Russia, 68, 73. *See also* Soviet Union

Sakakibara, Eisuke, 8
San Francisco Peace Treaty, 4, 5–6, 9
San Francisco System. *See* hub-and-spokes security relationships
Sarbanes-Oxley Act, 150
Sato, Yukio, 168–69
Schröder, Gerhard, 245
SCO. *See* Shanghai Cooperation Organization
SEATO. *See* Southeast Asia Treaty Organization
security architecture, East Asian: in Cold War era, 219–22; comparisons to Europe, 219, 240–41; drivers of change in, 218, 229; future alternatives, 247–51, 260–61, 266; rise of China and, 224–26; transition period in, 217. *See also* hub-and-spokes security relationships
security cooperation: Chinese role in, 30–31, 66–67, 180; in Cold War era, 18; Council for Security Cooperation in the Asia Pacific, 199, 211n2; five-power organization, 249–50, 265, 266; future need for, 10, 218, 225–26, 235–40; Japanese policies on, 169, 170, 180–82; in Northeast Asia, 199, 200, 210; Pacific Pact, 5, 18, 19, 20–21, 23–24; Shanghai Cooperation Organization, 67, 68, 118, 121; Southeast Asia Nuclear Weapon Free Zone treaty, 30–31; U.S. support of, 72, 170. *See also* ASEAN Regional Forum; Six-Party Talks
security issues: Japanese interests, 181, 235, 236, 238; trade route protection, 155–57, 160, 162; U.S. interests, 54, 175, 181–82. *See also* North Korean nuclear issue
Shanghai Cooperation Organization (SCO), 67, 68, 118, 121
Shanghai Five, 118
Singapore: foreign exchange reserves of, 70; free trade agreements of, 58, 59, 69, 86, 87, 92–93, 207; free trade agreement with Japan, 65, 173; free trade agreement with United States, 70, 80, 82, 97, 104n44; stock market, 148; trade of, 62, 73, 79, 96
Six-Party Talks, 40, 182, 249–50; abductions issue in, 186, 187; achievements of, 10, 260, 265; Bush administration views of, 52, 185, 186, 188, 235, 243; Chinese participation in, 68, 118, 132, 206, 243,